# Foods of
# Sicily & Sardinia
## and the Smaller Islands

# Foods of
# Sicily & Sardinia
## and the Smaller Islands

BY GIULIANO BUGIALLI

PHOTOGRAPHS BY JOHN DOMINIS

**RIZZOLI**
NEW YORK

This book is dedicated to
HENRY WEINBERG
for his support and without whom
the book could not have happened.

Thanks to:

John Dominis
Carole Lalli, my invaluable editor, and her assistant, Liana Fredley
The Four Musketeers at the Hotel Augustus—Florence
Hotel Politeama—Palermo
Hotel Excelsior—Catania
Hotel Villa Athena—Agrigento
Hotel Margherita—Cagliari
Hotel su Gologone—Nuoro
Hotel el Faro—Alghero
Hotel del Sole—Oristano
Charleston Restaurant—Palermo
Associazione Ceramisti di Caltagirone
Ente del Turismo Trapani
Ente del Turismo Favignana
Soprintendenza Monumenti Tharros
Florio Co.—Trapani
Cantine Sella & Mosca—Alghero
My patient, incredible assistant, Don Palazzo
Tessilarte Florence for all the linen and tableclothes

. . . and all the wonderful people I enjoyed speaking with who
enlightened me about so many island matters that I needed to
know.

First published in the United States of America in 1996 by
Rizzoli International Publications, Inc.
300 Park Avenue South
New York, NY  10010

Copyright © 1996 Giuliano Bugialli

Library of Congress Cataloging–in–Publication Data
Bugialli, Giuliano.
The foods of Sicily & Sardinia and the smaller islands/Giuliano Bugialli; photographs by John Dominis.
p.  cm.
Includes index.
ISBN 0-8478-1924-8 (hc)
1. Cookery, Italian.  2. Cookery—Italy—Sicily.  3. Cookery—Italy—Sardinia.
I. Title.
TX723.2.S55B84  1996
641.59458—dc20
96-18475
CIP

Designed by Nai Chang

Printed in Italy

# CONTENTS

◆ ◆ ◆

## INTRODUCTION
PAGE 8

◆

## APPETIZERS
PAGE 11

## PASTA, RICE AND POLENTA
PAGE 36

## SOUPS
### PAGE 88

## MAIN COURSES
### PAGE 105

## FISH
### PAGE 155

## VEGETABLES
### PAGE 186

## BREADS
### PAGE 229

## DESSERTS
### PAGE 249

◆

BASIC TECHNIQUES ◆ PAGE 294

CONVERSION CHART ◆ PAGE 296

INDEX ◆ PAGE 297

# INTRODUCTION

◆ ◆ ◆

For over 3,000 years, the Mediterranean has produced a steady stream of remarkable sailors and a succession of great naval powers who have found the beautiful and bountiful islands off Italy's coast a great temptation. Throughout their history the two largest, Sicily and Sardinia, as well as the smaller treasures of Elba, Giglio, Capri, Ischia and Pantelleria have experienced a continuous series of raids, invasions and occupations. In addition, cut off by the sea from their neighbors, the islands have been able to preserve their ancient Roman culinary traditions to a degree not possible on the mainland. This has produced a cuisine that is one of the most historically interesting to be found. The Phoenicians and the Greek city-states were among the early occupiers, for whom these islands became objects of the epic struggle between Rome and Carthage. When Roman power waned, there were the various Germanic tribes, the most influential of which were the Lombards. Then came the Byzantines, Arabs, Normans, medieval Swabian Germans, and most lastingly the great Italian sea powers of Pisa and Genoa and finally the Spanish Aragonese.

Sicily, the center of Mediterranean trade from the Roman period until the late Middle Ages, was the chief prize. It has become trendy in recent times to vastly overrate the Arab influence on Sicilian food. But a careful examination reveals facts that challenge this assumption.

The Phoenicians and Carthaginians followed the exact same route that the Arabs did well over a thousand years later, and many of the products credited to Arab influence almost certainly existed long before the relatively short Arab occupation of parts of the island. If we consider some of the most important ingredients of Sicilian cooking, we find the following: the cultivation of oranges and lemons did not begin until the Spanish occupation of the last few centuries and all beans and legumes, except favas, lentils and chick-peas (all three used by the Romans), came from the New World, as did peppers, zucchini and other squashes, tomatoes and potatoes. All types of broccoli and cauliflower were developed from cabbage, most likely in Italy, at some point. Lamb and kid were used by the Romans, as was a very important Sicilian meat, pork, which is, of course, forbidden to Islam. In addition, other pork products such as lard, often the shortening of choice, *pancetta* and *prosciutto* are essential to the island's cookery. By the time the Arabs arrived, olive oil was already being produced by the Etruscans and Romans. Dried pasta was made in Sicily for the entire late Roman world. It is unlikely that eggplant was brought in by the Arabs. The wide range of Indian spices was crucial to upper-class Roman Empire cooking.

The widespread attempts to prove Arab origins through the etymology of certain names is tricky. Some of these efforts remind one of the amateur etymologist, le curé, in Marcel Proust's *Remembrances of Things Past*, whose derivations are demolished by another character who is a real professional.

Ax grinders have even attempted to show Arabic origins of such an obviously Latinate name as *cassata*. Devoto, Italy's greatest etymologist, derives it from its main ingredient, ricotta (Latin: *caseus*). But even the origin of the name does not always prove the origin of the dish. *Couscous*, an undoubtedly Arabic word, became the name of a dish that was one of a group of coarsely ground cereals forming the mainstay of the working-class Roman diet. A similar case is that of *béchamel*, a sauce that was invented in Italy, renamed in France and came to be called by its French name in Italy. And *couscous* has continued to change in modern times, so that even in North Africa now, it includes vegetables such as squashes, peppers and potatoes, all of which come from the New World as does the hot red pepper of the main condiment, *harissa*. And so, a cookbook presenting the true Sicilian tradition cannot depend wholly or largely on alleged Arab influence.

Another point to bear in mind is that French cookery, which started in the early nineteenth century with Câreme, became a model for the wealthier classes in much of Europe. Even today some of the landed Sicilians do not eat Sicilian food at all. They have chefs called *monzù*, who are wholly trained in the French tradition. Indeed it is extremely difficult to get the really sophisticated restaurants on the island to cook the dishes of the older nobility, because for the restaurants, Sicilian food means working-class food, while food prepared in the French manner is more refined. This "refined" food, however, has little to do with Sicilian tradition.

Sardinia is not as big as Sicily, which is the second largest region of Italy after Tuscany, and does not provoke as much controversy about its traditions and origins. The different areas of the island reflect some previous occupiers more strongly than others. The west coast, facing the Balerics, retains a strong Spanish flavor; indeed many of the inhabitants still speak medieval Catalán. Pisa and Genoa are reflected more in other parts of the island. But in the interior, some of the most ancient Mediterranean traditions still survive.

The smaller islands which are closer to the penninsula or to a larger island, each share much with the respective neighboring region, as Capri does with Campania, or Elba and Giglio with the Tuscan coast or Pantelleria with Sicily. Nonetheless, they all have dishes that are specifically theirs.

From this rich and diverse cuisine, we have chosen from among the most authentic dishes in the hope of capturing the essential flavors of this old but still very vigorous and marvelous world.

# APPETIZERS

$N$owadays Sicily and Sardinia have the most varied and developed antipasto course in all of Italy. It is served as a series of dishes, both warm and at room temperature, with the emphasis on the simultaneous play of contrasting flavors. Various herbs and spices are used for the different preparations, and the main ingredient used covers the range of vegetable, fish, meat and pastries.

This type of antipasto table is modeled precisely on the old Renaissance antipasto, which was developed specifically for the noble families all over Italy. But it has survived best on the two islands, having been much simplified in other regions, except for the occasional great feasts of the year. In Sicily and Sardinia, whether in the noble houses, restaurants, trattorias or the simplest homes, the antipasto usually includes such a variety of dishes.

It is important to remember, however, that the modern noble Sicilian cooking, which originated in the nineteenth century and was prepared by the *monzù*, is not traditional Sicilian, but more closely follows the French style.

Dressed uncooked vegetables, preserved meats or cheese are not used in the true Italian antipasto, which comprises cooked preparations, some of which are allowed to cool. Marinated dishes are among the most characteristic. A rare exception is the Orange Salad, which is uncooked.

The most classic antipasto dishes are easily found, freshly prepared, being sold in the markets and by the colorful street vendors still so typical of these islands. These honest preparations are very far from modern "fast food." Any of the antipasto dishes may also be used traditionally as a main course or a vegetable course, but not at the same meal.

We include a representative sampling of some of the best, well known and little known or forgotten, of the hundreds of antipasto dishes from the islands.

# *Melanzane*

## EGGPLANT

Eggplant is the signature vegetable of Sicily. The type often called Sicilian is the white eggplant because it is the most widely used there, though the purple also exists. We include three antipasti based on this vegetable.

*Melanzane a beccafico* is one of the many stuffed eggplant dishes and the one that has the most typically Sicilian stuffing: breadcrumbs, grated *Pecorino*, raisins and pine nuts (*pignoli*). *Beccafico* is a fat bird and the eggplant or the fresh sardines with the same name and stuffing are humorously thought to resemble this overstuffed bird.

For *Melanzane arrosto al salmoriglio (sammorigghiu)* the thinly sliced eggplant is grilled and dressed with the basic *salmoriglio* sauce that Sicily shares with Calabria and uses on both fish and vegetables which are either grilled over hot ash or cooked in the oven or broiler. Originally a pesto in which the herbs were ground together with the garlic, anchovies, olive oil, lemon juice and black pepper with a mortar and pestle, it is now usually ground with more modern implements. A simple version may include only one herb—oregano. A more complex example is the sauce here, which includes rosemary and sage in addition to the oregano. The sauce may also be used as a marinade for raw fish or vegetables before they are cooked. The name *salmoriglio* derives from *sale*, the word for "salt," as the original version, still preferred by purists, uses a drop of seawater for the salting.

*Polpette di melanzane* are fritters made with chopped eggplant and seasonings. Modern cooks tend to lighten the dish by omitting the original lard, or *sugna* (a less refined version of lard), and substituting some cream. Cream and butter, of course, are not original to Sicilian cooking, but the lard, which is, has lost favor and these two are always substitutes for the original. Present-day Sicilians have also moved away somewhat from cooking in their own very full-bodied olive oil and tend to replace it with a vegetable oil or a lighter olive oil.

FROM SICILY

# *Melanzane Arrosto al Salmoriglio*

## GRILLED EGGPLANT IN *SALMORIGLIO* SAUCE

SERVES 8 TO 10.

4 thin eggplants *or* 4 Sicilian eggplants (about 3 pounds total)
    Coarse-grained salt
3 whole anchovies in salt, cleaned and boned (see Note, page 30), *or* 6 anchovy fillets in oil, drained

4 medium-sized cloves garlic, peeled
1 heaping tablespoon rosemary leaves, fresh or preserved in salt (see page 294)
15 sage leaves, fresh or preserved in salt (see page 294)

1 cup olive oil
6 tablespoons lemon juice
2 teaspoons dried oregano
    Salt and freshly ground black pepper to taste

Clean the eggplants, removing the stem, then cut them lengthwise into ½-inch-thick slices. Place eggplant slices on a large serving platter and sprinkle each layer with coarse salt. Place another heavy serving platter over the top layer as a weight. Let rest for about ½ hour. The salt causes the eggplant to expel the dark liquid that is responsible for the bitter taste of the vegetable. When this liquid is rinsed off later, the eggplant will taste much sweeter. While the eggplants are resting, make a wood fire to prepare the hot ash.

Meanwhile, finely chop anchovies, garlic, rosemary and sage all together on a board. Transfer the chopped ingredients to a large crockery or glass bowl and add the olive oil, lemon juice, oregano and salt and pepper to taste; mix very well with a wooden spoon.

When eggplants are ready, rinse them under cold running water to remove all the salt which has absorbed the dark liquid. Dry each slice very well with paper towels and place it in the bowl containing the marinade. When all the eggplant is in the bowl, let marinate for at least ½ hour, mixing several times to be sure all the slices are very well coated with the liquid.

Using tongs, transfer the eggplant slices onto a grill with abundant hot ash underneath. Grill for 2 minutes on each side, then transfer to a large serving platter. When all the slices are cooked and on the serving platter, pour the leftover marinade over the eggplant.

Serve immediately or at room temperature after a few hours.

NOTE: *If not using an open fire, you can cook the eggplant in single layers in one or more baking dishes in a preheated 400-degree oven for 15 minutes on each side or, even better, under a preheated broiler 7 to 8 minutes.*

# Melanzane a Beccafico

## STUFFED EGGPLANT *INVOLTINI*

SERVES 6 OR 12 AS AN APPETIZER OR VEGETABLE.

FOR THE STUFFING
- 1 large red onion, cleaned
- 2 cloves garlic, peeled
- 5 tablespoons olive oil
- 10 sprigs Italian parsley, leaves only
- 1 tablespoon raisins
  Salt and freshly ground black pepper
- 1 tablespoon pine nuts (*pignoli*)
- 5 tablespoons unseasoned very fine bread crumbs, lightly toasted, preferably homemade
- 1 tablespoon freshly grated *Pecorino*

PLUS
- 3 medium-sized eggplants (about 2½ pounds total)

Coarse-grained salt

TO BAKE THE *INVOLTINI*
- 4 tablespoons olive oil
  Salt and freshly ground black pepper
- 10 bay leaves
  Juice of 1 lemon

TO SERVE
  Italian parsley leaves

Prepare the stuffing: Finely chop onion and garlic together on a board. Place a medium-sized skillet with the oil over medium heat. When the oil is warm, add the chopped ingredients and sauté for 10 minutes, stirring every so often with a wooden spoon. Meanwhile coarsely chop the parsley and soak the raisins in 1 cup of lukewarm water. When onion is translucent, season with salt and pepper, then add the parsley and mix. Remove skillet from heat and immediately add the pine nuts, bread crumbs, cheese and the drained raisins. Mix very well and transfer mixture to a crockery or glass bowl and let it cool completely.

With the skin on, cut the eggplant lengthwise into less than ½-inch-thick slices. Each eggplant will yield about 5 slices. Use only the 12 widest slices. Set a medium-sized stockpot of cold water over medium heat. When the water reaches a boil, add coarse salt to taste, then the eggplant slices and boil them for about 4 minutes, by which time they should be soft. Transfer the eggplant onto paper towels and let cool for about 20 minutes.

Preheat the oven to 375 degrees. Divide the stuffing equally among the eggplant slices. Spread a thin layer of the stuffing over each slice and roll up the eggplant like *involtini*. Thread 6 prepared *involtini* onto each metal skewer. Even better, use skewers made from bay leaf branches. Alternate *involtini* and bay leaves. When both skewers are ready, place them in a very lightly oiled baking pan. Sprinkle salt and pepper over the skewers, then drizzle with the remaining oil and the lemon juice. Bake for 40 minutes.

Serve hot, at room temperature or cold, with fresh parsley leaves. A serving may consist of either 1 or 2 *involtini*.

# *Polpette di Melanzane*

## EGGPLANT FRITTERS

### SERVES 6 TO 8.

2 medium-sized eggplants (about 1 pound)
Coarse-grained salt
10 large sprigs Italian parsley, leaves only
1 small clove garlic, peeled

Scant ½ cup unbleached all-purpose flour
2 extra-large eggs
3 tablespoons heavy cream
Salt and freshly ground black pepper

TO COOK
1 quart vegetable oil (½ sunflower oil, ½ corn oil)

TO SERVE
Fine salt
Lemon wedges

Peel the eggplants, cut them into 2-inch cubes and place them on a serving dish. Sprinkle about 1 heaping tablespoon of coarse salt over them and let rest for about ½ hour. Meanwhile bring a medium-sized pot of cold water to a boil, add coarse salt to taste and, when ready, rinse the eggplant very well and add it to the boiling water for 3 minutes. Transfer eggplant onto paper towels to remove excess liquid and let rest until cold, about ½ hour.

Coarsely chop eggplant on a board then transfer to a crockery or glass bowl. Finely chop parsley and garlic together on a board and add it to the eggplant. Add flour, eggs and cream to bowl and season with salt and pepper. Mix very well with a wooden spoon.

Heat all the vegetable oil in a medium-sized skillet over medium-high heat. When the oil reaches 375 degrees, with a large spoon take about 2 tablespoons of the mixture and gently drop it into the hot oil. Continue until the skillet is moderately full. Fry fritters without letting them touch, for about 30 seconds; turn and cook until golden all over, about 2 more minutes. Transfer cooked fritters to a serving platter lined with paper towels. Repeat procedure until all the "batter" has been used up.

When all the fritters are on the platter, remove the paper towels, sprinkle with a little salt and serve hot with lemon wedges.

# Zucchine

## ZUCCHINI

The most common type of zucchini in Sardinia and Sicily, indeed in all of Italy, is very light green in color, long in shape, thin, serrated, with skin a little fuzzy and with very few seeds. It is sweeter than the dark-skinned smooth zucchini so common elsewhere. The two recipes that follow instruct you to first soak the zucchini in some salted water (as you normally do with eggplant). This is to remove the bitterness of the dark-skinned variety. If you are able to obtain the light-skinned type, which are much sweeter and do not have a bitter aftertaste, you do not need to soak them.

The *Zucchine marinate* come from the Campania islands, Capri and Ischia. They employ one of many different marinades that are used in that region for grilled or fried vegetables.

The flavoring of *Frittelle di zucchine*, like that of most Sardinian zucchini preparations, includes grated lemon peel and/or lemon juice. The strange part of this is that Sardinia, unlike Sicily or some other regions of Italy, has very few lemon trees. In fact, in my early trips through Sardinia, I was surprised that fried dishes were usually served without the lemon wedges that we take for granted to accompany fried dishes throughout most of Italy.

# Frittelle di Zucchine

## ZUCCHINI PANCAKES

SERVES 6 TO 8.

1 pound zucchini, cleaned
  Coarse-grained salt
1 lemon with thick skin, washed very
  well with lukewarm water (see Note)
10 sprigs Italian parsley, leaves only

1 small clove garlic, peeled
  Salt and freshly ground black pepper
2 extra-large eggs
½ cup unbleached all-purpose flour

PLUS
  About 1 cup olive oil
TO SERVE
  Salt and lemon wedges

Soak the zucchini in a bowl of cold water with a little coarse salt added for ½ hour. Drain the zucchini, rinse under cold running water and pat them dry with paper towels. Coarsely grate them, using a hand grater, into a crockery or glass bowl. Finely grate the lemon peel and finely chop parsley and garlic together on a board. Add lemon peel and the chopped ingredients to the bowl with the zucchini. Season with salt and pepper, then add the eggs, mix very well and start adding the flour, a little at a time, constantly mixing with a wooden spoon.

Heat ½ cup of the olive oil in a pan over medium heat. When the oil reaches about 375 degrees, scoop up about 3 tablespoons of the zucchini mixture with a small ladle and gently slide it into the pan. You can make 3 or 4 *frittelle* at a time. Using a spatula, turn the *frittelle* over when they are lightly golden on the bottom, after about 30 seconds. Cook the other side for 30 seconds more, then transfer the pancakes to a serving platter lined with paper towels. Before scooping up more zucchini batter to prepare the next pancakes, be sure to mix it very well because the liquid tends to stick to the bottom of the bowl. Add more oil to the pan as needed.

Sprinkle with salt and serve hot with lemon wedges.

This recipe can be prepared in advance, grating the zucchini and placing them in a colander until needed. In a different bowl prepare the batter and combine the zucchini and the batter when you are ready to cook.

NOTE: *It is important in this recipe that the lemon peel not be very bitter. The washing should remove most bitterness, but test it by tasting before adding it to the recipe.*

# *Zucchine Marinate*

# GRILLED MARINATED ZUCCHINI

SERVES 6 TO 8 AS AN APPETIZER.

4 very thin zucchini, but not the miniature ones
  Coarse-grained salt
2 tablespoons olive oil
  Salt and freshly ground black pepper

TO SERVE
10 large fresh basil leaves, torn into large pieces
20 large fresh mint leaves, left whole

Salt and freshly ground black pepper
3 tablespoons olive oil
2 tablespoons very good red wine vinegar

Prepare a wood fire.

Meanwhile, clean the zucchini, removing the two ends, then cut them lengthwise into slices less than ¼ inch thick. Put the slices in a large bowl of cold water with a little coarse salt added and soak for ½ hour.

Drain and rinse the zucchini, then dry them with paper towels. When the hot ash is ready, first lightly brush an iron grill with oil, then mix the 2 tablespoons of oil with salt and pepper and brush the zucchini slices on both sides. Broil them on the hot grill for about 1 minute on each side or until quite soft. Transfer the cooked slices to a serving dish.

When all the zucchini are cooked and on the serving dish, sprinkle them with the basil and mint leaves on top, season with salt and pepper and finally pour the oil and vinegar all over. Let the zucchini marinate for at least ½ hour, turning them twice. They are then ready to be served.

## Caponata

Although we now associate *caponata* and its derivative, *caponatina*, with Sicily, Sicilian *caponata* was originally a sailor's dish in which the cooked vegetables acquired at special osterie called *caupona* in the ports of call were seasoned with vinegar and sugar and eaten on the boat. Modern versions of *caponata* have come to include additional seasonings, such as anchovies, olives and capers, with the eggplant, peppers and celery, as the dish became a traditional antipasto for everyone. *Caponatina* is simply a more delicate version of *caponata* in which the ingredients are cut more finely. There are many variations with optional additional ingredients. Some versions of *caponatina* include pieces of shellfish.

The original sailor's version of *caponata* was based on sea biscuit softened by the vinegar and sugar. Sicilian *caponata* dispensed with the biscuit. The modern version closest to this original is the *cappon magro* of Genoa, which still has a layer of sea biscuit under vegetables and even more elaborate added ingredients, such as fish and eggs. *Caponata del marinaio* from Capri uses Campania's *friselle*, the dried, toasted bread rings with a hole in the center, in place of the sea biscuit. The hard bread is soaked, first in water and then in the traditional vinegar. The topping is fresh uncooked vegetables such as tomatoes, celery, onions and basil. In this recipe the old *caponata* has merged with the bread salads of other regions, especially that made in coastal cities like Livorno.

FROM SICILY

# Caponatina
## CAPONATA WITH PEPPERS

### SERVES 8 TO 10.

4 medium-sized eggplants (about 1½ pounds total)
  Coarse-grained salt
8 inner stalks celery
4 bell peppers of different colors
1 large red onion, cleaned
1 cup olive oil

1 heaping tablespoon tomato paste, preferably imported Italian
2 anchovy fillets in oil, drained
4 ounces pitted green olives in brine
4 tablespoons capers in wine vinegar, drained
6 tablespoons raisins

½ cup red wine vinegar, not very strong
¼ cup granulated sugar
  Salt and freshly ground black pepper to taste
OPTIONAL
2 tablespoons pine nuts (*pignoli*)

Clean the eggplants, discarding the stems, then cut them, with their skins, into 1-inch cubes. Place eggplant on a serving dish and sprinkle with coarse salt. Place another serving dish with a weight on it over the eggplant and let stand for at least ½ hour.

Cut the celery into 1½-inch pieces and if the stalks are very wide divide each piece into 2 or 3 strips. Soak the celery in a bowl of cold water for ½ hour. Clean the peppers, removing and discarding the stems, all the seeds and the inner membranes. Cut the peppers lengthwise into ½-inch strips and soak them in a second bowl of cold water. Slice the onion into thin rings and soak in a third bowl of cold water.

*Anchovies preserved in a barrel*

Bring a large pot of cold water to a boil, add coarse salt to taste, then drain the celery and add it to the pot. Cook for about 5 minutes until almost completely cooked. Drain the celery, cool it under cold running water and transfer it to a serving dish lined with paper towels.

Set a large skillet with ¼ cup of the oil over medium heat. When the oil is warm, drain the peppers, add them to the skillet and sauté for 5 minutes, stirring with a wooden spoon. Use a slotted spoon to transfer the peppers to a serving dish lined with paper towels. Discard the oil from the skillet.

Rinse the eggplant under cold running water to remove excess salt and dry it with paper towels. Heat ¼ cup of fresh oil over medium heat in the same skillet used before. When the oil is warm, add the eggplant and sauté for 5 minutes, continuously stirring the eggplant so it does not stick to the bottom of the skillet. Using a slotted spoon, transfer eggplant to a second serving platter lined with paper towels, and again discard the oil from the skillet. Repeat the same procedure again with the boiled celery and let it rest on a third towel-lined serving dish.

Heat the last ¼ cup of the oil in the same large skillet over medium heat. When the oil is warm, drain the onions, put them in the skillet, sauté for 5 minutes, then add tomato paste, anchovies, olives, capers and raisins and sauté for 10 minutes, adding a little cold water as needed. Return all the previously sautéed vegetables to the skillet and mix very well. Combine the vinegar with the sugar, making sure the sugar is completely dissolved, and pour into the skillet. Add the *pignoli*, if using, and season with salt and pepper. Cook for 15 minutes more, constantly stirring with a wooden spoon. The vegetables should be properly cooked and all the liquid absorbed.

Transfer mixture to a large serving dish and serve hot or at room temperature after a few hours. *Caponatina* may also be refrigerated and eaten cold.

# Caponata del Marinaio

## SAILOR'S CAPONATA

SERVES 4 TO 6.

2 *friselle* (about 1 pound total)

FOR THE *FRISELLE*

4 tablespoons olive oil
1 cup cold water
4 medium-sized cloves garlic, peeled
  Salt and freshly ground black pepper
2 large pinches dried oregano

FOR THE TOMATOES

1½ pounds very ripe fresh tomatoes

4 tablespoons olive oil
  Salt and freshly ground black pepper
  A large pinch of dried oregano

FOR THE TOPPING

8 celery stalks (the white ones from the heart)
4 whole anchovies in salt, cleaned and boned (see Note, page 30), *or* 8 anchovy fillets in oil, drained

8 tablespoons capers in wine vinegar, drained
2 or 3 cans tuna in olive oil, drained (yields about 7 ounces tuna)
  Salt and freshly ground black pepper to taste
10 large fresh basil leaves, torn into thirds
2 tablespoons olive oil

TO SERVE

Several fresh basil leaves

Hold the *friselle* in a bowl of cold water for 1 minute. Transfer the soaked bread, without breaking it, to a serving dish and place the *friselle* one next to the other. Combine the olive oil and the water in a small bowl. Coarsely chop the garlic on a board and sprinkle it all over the bread along with salt and pepper to taste and a large pinch of oregano. Start drizzling the oil/water mixture over the bread a little at a time and do not drizzle more until the previous quantity is completely absorbed by the bread.

Meanwhile, cut tomatoes into 1-inch cubes, transfer to a crockery or glass bowl, then season with oil, salt, pepper and oregano. Refrigerate, covered, until needed.

Cut the celery stalks into 1-inch pieces and place in a separate crockery or glass bowl. Cut anchovies into tiny pieces and add them to the bowl with the celery, along with the capers, tuna, salt and pepper to taste, basil and the olive oil. Mix very well and refrigerate, covered, until needed.

When the bread has absorbed all the water mixture, place serving dish in the refrigerator for at least ½ hour.

When ready, arrange tomatoes, with all their juices, over the bread, then top with the celery mixture also filling the hole of the bread. Serve with more fresh basil leaves, cutting the bread (by that time it should be very soft) together with all the stuffing and topping, like a pie. Or, all the ingredients can be mixed together and spooned out like a salad.

VARIATION: *Instead of chopping the garlic and sprinkling it over the soaked* friselle, *you can rub the* friselle *with the garlic before soaking it in water.*

# Frittata di Fave Fresche

## FRITTATA OF FRESH FAVA BEANS

SERVES 10 AS APPETIZER
OR 6 AS SIDE DISH.

The traditional large antipasto usually includes one or more *frittate*—large egg pancakes filled with a cooked fresh vegetable of the season and eaten at room temperature. A great favorite among fillings is very sweet young fresh fava beans, which have a short season. As a substitute, dried fava beans are also very popular, and after being soaked and cooked, make a very good *frittata*.

1 pound shelled very young fresh fava beans, with skins left on
Coarse-grained salt
1 large clove garlic, peeled

10 sprigs Italian parsley, leaves only
4 tablespoons olive oil
Salt and freshly ground black pepper
½ cup freshly grated *Pecorino*

PLUS
6 extra-large eggs
Salt and freshly ground black pepper
TO SERVE
Fresh basil and parsley leaves

Place the fresh fava beans in a bowl of cold water with a little coarse salt added to soak for ½ hour.

Bring a medium-sized casserole with cold water to a boil over medium heat. Add coarse salt, then drain the beans and add them to the casserole to boil for 5 minutes. Transfer the beans from the casserole to a strainer lined with paper towels to absorb all the extra moisture. Finely chop parsley and garlic together.

Heat the olive oil in a small saucepan over low heat. Add the chopped ingredients and sauté for 5 minutes, then add the beans, season with salt and pepper and cook for 5 minutes more. Transfer contents of saucepan to a bowl and let rest until cool, about ½ hour.

Mix *Pecorino* and eggs in a bowl and season with salt and pepper. Add the beans and mix thoroughly. Lightly oil a 12-inch omelette pan and set over medium heat. Add the egg mixture and cook until eggs are quite firm. Use a plate to reverse the *frittata* and cook for 2 minutes more. Transfer to a round serving platter and serve hot or cold as an appetizer.

# *Panelle*

## FLAT CHICK-PEA FRITTERS

MAKES ABOUT 25 FRITTERS.

Every market in Sicily has a *panillaru*, a vendor of this delicious snack. Made with a batter of chick-pea flour, these fritters resemble the Tuscan *cecina*, but are fried instead of baked. Chick-pea flour, which is very aromatic, remains in wide use in Sicily even to make a type of fresh pasta.

2 cups chick-pea flour
3½ cups cold water
   Scant ½ teaspoon fine salt

TO FRY THE *PANELLE*
1½ cups vegetable oil (½ corn oil,
   ½ sunflower oil)
½ cup olive oil

TO SERVE
Fine salt
OPTIONAL
Thin slices crusty country bread

Line 2 jelly-roll pans with plastic wrap and lightly oil them.

Place the flour in a small bowl, make a well in it and add ¼ cup of the water. Start mixing, incorporating some of the flour from the edges of the well, very little at a time, adding more water as that previously added is completely absorbed. By placing all the flour in a bowl and adding the water little by little you avoid creating a lot of lumps. When all the water is incorporated, add salt and mix again.

Transfer the rather thick batter to a medium-sized saucepan and set pan over medium heat, stirring constantly until batter begins to simmer. Continue to cook for at least 5 minutes.

By cooking, the batter may become very thick, so watch carefully to be sure it does not stick to the bottom of the pan. If the flour is very dry and old, you will need more water to prevent the batter from sticking. Transfer the batter to the prepared jelly-roll pans and use a spatula to spread it out quite thinly and evenly. Let the cooked batter rest until cold, for at least 5 hours or, even better, prepare the batter one day in advance and refrigerate until needed.

Heat the oil in a large skillet over medium heat. Meanwhile use a sharp knife to cut the solid batter into squares of about 3 inches. Line a serving dish with paper towels. When the oil is hot, about 400 degrees, transfer some of the squares to the hot oil and fry them until lightly golden on both sides. Use a strainer skimmer to transfer the cooked *panelle* to the serving dish lined with paper towels to absorb excess grease. When all the *panelle* are cooked and on the dish, remove the paper, sprinkle with some salt and serve hot. Sometimes *panelle* are served like sandwiches between 2 slices of crusty country bread.

NOTE: *Another way to prepare the* panelle *batter is to dissolve the flour slowly as above, but to add at least 3 times the amount of water. The batter rests in the refrigerator overnight and next morning the water sitting above the flour is poured off almost completely. The batter remaining underneath is then used to make the* panelle.

*The tiny port of Favignana. The two arches in the back center form the entrance to the area where the large boats used for the Tonnara are kept.*

# Pesce Alle Erbe Aromatiche

## SWORDFISH OR TUNA MARINATED IN AROMATIC HERBS

### SERVES 6 TO 8 AS AN APPETIZER.

*Pesce alle erbe aromatiche* from Favignana, the tiny island off Trapani, employs tuna, of course, since it is the center of tuna fishing, or swordfish, or the two together, since they really form the basis of the island's *cucina*. The fish are prepared in a fantastic marinade with many, many herbs: mint, basil, parsley, sage, rosemary, etc., but the one which is special to this recipe is lemon verbena. This herb was much more widely used in Italy in the nineteenth century, when almost every house had a required lemon verbena bush.

1 pound cleaned (bone and skin removed) swordfish or fresh tuna, cut in one slice
5 tablespoons olive oil
Salt and freshly ground black pepper

FOR THE MARINADE
10 large fresh mint leaves
10 fresh lemon verbena leaves *or* 1 teaspoon dried, or additional mint

15 large fresh basil leaves
30 sprigs Italian parsley, leaves only
10 large sage leaves, fresh or preserved in salt (see page 294)
1 heaping tablespoon rosemary leaves, fresh or preserved in salt (page 294)
4 heaping tablespoons capers in wine vinegar, drained

1 tablespoon fresh oregano leaves *or* 1 teaspoon dried oregano
1 small red onion, cleaned
1 tablespoon red wine vinegar
1½ tablespoons lemon juice
½ cup olive oil
Salt and freshly ground black pepper

Slice fish into strips ¾ inch wide and 4 inches long. Place a medium-sized skillet with the oil over medium heat. When the oil is warm, add the fish, raise the heat to high and sauté for 2 minutes, gently stirring with a wooden spoon, trying not to break up the strips. Season with salt and pepper. At the end of the 2 minutes, fish should be cooked but still very soft. Do not overcook swordfish or tuna; otherwise it becomes tough. Use a slotted spoon to transfer fish to a large serving platter. Discard all the juices in the skillet.

Prepare the marinade: Place mint, verbena, basil, parsley, sage, rosemary, capers, oregano and the onion in a blender or food processor and finely grind everything together. Transfer mixture to a crockery or glass bowl, then add the vinegar, lemon juice and olive oil and mix very well. Season with salt and pepper, mix again, then pour the marinade over the fish. Cover platter with plastic wrap and refrigerate for at least ½ hour before serving it. When fish is ready, remove platter from refrigerator and mix so that fish and sauce are well integrated. Transfer everything to a clean serving platter and serve.

# Acciughe Marinate con Patate

## MARINATED ANCHOVIES

SERVES 6 TO 8 AS AN APPETIZER.

The fresh anchovies that are so plentiful in Italy are marinated for this dish. A very close result can be achieved using whole anchovies preserved in salt or even anchovy fillets in oil if they are well soaked in milk. The fish are almost reconstituted and the taste of fresh fish somewhat restored. This dish is almost a must for the antipasto table of these islands. This version is one of the simplest; there are other versions with more ingredients.

15 whole anchovies in salt (see Note), or 30 anchovy fillets, packed in oil
1½ cups milk
3 medium-sized cloves garlic, peeled and finely chopped

6 tablespoons olive oil
4 tablespoons fresh lemon juice
2 tablespoons red wine vinegar
Freshly ground black pepper to taste
5 sprigs Italian parsley, leaves only, coarsely chopped

PLUS

1 pound all-purpose potatoes
Coarse-grained salt
5 tablespoons red wine vinegar
Capers in wine vinegar, drained

OPTIONAL

Hot red pepper flakes to taste

In a crockery or glass bowl, soak anchovy fillets in the milk for 1 hour.

Meanwhile peel the potatoes, cut them into 1-inch cubes and soak in a bowl of cold water until needed. Bring a medium-sized casserole with 6 cups of cold water to a boil over medium heat, add coarse salt to taste, then the vinegar. Drain potatoes, add them to casserole and cook until they are soft but still retain their shape, about 15 minutes. Drain potatoes, place them in a crockery or glass bowl and cover them with paper towels.

Drain milk from anchovies, lightly pat them with paper towels and arrange them on a plate or serving platter like the spokes of a wheel. Sprinkle with the garlic, then drizzle them evenly with the oil, lemon juice and vinegar. Season with freshly ground black pepper and hot red pepper, if using. Toss the parsley leaves over the top. Wrap the plate with plastic wrap and refrigerate for at least 3 hours before serving; the anchovies will be tastier if marinated overnight.

When ready to serve, arrange potatoes in the center of the platter and if using capers, distribute them all around. The potatoes do not need any dressing because they are eaten together with the anchovies and their sauce.

NOTE: *If using whole anchovies preserved in salt, rinse them under cold water to remove the bones and excess salt.*

# *Insalata di Arance*

## ORANGE SALAD

### SERVES 8.

One of Sicily's best known dishes, this salad and its many variations are used not only as part of the *antipasto*, but also as a side course or a refreshment. Oranges and other citrus fruits have become part of Sicilian cuisine only recently. They do not date back to the Romans, Byzantines or the Arabs but were introduced in the more recent period of Spanish domination, when Sicily's main crop, wheat, began to decline in production.

| | | |
|---|---|---|
| 4 large juicy oranges | 3 tablespoons olive oil | 4 walnuts, shelled and coarsely |
| 4 celery hearts | 1 teaspoon red wine vinegar | chopped |
| | 3 or 4 twists black pepper | |

Peel the oranges and carefully remove all the white pith under the rind. Cut the oranges crosswise into slices less than ½ inch thick and arrange them on a large serving platter.

Clean the celery hearts very well, removing all the threads, and cut them into ⅜-inch squares. Arrange the celery pieces over the oranges.

Mix the oil and vinegar together and drizzle it all over the oranges and celery, then season with a little pepper. Divide equally among individual salad plates and top each serving with a few walnut pieces.

# *Ricotta al Forno*

## BAKED RICOTTA MOLD

SERVES 8 TO 10 AS AN APPETIZER.

Sheep's milk ricotta is the most common type of ricotta throughout the Italian peninsula. This baked ricotta is completely wrapped in bay leaves, fresh or dried. Their flavor so permeates the dish that for some, this would be an acquired taste.

30 ounces whole-milk ricotta, drained very well
8 teaspoons black olive paste

Salt and freshly ground black pepper
4 extra-large eggs

TO BAKE
2 tablespoons (1 ounce) sweet butter
About 50 bay leaves, fresh if possible

Be sure the ricotta has been completely drained of excess water. Place ricotta in a bowl, add the olive paste, season with salt and pepper, then add the eggs and mix very well with a wooden spoon. The seasoned ricotta should be very smooth in texture. Refrigerate mixture, covered, for at least 1 hour before using it.

When ready, preheat the oven to 375 degrees and melt the butter in a double boiler. Brush the sides and bottom of a 10-inch spring-form pan with the melted butter. Carefully line bottom of pan with the bay leaves. Then completely line the sides, placing the leaves standing up and firmly pressed against the sides so they remain in place. Place the springform in the freezer for at least 1 hour.

Fill the mold with the prepared ricotta mixture and bake for 1 hour. Remove pan from oven, transfer to a rack and let rest until cool, about ½ hour. Place in the refrigerator for at least another ½ hour before serving.

*Ricotta al forno* is better if prepared one day in advance, removed from the mold once cool, and kept in the refrigerator. To serve, slice it like a pie. Bay leaves are removed and discarded individually.

# *Pastiere Siciliane*

## LAMB IN CRUST, SICILIAN STYLE

MAKES 16 SMALL "PIES."

A significant part of the Renaissance *antipasto* course, pastries filled with meat or vegetables have retained a strong presence in the modern Sicilian *antipasto*. When the pastry is a main course, it is made as a large pie. For this *antipasto*, they are made into small individual pastries. The ground lamb is seasoned with the famous *Pecorino pepato*, the sheep's cheese containing whole black peppercorns.

FOR THE CRUST

- 2 cups unbleached all-purpose flour
- ¼ cup very fine semolina flour
- ½ cup lukewarm water
- 8 tablespoons (4 ounces) sweet butter, at room temperature
  A pinch of salt

FOR THE STUFFING

About 3 pounds shoulder lamb chops (to yield 1½ pounds meat)
- 15 sprigs Italian parsley, leaves only
- 4 large cloves garlic, peeled
- 3 ounces fresh grated Sicilian *Pecorino* with black peppercorns or 3 ounces

*Pecorino Romano* with about 10 cracked black peppercorns
- 4 extra-large eggs
  Salt and freshly ground black pepper

TO BAKE

- 16 pats of sweet butter

Prepare the crust: Combine 1½ cups of the flour and all of the semolina flour in a bowl and mix very well. Make a well and add the butter, water and pinch of salt. Use a wooden spoon to incorporate the butter completely into the flour, then transfer pastry to a board and knead it for 30 seconds or until a ball of dough is formed. Wrap dough with plastic wrap and refrigerate for at least ½ hour.

Meanwhile, prepare the filling. Remove the meat from the bones and discard bones along with some of the thicker fat. Coarsely grind the meat, using an electric meat grinder, and finely chop the parsley and the garlic together on a board. Mix the ground meat and the chopped herbs together in a crockery or glass bowl, then add the cheese, eggs and salt and pepper to taste and mix very well.

*The still unbaked pastiere*

*Elaborate baroque balconies line the streets of Noto.*

Preheat the oven to 400 degrees and line 1 or 2 cookie sheets with parchment paper.

When the pastry is ready, place the remaining ½ cup of flour on a pastry board. Unwrap the pastry and place on the board. Knead the pastry for less than 1 minute, incorporating a little bit of the flour. With a rolling pin stretch the pastry into a large sheet less than ¼ inch thick. Use a 5-inch cookie cutter with scalloped edges to cut out 16 discs. Place a scant ¼ cup of the filling in the center of each disc. Pull the ends of the dough all around up to the level of the stuffing and pinch it all around to make the dough into small "containers" for the stuffing. These form individual *pastiere*.

Transfer all the *pastiere* to the prepared cookie sheets, making sure they do not touch one another. Place a pat of butter on top of the stuffing in each "container" and bake for about 35 minutes or even less if you prefer the lamb less than well done.

Remove from oven, transfer to a large serving platter and serve hot.

# PASTA · RICE · POLENTA

$S$icily has perhaps the longest tradition of dried pasta. It is also very likely the place where its consumption in the Western world originated, because from Roman times onward, it was the center of wheat production in the Mediterranean. Today, Sicilians eat a great deal of pasta, most often dried, though they also prepare fresh pasta versions of some of the same dishes. Often combined with meat, fish or vegetables, these pasta dishes can easily serve as one-course meals.

Western Sicily stresses the combination of contrasting tastes—sweet, sour, savory—which some think reflects the influence of a series of invaders who came all the way from the Middle East through North Africa. These included not only medieval Arabs but predecessors such as the Phoenicians and Carthaginians. There was even a strong Jewish presence in medieval Sicily. In contrast, the cooking of eastern Sicily, which had a history of Greek and Byzantine domination, has simpler, more classically balanced dishes with fewer ingredients. It is these simpler dishes which many feel also represent the older native cooking of the Siculi.

Of the Sardinian pastas, we are emphasizing the lesser known native ones, such as both types of *fregola* and *malloreddus*.

Although introduced to these ancient islands only in recent centuries, both rice and cornmeal have been given their place in the native cuisine. Real *risotto* is a novelty on both islands, so the rice is more often slowly boiled together with its seasonings and other ingedients. Cornmeal, a product of the New World, was probably substituted for some older, coarsely ground grains such as millet and barley, which were the basis of many simple dishes in the ancient world.

We present varied versions of *gnocchi* from Sicily, Sardinia and Elba, and end the chapter with a remarkable couscous from Sardinia. With just its own sauce and no meat, fish or vegetables, it is more classical than North African versions. This variation probably reflects the ancient Roman use of coarsely ground wheat before the medieval Arab invasions.

## Al Dente

As the term relates to dried pasta in southern Italy and the islands, *al dente* means cooked less than is usual for the rest of Italy and less than the cooking times in the recipes here. For many, the pasta would barely seem cooked, so we leave the adjustment to the reader.

FROM SICILY

# *Pasta all'Aglio*

## PASTA WITH BOILED GARLIC CLOVES

SERVES 4 TO 6.

In *Pasta all'aglio,* an entire head of garlic is separated into cloves, which are then boiled. The boiled cloves, left whole, are combined with cooked dried pasta and dressed with warmed olive oil.

1 large head garlic (not elephant garlic) peeled (about 2 ounces)
3 quarts cold water
  Coarse-grained salt
½ cup olive oil

1 pound dried pasta, such as vermicelli (thick spaghetti) or perciatelli (bucatini), preferably imported Italian
  Salt
  Freshly ground black pepper

TO COOK THE PASTA
  Coarse-grained salt
TO SERVE
½ cup freshly grated *Pecorino Romano*
  A large quantity of fresh basil leaves
  Freshly ground black pepper

Place the peeled garlic in a medium-sized stockpot of water and set over medium heat. When the water reaches a boil, add 2 tablespoons of the oil and coarse salt to taste. Lower heat and simmer for about 30 minutes or until garlic is soft. Put in the pasta and cook it for 11 to 13 minutes, depending on the brand, until *al dente.* Meanwhile, heat the remaining oil in a small saucepan over low heat, seasoning with salt and pepper.

   Drain the pasta together with the garlic and transfer the pasta to a serving platter. Pour the heated oil over the pasta, mix well, then sprinkle with the cheese and basil leaves. Mix again and serve hot with more freshly ground black pepper.

*Freshly harvested garlic*

For these very old island cultures, the tomato is a recent addition to their cuisine. We include two recipes from Trapani which indicate how successfully this new ingredient has been adapted to the older approaches.

Spaghetti al pomodoro crudo combines diced tomatoes, basil, parsley and grated Pecorino, all uncooked, with just-cooked piping-hot pasta. The heat from the pasta releases the flavors of the herbs in this simple and beautiful dish.

Grinding with the mortar and pestle gave rise to the name pesto for numerous herb sauces. For this recent Pasta al pesto from Trapani, the tomato is ground together with garlic and basil, less of which is included than in the famous Genoese sauce.

## FROM SICILY (TRAPANI)
# Spaghetti al Pomodoro Crudo
## SPAGHETTI WITH TOMATO PESTO

### SERVES 6 TO 8.

6 large cloves garlic, peeled
10 sprigs Italian parsley, leaves only
40 large fresh basil leaves
1 pound fresh tomatoes, ripe but not overripe, blanched (see Note)
2 ounces freshly grated Pecorino

Romano cheese
1 cup olive oil
Salt and freshly ground black pepper
1 pound dried pasta, such as thick spaghetti, perciatelli or bucatini, preferably imported Italian

TO COOK THE PASTA
Coarse-grained salt
TO SERVE
15 fresh basil leaves

Finely chop garlic, parsley and basil all together on a board. Transfer the chopped ingredients to a crockery or glass bowl.

Remove and discard skin and seeds from tomatoes. Cut tomatoes into small pieces and add them to the chopped herbs, along with the grated cheese, oil and salt and pepper to taste. Mix well and refrigerate, covered, until needed.

Bring a large pot of cold water to a boil over medium heat. Add coarse salt to taste, then the pasta and cook it for 11 to 13 minutes, depending on the brand. Pasta should have a rather strong bite.

Meanwhile, remove sauce from refrigerator and ladle half of it onto a large serving platter. Drain the pasta and transfer it to the platter. Pour the remaining cold sauce over the pasta and mix very well. Sprinkle the basil on top and serve, with the pasta still hot.

NOTE: Blanch tomatoes in salted boiling water for 2 minutes. The skins will easily slide off.

# Pasta con Pesto alla Trapanese

## PASTA WITH SICILIAN PESTO

SERVES 6 TO 8.

1½ pounds ripe, fresh tomatoes, blanched (see Note, page 40)

4½ ounces almonds, blanched for about 2 minutes in boiling water

4 medium-sized cloves garlic (about ¼ ounce), peeled

25 large fresh basil leaves

10 sprigs Italian parsley, leaves only

10 leaves fresh mint

Salt and freshly ground black pepper

A large pinch of hot red pepper flakes

¾ cup olive oil

FOR THE PASTA

4 cups unbleached all-purpose flour

5 extra-large eggs

Pinch of salt

OR

1½ pounds dried bucatini, linguini or spaghetti, preferably Italian

TO COOK THE PASTA

Coarse-grained salt

TO SERVE

About 25 large fresh basil leaves

Remove the seeds from the tomatoes and put the tomatoes in a crockery or glass bowl until needed.

With a mortar and pestle, finely grind the almonds with the garlic (any green sprouts removed). When the texture is very creamy, add the basil, parsley and mint and grind until herbs are completely incorporated. Transfer mixture to a large crockery or glass bowl. Pass the tomatoes through a food mill, using the disc with the smallest holes, into the bowl containing the almond-herb mixture. Season with salt, pepper and hot pepper to taste, add the olive oil and mix all the ingredients with a wooden spoon. Cover the bowl and refrigerate until needed. (The pesto sauce can be prepared several hours before serving and kept, covered, in the refrigerator.)

If using fresh pasta, prepare it with the ingredients listed. Stretch the layer of pasta to a little less than ⅛ inch thick; on the pasta machine, take it to the notch 2 from the last. Cut into spaghetti. Let pasta rest on cotton dish towels or paper towels until needed.

Bring a large pot of cold water to a boil. When the water reaches a boil, add coarse salt to taste, then add the pasta and cook until *al dente*, 9 to 12 minutes, depending on the brand. (If using fresh pasta, cook for 1 to 3 minutes, depending on dryness.) As the pasta cooks, line a large serving platter with the basil leaves and pour 1 cup of the pasta water into the sauce. Mix very well. Drain the pasta and transfer it to the prepared serving platter; pour the sauce over, mix very well and serve immediately.

NOTE: *The pesto can be made in a food processor. Place the almonds, garlic and olive oil in the bowl and, using the metal blade, grind until very fine. Then add the basil, parsley, mint, salt, pepper and hot pepper flakes and grind again until texture is very creamy. Transfer mixture to a crockery or glass bowl, add the passed tomatoes and mix again.*

# Calamari Ripieni di Pasta

## PASTA BAKED IN A SQUID

### SERVES 6.

If you wish to eat this dish, it is unlikely you would find it in a restaurant. It comes from the tiny island of Favignana, off Trapani, and you must make it yourself. It makes a beautiful presentation, but the baking of the cooked, already-sauced pasta inside the squid body also produces a new flavor, and it is this flavor rather than the presentation that is most important to the islanders.

6 very large squid bodies (about 4 ounces each), cleaned and with no holes
1 lemon
Coarse-grained salt
About 8 ounces of the leafy parts of a fennel bulb
2 large stalks of dried wild fennel or 2 additional ounces of the leafy parts of the fennel bulb
20 fresh dill sprigs

1 wine bottle cork, unused if possible
4 large cloves garlic, peeled
10 tablespoons olive oil
2 large pinches ground saffron
Salt and freshly ground black pepper
20 sprigs Italian parsley, leaves only, coarsely chopped
1 pound dried perciatelli, bucatini or spaghetti, preferably imported Italian, broken in half

TO COOK THE STUFFED *CALAMARI*
1 cup dry white wine
1 tablespoon olive oil
Salt and freshly ground black pepper to taste
2 cloves garlic, peeled but left whole

TO SERVE
½ cup unseasoned very fine bread crumbs, lightly toasted, preferably homemade
1 tablespoon olive oil
Pinch of coarse-grained salt

Soak the cleaned *calamari* in a bowl of cold water with the lemon, cut in half, and a little coarse salt for 30 minutes. Meanwhile, cut the leafy parts of the fennel bulbs and the dill into 1-inch pieces and soak them in a bowl of cold water for 30 minutes. Place a medium-sized casserole of cold water over medium heat. When the water reaches a boil, add coarse salt to taste, the lemon from the squid and the cork. Drain squid, add them to the casserole, lower heat and let squid simmer for 1 hour. If you cannot obtain the very large squid and you use slightly smaller ones, simmer for 30 to 45 minutes, depending on size. Squid should be completely cooked but still quite chewy, as they will be cooked further in the oven. Transfer squid to a bowl of cold water to rest until needed.

Place a large pot of cold water over medium heat. Meanwhile, coarsely chop the garlic. Set a skillet with the oil over medium heat and when the oil is warm, add the garlic and sauté for 5 to 6 minutes. When the water in the pot reaches a boil, add coarse salt to taste, then drain the fennel and dill and add them to the pot along with the dried wild fennel; cook for 5 minutes. With a strainer-skimmer transfer the greens from the pot to the skillet and discard the fennel stalks. Sauté for 5 minutes, then add 1 cup of the cooking water; reserve the remaining water. Season the sauce with the saffron, salt and pepper; lower heat and simmer sauce for 20 minutes more, adding another cup of the cooking water.

When sauce is ready, bring the pot with the remaining water back to a boil, then add the pasta and cook it for 7 to 10 minutes—2 minutes less than for normal *al dente*. Drain pasta and add it to the skillet containing the sauce. Mix very

well, then add the parsley, taste for salt and pepper and sauté for 1 minute.

Preheat the oven to 375 degrees. Pour the wine and olive oil into a 13½-by-9¾-inch glass baking pan, season with salt and pepper and add the garlic. Remove squid from the water and use a pastry bag without its tip, tongs or a fork to fill them with pasta and sauce from the skillet. If there is some leftover sauce, pour it into the baking dish. If the squid are really very large, as they should be, the pasta should be all used up. Close the squid with a toothpick and place them in the prepared baking dish. Bake for 20 minutes.

Transfer baking pan from the oven to a board. Divide *calamari* and juices among individual plates; remove toothpicks. Using a fork, pull out some strands of the pasta (to resemble tentacles) and sprinkle each serving with bread crumbs. The pasta, which has absorbed the flavor of the *calamari,* is the primary attraction, though the *calamari* themselves may be eaten if they are sufficiently tender.

# Linguette alla Bottarga

## FRESH *LINGUETTE* WITH *BOTTARGA* SAUCE

SERVES 6 TO 8.

*Bottarga* is mullet or tuna caviar, salted and pressed to become firm enough to slice. Used for many dishes, especially in Sardinia, its classic and original form is the solid piece, held together by the sac, very thinly sliced, which, when tossed with pasta, breaks up by itself. It is usually combined with only butter, so that nothing interferes with its flavor. Recently, pre-grated *bottarga* in jars has appeared on the market in Italy. It is inferior in flavor to the original form.

To make *bottarga*, the eggs are removed from the female mullet or tuna, still in the sac. They are sprinkled freely with salt and placed between two pieces of aged wood, like a sandwich. A weight is placed on the "sandwich" for several days until it is pressed to a thickness of little more than 1½ inches. After it is freed from the pieces of wood, it is left to dry until it turns the color of a light orange rind. The mullet *bottarga* is considered superior to that of tuna, but both are delicious.

The traditional pasta for this dish is a fresh homemade pasta, in the form of 2-by-4-inch rectangles, but a dried pasta such as spaghetti or tagliatelle is often substituted. We sprinkle the dish with parsley and mint, but we have seen other fresh herbs, such as tarragon or marjoram, used instead.

4 ounces *bottarga*
12 tablespoons (6 ounces) sweet butter, at room temperature
Freshly ground black pepper

FOR THE PASTA
1½ cups finely ground semolina flour
1½ cups unbleached all-purpose flour

4 extra-large egg whites
1 extra-large egg
A pinch of salt

OR

1 pound dried commercial pasta, spaghetti or tagliatelle, preferably imported Italian

TO COOK THE PASTA
Coarse-grained salt

TO SERVE
15 sprigs Italian parsley, leaves only
20 fresh mint leaves

Prepare the sauce: Remove the skin from the *bottarga* and cut it into pieces. Place the butter along with the *bottarga* in a blender or food processor and blend until very smooth. Remove from the blender, add a large pinch of pepper and refrigerate in a glass or crockery bowl, covered, until needed.

Prepare the pasta with the ingredients and quantities listed above (see page 294). Let the dough rest, wrapped in plastic wrap, for 30 minutes in a cool place or on the bottom shelf of your refrigerator. When ready, stretch the layer of pasta a little thicker than usual, to 1/16 inch; on the pasta machine, take it to the next to last setting. Cut the layer of pasta into 4-by-2-inch rectangles using a pastry wheel.

Linguine alla bottarga *in a wonderful ceramic dish, sitting on an ancient Roman bridge near Alghero on Sardinia's northwest coast*

Bring a large quantity of cold water to a boil, add coarse-grained salt to taste, then the pasta and cook it for 3 to 5 minutes, depending on dryness.

Meanwhile, remove the *bottarga* butter from the refrigerator, cut it into pieces and place it on a large serving platter. When the pasta is ready, drain it and transfer to the prepared platter. Mix very well to melt the butter completely. Sprinkle with parsley and mint, mix again and serve.

# Pasta con Ceci ai Finocchi

## WHOLE-WHEAT PASTA WITH CHICK-PEAS AND FENNEL

SERVES 8 TO 10.

In Sardinia, to impart a fennel flavor to soups or sauces, the fresh fennel bulb is used more often than wild fennel as is done in Sicily.

FOR THE SAUCE

1¼ cups dried chick-peas
   Coarse-grained salt
1 large fennel bulb with some stems and leaves
1 large red onion, cleaned
15 sprigs Italian parsley, leaves only
4 ounces pancetta or prosciutto, in one piece

3 tablespoons olive oil
¾ pound very ripe fresh tomatoes or ¾ pound drained canned tomatoes, preferably imported Italian
   Salt and freshly ground black pepper to taste
3 cups lukewarm water

FOR THE PASTA

2 cups whole-wheat flour, sifted
1½ cups unbleached all-purpose flour
4 extra-large eggs
   A pinch of salt

TO COOK THE PASTA

   Coarse-grained salt

TO SERVE

15 sprigs Italian parsley, leaves only

Soak the chick-peas in a bowl of lukewarm water overnight. Next morning, drain the peas, rinse very well under cold running water and place them in a medium-sized casserole with 3 quarts of cold water. Set the casserole over low heat, cover and let simmer for about 45 minutes. By that time the peas should be cooked but still firm. Add coarse salt to taste and simmer for 2 minutes more. Drain the peas, discarding the water, transfer them to a crockery or glass bowl, cover with a wet cotton towel or some paper towels and set aside until needed.

Prepare the fennel sauce: Discard only the top stems if they are a little bit dark. Cut the fennel bulb and the stems into 1-inch pieces and soak in a bowl of cold water for 30 minutes.

Meanwhile, coarsely chop onion and parsley together on a board. Cut pancetta into tiny pieces. Heat the oil in a medium-sized casserole over low heat. When the oil is warm, add the pancetta and sauté for 15 minutes, mixing every so often with a wooden spoon. Add the chopped ingredients, sauté for 5 minutes more, then drain the fennel and add it to the casserole. Mix very well and cook for 5 more minutes. If using fresh tomatoes, cut them into small pieces. Add fresh or canned tomatoes to casserole and cook for another 10 minutes, seasoning with salt and pepper. Add 1 cup of the lukewarm water and cook for 40 minutes, adding the remaining water as more liquid is needed. By that time the fennel should be soft.

Transfer the cooked chick-peas to a second casserole, then pass the fennel sauce in the first casserole through a food mill, using the disc with smallest holes, directly into the new casserole containing the peas. Do *not* mix. Cover and set aside until needed.

As the sauce cooks, prepare the pasta with the ingredients and quantities listed above, mixing the two flours together at the beginning (see page 294). Prepare tagliatelle, but only 8 inches long. The pasta should be rolled out to a thickness of less than 1/16 inch; on the hand pasta machine take roller to the last setting. Let pasta rest on cotton towels until needed.

Bring a large pot of cold water to a boil over medium heat. Meanwhile, coarsely chop the parsley for serving. When the water boils, add coarse salt to taste, then the pasta and cook for 2 to 4 minutes, depending on the dryness.

Meanwhile, heat the sauce to a simmer, taste for salt and pepper and let it cook as the pasta cooks, mixing every so often. Drain the pasta, transfer it to a large warm serving dish. Pour the sauce over the pasta and mix very well. Sprinkle with the chopped parsley and serve hot.

### FROM SARDINIA

# Spaghetti allo Zafferano o alla S. Gavino

## SPAGHETTI WITH SAFFRON, IN THE STYLE OF SAN GAVINO

### SERVES 4 TO 6.

Saffron, long one of the Mediterranean's most treasured spices, has been used in Italy since ancient and medieval times. The most famous Italian saffron comes from Abruzzi, but the lesser known Sardinian saffron is magnificent and widely used in the island's cookery. It is extremely aromatic, and the small town of San Gavino is the center of its cultivation.

1 pound very ripe fresh tomatoes, blanched (see Note, page 40)
A large pinch of ground saffron
4 ounces very well-aged *Pecorino*, freshly grated

½ cup olive oil
Salt and freshly ground black pepper
PLUS
1 pound spaghetti, preferably imported Italian

TO COOK THE PASTA
Coarse-grained salt
TO SERVE
15 sprigs Italian parsley, leaves only
10 large fresh basil leaves

Remove skin and seeds from tomatoes and cut them into large pieces. Place tomatoes in a crockery or glass bowl and coarsely mash them, using a fork. Add the ground saffron, half of the cheese, the olive oil and salt and pepper to taste. Mix very well with a wooden spoon and refrigerate, covered, for at least a half hour or until needed.

Bring a large pot of cold water to a boil, add coarse salt to taste, then the pasta and cook it from 9 to 12 minutes, depending on the brand.

Meanwhile, coarsely chop the parsley and tear the basil leaves into thirds. When the pasta is ready, drain it and transfer to a large serving dish. Pour the cooled sauce over the pasta, mix very well, and sprinkle with the remaining cheese, the parsley and the basil.

# Pasta con i Peperoncini Verdi

## PASTA WITH ITALIAN HOT GREEN PEPPERS

SERVES 6.

The long, thin, hot green peppers known as Neapolitan, frying or wax peppers are also used in Elba for this pasta sauce. The island is just across from the southern Tuscan coast, which is as known for its peppery cooking as Calabria or Abruzzo in the south.

2 Italian hot green peppers*

8 Italian frying peppers (also called Neapolitan, Hungarian or wax peppers)

¼ cup olive oil

2 large cloves garlic, peeled and cut into 3 pieces each

2 large ripe fresh tomatoes (about 1½ pounds) or 1½ pounds drained canned tomatoes, preferably imported Italian

Salt and freshly ground black pepper

OPTIONAL

A large pinch of hot red pepper flakes if the hot green peppers are not spicy enough**

FOR THE PASTA

3 cups unbleached all-purpose flour

3 extra-large eggs

3 tablespoons cold water

A pinch of salt

OR

1 pound dried pasta, such as spaghetti, preferably imported Italian

PLUS

10 large fresh basil leaves

TO COOK THE PASTA

Coarse-grained salt

Cut the hot green peppers in half lengthwise and discard stems, seeds and all the membranes. Cut the peppers lengthwise into thin strips and soak them in a bowl of cold water. Also prepare the frying peppers in the same way, but cut into 1-inch strips. Add them to the bowl with the hot peppers.

Heat the oil in a large skillet over medium heat. When the oil is warm, add the garlic and sauté for 1 minute. Drain the peppers and add them to skillet; sauté for 20 minutes, stirring every so often with a wooden spoon.

If fresh tomatoes are used, cut them into small pieces, without removing skin or seeds. Add fresh or canned tomatoes to skillet, season with salt and pepper, cover and cook for 25 minutes more, stirring the first time after 10 minutes. Sometimes fresh tomatoes are not very juicy, in which case add a little chicken broth.

If using fresh pasta, prepare it with the ingredients and quantities listed above (see page 000). Stretch the layer of pasta to a thickness of a little less than ⅛ inch; on the pasta machine, take it to the notch 2 from the last. Cut the pasta into strands for spaghetti.

Bring a large pot of cold water to a boil over medium heat, add coarse salt to taste, then the pasta and cook until *al dente*, 9 to 12 minutes, depending on the brand, or 30 seconds to 1 minute for fresh. The sauce is ready when all the peppers are completely cooked. Drain the pasta, transfer it to the skillet with all the sauce and mix well. Add the basil and mix. Transfer the contents to a large warm serving platter and serve.

\* It is often more convenient to obtain the long, thin green peppers at Korean or Chinese markets; these are very similar to the Italian ones and more commonly available.

\*\* The hot green peppers vary considerably in spiciness.

# Spaghetti ai Frutti di Mare
## SPAGHETTI WITH SEAFOOD
### SERVES 8.

Porticello, a tiny fishing port near Palermo on the road to Messina, has more fish restaurants than inhabitants. The eateries range from very simple and inexpensive to luxurious. In the evening it is easy to observe the restaurant owners bidding for the best fish from the incoming fishing boats. The seafood sauce for this dish is more complicated than usual in that it has as many ingredients as a traditional *zuppa di pesce* (a fish soup) rather than the simple combination, with or without tomato, that is most common for pasta with seafood. I often go to the restaurant of Nello Il Greco, for the food, of course, but also for Nello's great personality. His longhaired ascetic appearance is belied by his sparkling eyes so full of fun.

1 medium-sized yellow onion, cleaned and finely sliced

½ cup of olive oil

1 pound of pieces of different types of fish, even very inexpensive fish with some heads with a little flesh attached

4 large cloves garlic, peeled

15 sprigs Italian parsely, leaves only

2 pounds fresh and very ripe tomatoes *or* 2 pounds drained canned tomatoes, preferably imported Italian

Salt and freshly ground black pepper

A large pinch of dried oregano

A large pinch of hot red pepper flakes

THE SHELLFISH

1 pound *calamari*, cleaned and cut into 1-inch rings

1 pound medium-sized shrimp, shelled and deveined

3 tablespoons olive oil

2 medium-sized cloves garlic, peeled and cut into slivers

2 pounds clams and mussels, very well scrubbed

1 cup dry white wine

1 lemon
Salt and freshly ground black pepper
Coarse-grained salt

PLUS

1 pound dried spaghetti, preferably imported Italian

TO COOK THE PASTA
Coarse-grained salt

TO SERVE

10 sprigs Italian parsley, leaves only

Soak the *calamari* and shrimp in a bowl of cold water with the lemon, cut in half and squeezed, and a little coarse salt for ½ hour. Soak the sliced onion in a bowl of cold water for 5 minutes. Place a casserole with the oil over medium heat. When the oil is warm, drain the onion and add it to the casserole; sauté for 5 minutes, stirring every so often.

Rinse all the fish for the sauce very well, then add it to the casserole and sauté for 5 minutes more. Meanwhile, finely chop garlic and parsley together on a board and add them to the casserole; sauté 2 to 3 minutes—if using fresh tomatoes, cut them into large pieces, add them to the casserole and cook for 30 minutes. Pour in some lukewarm water if the sauce becomes too thick.

Transfer the sauce to a large bowl. Discard all the fish bones and pass the remaining sauce through a food mill, using the disc with medium-sized holes, into a clean casserole. Set casserole over low heat, season with salt, pepper, oregano and hot pepper and simmer for 5 minutes. Add the *calamari* and simmer gently for 30 to 35 minutes, depending on their size. When they are soft, add the shimp and

cook for 1 minute, then remove casserole from the heat.

Set a large stockpot of cold water over medium heat and a skillet with oil over low heat. When the oil is warm, add the prepared garlic, then drain the clams and mussels and add them to the skillet. Season with salt and pepper and cover skillet. After 2 minutes, discard unopened clams and mussels and add the wine to the casserole. Raise the heat and let the wine evaporate for 4 or 5 minutes.

When the water in the stockpot reaches a boil, add coarse salt to taste, then the pasta and cook it until *al dente*, 11 to 13 minutes, depending on the brand.

Reheat the sauce in the casserole. When the pasta is cooked, drain it, then transfer it to the casserole along with the contents of the skillet—clams, mussels and all their juices. Combine all the ingredients over high heat, mixing very well.

Sprinkle with parsley and serve hot.

## Festive Pastas

The following five recipes are *alta cucina* of the more refined tradition that are used for special occasions or holidays. Feasts generally feature a more elaborate pasta dish than usual, with more ingredients and an impressive presentation. Traditionally these dishes were made just for that holiday, but now the restriction has given way before the desire to eat these special plates more often.

FROM SICILY

# Cannelloni delle Feste
## CANNELLONI FOR THE HOLIDAYS

SERVES 8 TO 16.

According to Sicilian taste, these *cannelloni* are more festive than is usual because the stuffing is made of meat. The cheese used is grated *provolone*. The *cannelloni* are layered in the baking dish and cut through, much the way *lasagne* is served.

FOR THE SAUCE

- 2 pounds rump roast of beef, preferably in one piece
- 2 large red onions, cleaned
- 6 tablespoons olive oil
- 1 cup dry red wine
- 12 basil leaves, fresh or preserved in salt (see page 294)
- 15 sprigs of Italian parsley, leaves only
- 4 celery stalks
- 1 tablespoon rosemary leaves, fresh or

preserved in salt or dried and blanched for a few seconds
Salt and freshly ground black pepper
- 2 pounds canned tomatoes, juice and pulp
About 6 cups chicken or beef broth, preferably homemade

FOR THE PASTA

- 2 cups unbleached all-purpose flour
- 3 extra-large eggs
Pinch of coarse-grained salt

TO COOK THE PASTA

Coarse-grained salt
- 2 tablespoons vegetable oil or olive oil

PLUS

- 2 extra-large egg yolks
Salt and freshly ground black pepper to taste
- 8 tablespoons grated *provolone*, preferably imported Italian

Prepare the sauce: Remove the extra fat from the meat. Finely slice the onions. Pour the oil into a medium-sized casserole and set over medium heat. When the oil is warm, add the onions, place the meat over the onions and sauté for 20 minutes, turning the meat twice. Add the wine and let cook for 15 minutes.

Meanwhile, coarsely chop basil, parsley, celery and rosemary all together on a board. Pass tomatoes and all their juices through a food mill, using the disc with the smallest holes, into a crockery or glass bowl. Add the chopped ingredients, salt and pepper to taste and tomatoes to casserole and enough cold broth to cover the meat completely; simmer, half covered, for 2½ hours.

Meanwhile, prepare the pasta with the ingredients and quantities listed above (see page 294). Stretch the layer of pasta to a thickness less than ¹/₁₆ inch; on the pasta machine, take it to the last setting. Cut into squares as for *lasagne*. Parboil the pasta squares in salted boiling water, cool them in a bowl of cold water mixed with the oil and let the pasta rest on wet towels until needed.

When the sauce is ready, transfer the meat to a chopping board and cut it into pieces. Use a meat grinder to finely grind the meat into a crockery or glass bowl. Take 3 cups of the sauce and pour it into the bowl with the meat. Taste for salt and pepper and mix very well. Add the egg yolks and mix again. Meanwhile, place the remaining sauce over medium heat, taste for salt and pepper and reduce it by half. Preheat the oven to 375 degrees.

Stuff each pasta square with ⅓ cup of the meat stuffing, trying to place the stuffing in the center part of the pasta, so both ends of the *cannelloni* are completely empty. If some stuffing is left over, incorporate it into the sauce. Pour 4 tablespoons of the sauce on the bottom of a 13½-by-8¾-inch glass baking dish. Place 8 *cannelloni* in the prepared dish, sprinkle with 4 tablespoons of the cheese, then one-half of the reduced sauce. Make one more layer of *cannelloni,* cheese and sauce. Bake for 25 minutes.

Remove dish from oven and cool for a few minutes before serving. No extra cheese should be added. Do not serve the individual *cannelloni,* but rather cut through both layers and serve like *lasagne.*

## FROM SARDINIA

# Lasagne alla Sarda con Salsa Noci

## SARDINIAN *LASAGNE* PASTA WITH WALNUT SAUCE

### SERVES 4 TO 6.

In Sardinia, the pasta term *lasagne* does not mean the layered baked pasta, but mostly refers to what is called elsewhere tagliatelle. Here, the humble bread-crumb sauce, found all over Italy, is elevated by the addition of different aromatic herbs, such as parsley, basil and mint, and especially by ground walnuts. The effect is that of a cooked pesto, but without cheese.

FOR THE SAUCE
- 8 ounces shelled walnuts
- 20 sprigs Italian parsley, leaves only
- 10 basil leaves
- 5 mint leaves
- 4 large cloves garlic, peeled

- 1 pound dried tagliatelle, preferably imported Italian
- From ¾ cup to 1 cup olive oil
- Salt and freshly ground black pepper
- 5 tablespoons unseasoned very fine bread crumbs, lightly toasted, preferably homemade

OPTIONAL
- Hot red pepper flakes
TO COOK THE PASTA
- Coarse-grained salt
TO SERVE
- Basil leaves

Finely chop walnuts, parsley, basil, mint and garlic all together or grind them in a blender or food processor.

Bring a large amount of cold water to a boil, add coarse salt to taste, then the pasta and cook until *al dente,* 11 to 13 minutes, depending on the brand.

Meanwhile, set a skillet with the oil over low heat. When the oil is warm, add the chopped ingredients and lightly sauté for 2 minutes. Season with salt and pepper. One minute before the pasta is ready, add the bread crumbs and mix very well.

Drain pasta, transfer it to the skillet and add ½ cup of the cooking water from the pasta. Mix very well and taste for seasoning. Be sure the sauce completely coats the pasta; otherwise add a little more water.

Transfer to a warmed serving dish, sprinkle everything with basil leaves and serve immediately.

# Lasagne per Capo d'Anno

## LASAGNE FOR NEW YEAR'S DAY

### SERVES 8 TO 10.

This dish from Palermo celebrates the New Year with a sauce made with three meats and the wonderful local sheep's milk ricotta, which is incorporated last.

FOR THE PASTA
- 3 cups unbleached all-purpose flour
- ¾ cup very fine semolina flour
- 5 extra-large eggs
- A pinch of salt

TO COOK THE PASTA
- Coarse-grained salt

FOR THE SAUCE
- 8 ounces ground pork
- 8 ounces ground beef
- 3 hot sausages with hot pepper but no fennel seeds, skins removed and crumbled, *or* 9 ounces ground pork mixed with ½ teaspoon of hot red pepper flakes
- 2 tablespoons olive oil
- 4 tablespoons (2 ounces) sweet butter or lard, very soft
- ½ cup dry red wine
- Salt and freshly ground black pepper
- 1½ pounds ripe tomatoes, blanched and seeded (see Note, page 40) or 1½ pounds drained canned tomatoes, preferably imported Italian, seeded
- About 1 cup chicken or meat broth, preferably homemade

PLUS
- 15 ounces ricotta, very well drained
- Salt and freshly ground black pepper to taste

TO SERVE
- Abundant freshly grated ricotta salata or *Pecorino Romano* and *Parmigiano*, mixed

Prepare the pasta with the ingredients and quantities listed above, placing the semolina flour in the well of the all-purpose flour along with the eggs and salt (see page 294). Stretch the layer of pasta, by hand or with a pasta machine, to a thickness of less than $^1/_{16}$ inch. On the pasta machine take the layer of pasta to the last notch. Cut the layer into 12-inch pieces, then use a scalloped pastry wheel to cut each piece lengthwise into thirds. The 3 strips, each about 2 inches wide, must have both long sides cut with the scalloped wheel for, as it is said, *arricciate*. Let the pasta rest on cotton towels until needed.

Prepare the sauce: Mix the ground pork, ground beef and the sausages all together in a small bowl. Place a medium-sized casserole with the oil over medium heat. When the oil is warm, add the meats and sauté for 2 minutes. Mix the butter with the wine and add it to casserole. Mix very well, season with salt and pepper and sauté for 15 minutes more. Add tomatoes, lower the heat and simmer for 40 minutes, adding the broth as needed.

When the sauce is ready, place a large pot of cold water over medium heat. When the water reaches a boil, add coarse salt to taste, then the pasta and cook it for 3 to 5 minutes, depending on the dryness.

Meanwhile, combine the ricotta, 4 or 5 tablespoons of boiling water and salt and pepper to taste in a large serving bowl; mix very well to make the ricotta very creamy. If you are able to get ricotta made from sheep's milk, do not season it with salt and pepper. Drain the pasta, transfer it to the bowl with the ricotta, mix very well and serve immediately. Each serving will be sauced with an abundant portion of the prepared meat sauce, poured over the pasta, and sprinkled with plenty of cheese.

*The cloister of the cathedral at Monreale, the greatest Norman church in Sicily, with famous Byzantine mosaics*

# Timballo di Anellini
## SICILIAN PASTA TIMBALE

SERVES 8 TO 10.

One of Sicily's signature dishes, it exists in several forms, even a modern "fast-food" version. This is a dish from the genuine *alta cucina* of the older nobility, predating the French influence. Here, the *timballo* is wrapped in lettuce leaves and is lighter than one of the more modern versions in which it is wrapped in fried eggplant slices. The pasta on the inside of the *timballo* should be tender, not compacted, which causes it to become tough.

FOR THE *BALSAMELLA*

6 tablespoons (3 ounces) sweet butter

7 tablespoons unbleached all-purpose flour

3 cups whole milk
  Salt and freshly ground black pepper
  A large pinch freshly grated nutmeg

¾ cup freshly grated *Parmigiano*

PLUS

2 extra-large egg yolks

FOR THE MEAT SAUCE

2 medium-sized red onions, cleaned

4 medium-sized carrots, scraped

4 medium-sized celery stalks

½ cup olive oil

2 pounds ground beef

1½ cups dry red wine
  Salt and freshly ground black pepper

6 tablespoons tomato paste

2 cups chicken or meat broth, preferably homemade

1 whole clove

FOR THE LETTUCE LEAVES

2 large heads Romaine lettuce

Coarse-grained salt

FOR THE PEAS

10 ounces fresh peas, shelled *or* 10 ounces frozen "petite" peas
  Coarse-grained salt

1 large clove garlic, peeled

1 pound dried *anellini* (small ring-shaped pasta, about ¼ inch in diameter), preferably imported Italian

TO BAKE THE *TIMBALLO*

4 tablespoons (2 ounces) sweet butter

1 tablespoon olive oil

Prepare the *balsamella* with the butter, flour and milk and season with salt, pepper and nutmeg (see page 295). Transfer the cooked *balsamella* to a crockery or glass bowl and press directly over it a piece of buttered wax paper to prevent a skin from forming. Let the *balsamella* rest until cold, about ½ hour.

Prepare the meat sauce: Finely chop onion, carrots and celery all together on a board. Place a medium-sized casserole with the oil over medium heat. When the oil is warm, add the chopped ingredients and sauté for 5 minutes, stirring with a wooden spoon. Add the meat and sauté for 5 minutes more. Add the wine and season with salt and pepper. Let the wine cook for 15 minutes, then dissolve the tomato paste in the broth and add it to casserole along with the clove. Simmer for 45 minutes, stirring every so often with a wooden spoon.

Meanwhile, blanch the lettuce leaves in boiling salted water for 30 seconds, then transfer them to a bowl of cold water. When cooled, carefully spread them out on paper towels dampened in cold water.

Prepare the peas and the pasta: Bring a large pot of cold water to a boil over medium heat, add coarse salt to taste and the whole clove of garlic. Add the peas and cook them for 10 minutes. Strain peas and transfer them to a large crockery or glass bowl, saving their water. Discard the garlic and set this water back on the heat. When it returns to a boil, add the pasta and cook it for 5 minutes. Drain pasta and add it to the bowl with the peas.

When the *balsamella* is cool, add the *Parmigiano* and the egg yolks and season

*Walking shoeless down the hill from Monreale, as thanks for grace received ("grazia recevuta"), a custom still alive in Palermo*

again with salt, pepper and nutmeg; mix very well.

Lightly butter bottom and sides of a 12-inch spring-form pan and preheat the oven to 375 degrees. Line the spring-form with the blanched lettuce leaves, first placing the leaves over the sides with the bottom part of each leaf overhanging, and then lining the bottom of the form.

When the meat sauce is ready, transfer half of it to a crockery or glass bowl and let rest until cool. Let the other half of the meat sauce rest in the casserole.

Meanwhile, add the *balsamella* to the pasta with the peas, then add ¾ cup of the meat sauce and mix very well. Drain the meat sauce, letting the excess juices pass through the strainer directly into the pasta mixture, then stir to combine everything very well. Arrange half of the pasta on the bottom of the form, top with all of the remaining meat sauce and cover everything with the remaining pasta. Distribute the remaining butter over the top of the pasta, then cover with the overhanging lettuce leaves. Fold the overlapping leaves inward and brush the top with the tablespoon of oil. Wrap the spring-form with aluminum foil to prevent any leakage and bake for 30 minutes. Remove pan from oven, transfer to a large serving platter and let rest for at least 15 minutes before opening.

To serve, reheat the sauce in the casserole. Slice the mold like a pie and serve with some of the reheated meat sauce. Do not expect the slices to hold together; the purpose of wrapping the pasta mixture in the lettuce leaves is to preserve the full flavor of the pasta and its ingredients, not to keep it together when cut. The wedges are expected to fall apart, to be served as a normal pasta with its sauce.

VARIATIONS: *The pasta may be wrapped with thin slices of eggplant, grilled or fried. With fried eggplant the* timballo *will turn out a bit heavier than when lettuce leaves or grilled eggplant are used.*

# *Triangolone alle Verdure*

## PASTA TRIANGLES WITH VEGETABLE STUFFING

### SERVES 8 TO 10.

The oversized stuffed pasta triangles from Capri and the Campania region contain a stuffing that is made by reducing its own sauce.

FOR THE STUFFING AND THE SAUCE

1 pound cleaned Savoy cabbage
  Coarse-grained salt
3 medium-sized carrots, scraped
2 large yellow onions, cleaned
4 ounces prosciutto or pancetta, sliced
2 tablespoons (1 ounce) sweet butter
3 cups chicken or meat broth, preferably homemade

Salt and freshly ground black pepper
½ cup freshly grated *Pecorino Romano*
2 extra-large egg yolks
½ tablespoon fresh marjoram leaves

FOR THE PASTA

2¼ cups unbleached all-purpose flour
4 extra-large egg yolks
2 tablespoons olive oil
¼ cup cold water

Pinch of coarse-grained salt

TO COOK THE PASTA

Coarse-grained salt
2 tablespoons olive oil or vegetable oil

PLUS

4 tablespoons (2 ounces) sweet butter

TO SERVE

Fresh marjoram leaves

Cut the cabbage into thin strips and soak it in a bowl of cold water for ½ hour.

Place a large pot of cold water over medium heat. When the water reaches a boil, add coarse salt to taste, then drain the cabbage and add it to the pot to cook for 5 minutes. Drain cabbage and cool it under cold running water. Let rest until needed.

Coarsely chop carrots and onions together. Line the bottom of a heavy casserole with prosciutto or pancetta, then cut the butter into pats and place them over the prosciutto. First make a layer of the chopped ingredients over the butter, then a layer of the parboiled cabbage. Pour the broth over and season with salt and pepper. Cover the casserole, place it over medium heat and cook for 1 hour, without mixing, but shaking the casserole every so often to be sure that nothing sticks to the bottom.

Pass contents of casserole through a food mill twice, first using the disc with the largest holes, then the one with the smallest holes, into a crockery or glass bowl. Let rest until cold, about ½ hour.

When ready, take 1½ cups of the sauce, transfer it to a small saucepan and reduce it over medium heat until rather thick. Transfer the sauce to a crockery or glass bowl and then let rest until cool. Add the cheese, taste for salt and pepper, then put in the egg yolks and mix very well. This will be the stuffing for the pasta.

Prepare the pasta with the ingredients and quantities listed above (see page 294). Stretch the layer of pasta to a thickness of less than ¹⁄₁₆ inch; on the pasta machine, take it to the last setting.

Cut the layer of pasta into squares (about 6 inches), place 1 heaping tablespoon of the stuffing in the center of each square and fold over one side in order to form a large triangle. Press the edges firmly to seal and immediately put them into the salted boiling water for 2 seconds, then quickly into the cold water with

the oil, and finally onto dampened dish towels. When all the pasta squares are stuffed and in place on the wet towels, prepare the sauce.

Heat the remaining sauce/stuffing in a skillet over medium heat. Add the marjoram and 3 tablespoons of the butter and cook for 5 minutes, seasoning with salt and pepper.

Heavily grease 2 glass baking dishes, using the remaining tablespoon of butter, and preheat the oven to 375 degrees. Arrange all the triangles in the baking dishes and pour the sauce over. Cover pans with aluminum foil and bake for 20 minutes. Serve hot with more fresh marjoram leaves sprinkled on top.

## Pasta with Eggplant

Eggplant is Sicily's favorite vegetable, so much so that the name of a group of favorite pastas is *Pasta alla norma*, which means "pasta in the normal way." (It is not named after Bellini's opera.) *Spaghetti alla siracusana* and the version of *Pasta alla norma* included here are two of the many eggplant and pasta dishes on the island.

FROM SICILY (RAGUSA)
# *Pasta alla Norma*
## PASTA WITH EGGPLANT AND PEPPERS

SERVES 4 TO 6.

2 eggplants (about 2 pounds total)
Coarse-grained salt
2 yellow bell peppers
2 large cloves garlic, peeled
6 large fresh basil leaves
10 sprigs Italian parsley, leaves only
2 medium-sized celery stalks

¼ cup olive oil
2 pounds ripe tomatoes *or* 2 pounds drained canned tomatoes, imported from Italy
Salt and freshly ground black pepper
A large pinch of hot red pepper flakes

PLUS
1 pound dried pasta, such as rigatoni, preferably imported Italian
TO COOK THE PASTA
Coarse-grained salt
TO SERVE
A large amount of fresh basil leaves
½ cup freshly grated *Pecorino Romano*

Peel the eggplants, cut them into 2-inch cubes and place them on a serving platter. Sprinkle with 2 tablespoons of coarse salt and cover eggplant with a weight. Let rest for ½ hour.

Clean the peppers, discarding stems, seeds and inner membranes, and cut them into 2-inch strips. Place in a bowl of cold water. Add basil, garlic, parsley and the celery stalks cut into large pieces to the bowl containing the peppers.

When eggplants are ready, rinse several times under cold running water to remove all the salt, then pat them dry. Drain all the vegetables in the bowl and mix them with the eggplant. With an electric grinder coarsely grind everything together, using the disc with medium-sized holes, into a crockery or glass bowl.

In a medium-sized casserole heat the olive oil over medium heat. When the oil is warm, add the ground ingredients and sauté for 15 minutes, stirring every so often with a wooden spoon. Meanwhile, pass fresh or canned tomatoes through a food mill, using the disc with the smallest holes, into a crockery or glass bowl. Add the tomatoes to the casserole and season with salt, pepper and hot pepper. Cook for 25 minutes or until a thick sauce forms.

Bring a large quantity of cold water to a boil, add coarse salt to taste, then the pasta and cook until a little bit harder than *al dente*, 10 to 11 minutes depending on the brand. Drain the pasta, add it to the casserole containing the sauce and keep cooking, stirring constantly with a wooden spoon, until the pasta absorbs all the sauce and it is perfectly *al dente*.

Transfer the contents of the casserole to a large serving platter and sprinkle everything with the basil leaves and the cheese. Serve immediately.

# Spaghetti alla Siracusana
## SPAGHETTI SYRACUSE STYLE

SERVES 6 TO 8.

2 medium-sized eggplants (not miniature Oriental ones), about ¾ pound total
Coarse-grained salt
½ cup olive oil
2 large cloves garlic, peeled
1½ pounds ripe fresh tomatoes *or* 1½ pounds drained canned tomatoes, preferably imported Italian
4 anchovy fillets preserved in oil, drained

2 heaping tablespoons capers in wine vinegar, drained
2 large yellow bell peppers
2 ounces pitted black Greek olives
20 leaves fresh basil, torn into thirds
Salt and freshly ground black pepper

FOR THE PASTA

3 cups unbleached all-purpose flour
¾ cup very fine semolina
3 extra-large eggs
3 teaspoons olive oil

3 tablespoons cold water
Pinch of salt

OR

1 pound dried spaghetti, preferably imported Italian or

TO COOK THE PASTA

Coarse-grained salt

TO SERVE

Freshly grated *Pecorino Romano*
Fresh basil leaves

Peel the eggplants and cut them into 1-inch cubes. Place the cubes on a serving dish and sprinkle evenly with about 2 tablespoons of coarse salt. Place a second serving platter over the eggplant as a weight and let rest for at least ½ hour.

Rinse the eggplant cubes under cold running water to remove excess salt and pat them dry with paper towels. Place a casserole with the oil over medium heat. When the oil is warm, add the whole cloves of garlic and sauté until lightly golden all over, about 20 seconds. Discard the garlic and put the eggplant in the casserole to cook for about 15 minutes, stirring every so often with a wooden spoon.

Meanwhile, if fresh tomatoes are used, cut them into pieces. Pass fresh or canned tomatoes through a food mill, using the disc with the smallest holes, into a crockery or glass bowl. When eggplant pieces are lightly golden, add the tomatoes and simmer for about 10 minutes.

Cut anchovies into ½-inch strips, rinse capers and cut the peppers lengthwise into less than ½-inch strips, discarding stems, seeds and the inner membranes. Rinse peppers very well under cold running water. Add anchovies, capers, peppers and the pitted olives to the casserole, mix very well and cook for about 15 minutes, adding some lukewarm water as needed. The sauce should be quite homogeneous. Season with salt and pepper.

If using fresh pasta, prepare it with the ingredients and quantities listed above (see page 294). Stretch the layer of pasta to a thickness of a little less than ⅛ inch; on the pasta machine, take it to the notch 2 from the last. Cut the pasta into strands for spaghetti.

Meanwhile, bring a large pot of cold water to a boil over medium heat. Add coarse salt to taste, then the pasta and cook it for about 12 minutes or until *al dente*. If using fresh pasta, the cooking time will be shorter than for dried, but longer than that needed for normal fresh spaghetti made without semolina.

As the pasta cooks, add the basil to the sauce and taste for salt and pepper, then transfer all the sauce to a casserole large enough to contain all the sauce and the pasta. Add 1 cup of the boiling water from the stockpot with the pasta and set casserole over medium heat.

Drain pasta, add it to the larger casserole containing all the sauce, mix very well and cook for 20 seconds more. Transfer contents of casserole to a large serving platter and serve hot, sprinkled with grated *Pecorino* and the basil leaves.

# Vermicelli al Tonno e Capperi

## VERMICELLI IN SICILIAN TUNA SAUCE

SERVES 4 TO 6.

Vermicelli, a long, thick type of spaghetti, is the pasta of choice for fish and seafood dishes in Southern Italy and Sicily. Even the canned tuna in Italy is special, particularly as one gets it from the large chunks (*trancia*) kept preserved in pure olive oil in barrels. It is frequently used for pasta sauces, for stuffings or together with beans; it is not considered a substitute for the plentiful fresh tuna. The especially flavorful capers of Sicily, preserved in either salt or wine vinegar, are world famous, especially those coming from the small island of Pantelleria, which is also famous for its dessert wine *Moscato*.

1 medium-sized red or white onion, cleaned
2 large cloves garlic, peeled
20 sprigs Italian parsley, leaves only
5 tablespoons olive oil
1½ pounds fresh ripe tomatoes *or* 1½ pounds drained canned tomatoes, preferably imported Italian
6 heaping tablespoons capers in wine vinegar, drained
1 (3¼-ounce) can tuna
Salt and freshly ground black pepper

PLUS

1 pound dried long pasta, such as vermicelli (thick spaghetti) or perciatelli (bucatini), preferably imported Italian

TO COOK THE PASTA
Coarse-grained salt

TO SERVE
Fresh basil leaves

Finely slice the onion. Finely chop the garlic and coarsely chop the parsley on a board. Place a medium-sized skillet with the oil over medium heat. When the oil is warm, add the onion and garlic and sauté for 5 minutes, stirring constantly with a wooden spoon. If fresh tomatoes are used, cut them into large pieces. Pass fresh or canned tomatoes through a food mill, using the disc with the smallest holes, into a crockery or glass bowl. Add tomatoes to skillet, along with the parsley and capers. Drain tuna, put it in the skillet and break it up with a fork; let mixture simmer for 15 minutes, seasoning with salt and pepper.

Place a large pot of cold water over medium heat. When the water reaches a boil, add coarse salt to taste, then the pasta and cook for 11 to 13 minutes, depending on the brand, until *al dente*. Drain pasta, add it to skillet containing the sauce, mix well over medium heat for a few seconds, then transfer contents to a large serving platter. Sprinkle evenly with basil and serve hot.

# Culingionis di Patate

## POTATO RAVIOLI

SERVES 6 TO 8.

FOR THE STUFFING
- 1½ pounds all-purpose potatoes
  Coarse-grained salt
- ½ cup olive oil
- 5 sprigs Italian parsley, leaves only
- 3 medium-sized cloves garlic, peeled
- 15 fresh mint leaves
  Pinch of freshly grated nutmeg
  Salt and freshly ground black pepper

- 5 tablespoons freshly grated *Pecorino Romano*

FOR THE PASTA
- 2½ cups unbleached all-purpose flour
- ¼ cup very fine semolina
- 3 extra-large eggs
- ⅓ cup lukewarm water
  A pinch of salt

OPTIONAL
  A pinch of ground saffron

TO COOK THE PASTA
  Coarse-grained salt

TO SERVE
- 8 tablespoons (4 ounces) sweet butter
- 8 tablespoons freshly grated *Pecorino Romano*
  About 20 leaves fresh mint
  Freshly ground black pepper

Boil potatoes in salted water until tender, about 30 minutes.

Peel potatoes and, using a potato ricer, immediately mash them into a crockery or glass bowl. Add the oil and mix very well. Let potatoes rest until cold, about ½ hour.

Meanwhile, prepare the pasta with the ingredients and quantities listed above (see page 294), dissolving the pinch of salt in the lukewarm water and adding the saffron, if using, as the last ingredient. Let the dough rest, wrapped in a lightly dampened towel, for ½ hour.

Finish the stuffing: Finely chop parsley and garlic together on a board and tear the mint leaves into 2 or 3 pieces. Add everything to the potatoes and season with nutmeg and salt and pepper to taste. Add the cheese and mix very well with a wooden spoon.

When the dough for the pasta is ready, knead it for 1 minute more to incorporate some of the leftover flour. Prepare the *culingionis* by stretching the dough to a thickness of less than ⅟₁₆; on the pasta machine, take it to the last setting. Cut the layer of pasta into discs about 2½ inches in diameter. Place a flat tablespoon of the stuffing in the center of half of the discs. Fit a second disc of pasta over stuffing and press the edges of the 2 discs together, closing them firmly. Let the *culingionis* rest on cotton towels until needed.

Set a large pot of cold water over medium heat and place a large oven-proof serving dish on the pot. Cut the butter into pats and place some of them on the dish.

When the water reaches a boil, add coarse salt to taste, then gently drop in the *culingionis*, a few at a time, and cook for 3 to 4 minutes, depending on their dryness, or until they are soft. Use a skimmer to transfer the ravioli to the dish. Be sure no cooking water remains inside the *culingionis*. Make layers of ravioli, adding more pats of butter and sprinkling with mint leaves, cheese and freshly ground pepper. Serve hot.

## Riso—Rice

Rice production in Italy was introduced in the early Renaissance to the misty northern Padana plain by the Venetians and to Naples by the Aragonese Spanish. The Sicilian and Sardinian climates are not suited to this crop and there is no evidence that the Arabs brought rice to Sicily. It is said that the areas of Italy that do not grow rice have created the rice dishes most full of fantasy: the *Sartú* of Naples, the *Supplí* of Rome, the *Bomba di riso* of Tuscany, and finally the *Arancine* of Sicily. But we must not forget the great achievement of the northern Italians, the invention of the risotto method. Originally all Sicilian and Sardinian rice dishes were made with a basis of boiled rice and did not evolve into *risotti* until much later. Resistance to the *risotto* method persists only with the stuffed rice *Arancine*, which to this day are still prepared with the traditional boiled rice.

We present the *Arancine* with several variations of stuffing. Two *risotti* from Sicily follow: *Risotto ai carciofi con piselli*, with artichokes and peas, and *Risotto alla palermitana*, in which the *risotto*, once made, is wrapped in eggplant slices and then baked. From Sardinia we have *Risotto all'aragosta*, with lobster, and *Risotto con rapini*, with *rape* (*broccolirab*).

FROM SICILY

# *Arancine*

## SAVORY RICE BALLS

FOR THE RICE

About 2½ cups chicken or meat broth, preferably homemade, completely defatted
½ pound raw rice, preferably Italian Arborio
2 extra-large eggs
1 extra-large egg yolk
Salt and freshly ground black pepper to taste
4 tablespoons freshly grated *Pecorino Romano* or *Caciocavallo*

FOR THE STUFFING

1 medium-sized red onion, cleaned
2 large sage leaves
4 tablespoons olive oil
4 ounces ground beef (preferably chuck) or veal
½ cup dry white wine
8 ounces ripe fresh tomatoes *or* 8 ounces drained canned tomatoes preferably imported Italian
6 ounces tiny fresh peas *or* 6 ounces frozen "petite" peas

1 cup chicken broth or meat broth, preferably homemade
Salt and freshly ground black pepper

TO FRY THE *ARANCINE*

3 cups vegetable oil (½ sunflower oil, ½ corn oil)
3 extra-large egg whites
1 cup unbleached all-purpose flour
1 cup unseasoned very fine bread crumbs, lightly toasted, preferably homemade
A pinch of salt

Place a medium-sized casserole with the broth over medium heat. When the broth reaches a boil, add the rice and cook for about 14 minutes. The rice should be completely cooked and all the broth absorbed. Let the rice rest in the casserole.

Prepare the stuffing: Finely chop onion and sage together. Heat the oil in a medium-sized saucepan over medium heat. When the oil is warm, add the chopped ingredients and sauté for 5 minutes, stirring with a wooden spoon. Add the meat and cook for 5 minutes more, then pour in the wine and let it evaporate for 5 minutes. Pass tomatoes through a food mill, using the disc with the smallest holes, and add them to saucepan. Simmer for 10 minutes. Add the peas and the broth, season with salt and pepper and cook for 20 minutes more.

*Besides the pyramid-shaped* arancine, *the classic shape used in Siracusa, are various stuffed* focacce *and breads known as* guastelle *or* guastedde, *stuffed mainly with liver and spleen;* inpanade *or* empanade *with vegetable or meat stuffings and a type of the most famous* calzoni *from Naples. In the background is the celebrated cathedral of Siracusa, which incorporated the ancient Greek temple of Athena, whose graceful columns show through the Baroque architecture.*

Strain the sauce, letting the juices drain onto the cooked rice. Leave the strainer with the solids of the sauce suspended over the rice, so any remaining liquid will drain onto it. Add the cheese to the rice and season with salt and pepper.

Heat the vegetable oil in a deep-fat fryer over medium heat, then place the egg whites in a bowl and the flour and the bread crumbs on 2 separate plates. Line a serving platter with paper towels.

When the oil is hot (about 400 degrees) shape 3 almost heaping tablespoons of the rice mixture into a ball. Then, holding the rice in your right hand, with the fingers of your left hand make a well in the rice. Place a heaping tablespoon of the prepared stuffing in the well, then cover the stuffing completely with 1 more heaping tablespoon of the rice. Shape the rice into a ball again, lightly flour it, then dip it in the lightly beaten egg whites and roll it in the bread crumbs.

Fry *arancine* for about 1 minute, making sure the oil completely covers them. When they are golden all over, transfer them to the towel-lined serving platter. Repeat until all the balls are on the dish. Remove the paper towels and serve immediately, still very hot.

## VARIATIONS

1. FOR THE RICE:
a. Boil in salted water instead of broth.
b. Season rice with salt, black pepper and ground saffron or boil with saffron threads, then season with salt and pepper.
c. Mix rice, once boiled, with *balsamella* (see page 295).
d. Use only 1 egg but add a little butter and mix with *balsamella* or not.

2. FOR THE STUFFING:
a. *Balsamella* and peas
b. Mozzarella cut into small cubes
c. *Caciocavallo* cut into small cubes
d. Fontina cut into small cubes
e. Meat ragù with or without peas
f. Vegetables, such as artichokes or asparagus, with a *balsamella* binder

3. FOR FRYING:
a. Fry without any coating.
b. Roll balls in flour.
c. Roll balls in flour, then in lightly beaten egg whites.
d. First dip balls in lightly beaten egg whites, then in bread crumbs.

4. SHAPE:
The *arancine* in Siracusa are egg-shaped.

# Risotto all'Aragosta

## RISOTTO WITH LOBSTER

SERVES 6 TO 8.

1 lobster to yield, once boiled,
½ pound lobster meat
Coarse-grained salt

FOR THE SAUCE

15 sprigs Italian parsley, leaves only

2 medium-sized cloves garlic, peeled
8 tablespoons olive oil

FOR THE RISOTTO

A large pinch of ground saffron

2 cups raw rice, preferably Italian
Arborio
Salt and freshly ground black pepper

TO SERVE

Italian parsley leaves

Cook the lobster in salted boiling water, or if using already cooked lobster, place the meat in a colander and let the colander sit in 6 cups of salted simmering water for 2 minutes. Drain the lobster and save the water. Take half of the meat and finely chop it together with the parsley and garlic.

Heat the olive oil in a medium-sized casserole over low heat. When the oil is warm, add the chopped ingredients and lightly sauté for 2 minutes. Meanwhile, bring the reserved water back to a boil, adding the saffron to it. Add the rice to the casserole containing the sautéed ingredients and sauté the rice for 2 minutes, stirring constantly with a wooden spoon. Start adding the lobster-flavored boiling water, ½ cup at a time, mixing constantly with a wooden spoon. Do not add more liquid until that previously added is absorbed by the rice. You should use a total of 4 cups of the liquid. Season with salt and pepper.

When the risotto is almost ready, about 18 minutes after the rice was added, cut up the remaining lobster meat and add it to the casserole. Mix very well, transfer risotto to a large warmed serving platter and serve hot, sprinkled evenly with parsley leaves.

# Risotto ai Carciofi con Piselli

## ARTICHOKE RISOTTO WITH PEAS

SERVES 6 TO 8.

2 large artichokes
1 lemon
20 sprigs Italian parsley, leaves only
2 medium-sized cloves garlic, peeled
¼ cup olive oil
Salt and freshly ground black pepper
About 7 cups very light chicken broth, preferably homemade

3 cups raw rice, preferably Italian
Arborio

FOR THE PEAS

3 ounces pancetta or prosciutto, in one piece
10 sprigs Italian parsley, leaves only
¼ cup olive oil

½ pound shelled fresh peas *or* ½ pound frozen "petite" peas
Salt and freshly ground black pepper
About 1 cup light chicken broth, preferably homemade

TO SERVE

Freshly grated *Parmigiano*

*The normal size of artichokes in Italy is not very large.*

Soak the artichokes in a bowl of cold water with the lemon, cut in half and squeezed, for ½ hour. Clean the artichokes (see Note, page 190). Finely chop parsley and garlic together on a board.

Place a heavy medium-sized casserole with the oil over medium heat. When the oil is warm, add the chopped ingredients and sauté for 1 minute. Drain artichokes and add them to casserole; sauté for 2 minutes, stirring with a wooden spoon. Add 1 cup of the broth, cover and cook for about 15 minutes or until artichokes are very soft, adding more broth if needed. Season with salt and pepper.

Meanwhile, prepare the peas. Cut pancetta or prosciutto into tiny pieces and coarsely chop parsley on a board. Place a medium-sized skillet with the oil over medium heat. When the oil is warm, add the pancetta and parsley and sauté for 1 minute. Add the peas, mix very well and season with salt and pepper. Add ½ cup of the broth and keep cooking, adding broth, until peas are almost cooked, about 15 minutes. Let peas rest until needed.

When the artichokes in the casserole are very soft and almost dissolved into a rather thick sauce, add rice and sauté for 3 minutes, constantly mixing with a wooden spoon. Heat the remaining broth. Start adding the hot broth ½ cup at a time, constantly mixing and adding more broth only when that previously added is completely absorbed by the rice. You will need about 6 cups of broth in all.

When all the broth but 1 cup is used, transfer contents of skillet, with the peas and all their juices, to the casserole. Mix gently, incorporating the remaining broth. Taste for salt and pepper. Rice should be cooked, but still have a "bite." Transfer *risotto* to a large warmed serving platter and serve hot, accompanied by the *Parmigiano*.

# Risotto alla Palermitana
## RISOTTO WITH EGGPLANT, PALERMO STYLE

SERVES 8 TO 10.

FOR THE SAUCE

1 large red onion, cleaned and thinly sliced
¼ cup olive oil
20 sprigs Italian parsley, leaves only
10 large fresh basil leaves
1 small clove garlic, peeled
2 pounds fresh tomatoes *or* 2 pounds drained canned tomatoes, preferably imported Italian
   Salt and freshly ground black pepper

FOR THE EGGPLANT

3 pounds cleaned peeled eggplant, cut crosswise into slices less than ½ inch thick
   Coarse-grained salt
1 quart vegetable oil (½ corn oil, ½ sunflower oil)
½ cup olive oil

FOR THE *RISOTTO*

1 medium-sized red onion, cleaned
5 sprigs Italian parsley, leaves only
5 fresh basil leaves
¼ cup olive oil

2 tablespoons (1 ounce) sweet butter
1 pound raw rice, preferably Italian Arborio
6 cups boiling chicken or meat broth, preferably homemade
   Salt and freshly ground black pepper

PLUS

1 tablespoon olive oil
8 tablespoons freshly grated *Pecorino Romano* or *Caciocavallo*
40 fresh basil leaves

TO SERVE

Fresh basil leaves

Place the onion in a bowl of cold water for ½ hour. Heat the oil in a saucepan over low heat. When the oil is warm, drain the onion, add it to pan and cook for 15 minutes, stirring every so often with a wooden spoon. Meanwhile, finely chop parsley, basil and garlic all together on a board. Add chopped vegetables to the onion, raise heat to medium and cook for 10 minutes more.

If using fresh tomatoes, blanch them in salted water (see Note, page 40), removing skin and seeds, then cut them into small pieces. If canned tomatoes are used, pass them through a food mill, using the disc with the smallest holes, into a crockery or glass bowl. Add fresh or canned tomatoes to pan and cook for 15 minutes, stirring every so often with a wooden spoon. Season with salt and pepper and cook until a rather thick sauce forms.

Meanwhile, place the sliced eggplant on a serving platter and sprinkle evenly with a tablespoon of coarse salt. Place a second serving platter on top and place weights on the platter. Let rest for at least ½ hour.

When ready, drain the eggplant slices, rinse them under cold running water and pat them dry with paper towels. Heat the vegetable oil and olive oil together in a skillet over medium heat. When the oil is hot (about 375 degrees), fry the eggplant, a few slices at a time, until soft and golden on both sides. Transfer the fried eggplant to a serving platter lined with many layers of paper towels. Let the eggplant rest until needed.

By this time, the tomato sauce should also be ready; transfer the sauce to a crockery or glass bowl and let rest until needed. (The eggplant and the tomato sauce may be prepared as much as several hours in advance.)

About 45 minutes before serving, prepare the *risotto*. Finely chop onion, parsley and basil all together. Heat the oil and the butter in a heavy medium-sized casserole over medium heat and preheat the oven to 375 degrees. Add the chopped

*Eggplants*

ingredients to the casserole and sauté for 2 minutes, mixing with a wooden spoon. Add the rice and sauté for 3 minutes, mixing constantly with a wooden spoon. Start adding the boiling broth, ¾ cup at a time, stirring constantly with a wooden spoon. Do not add more broth until that previously added is completely absorbed by the rice. Season with salt and pepper. When the broth is all used up, *risotto* should be ready, cooked but with a very light bite.

Immediately use the tablespoon of oil to coat a 13½-by-8¾-inch glass baking dish. Arrange half of the fried eggplant in a single layer. Distribute half of the tomato sauce over it, then half of the basil. The next layer uses half of the *risotto*. Then sprinkle all the grated cheese over that as the middle layer. Repeat the layering in reverse order, using the remaining quantities of basil, then *risotto*, tomato sauce and, as the top layer, the eggplant slices. Bake for 20 minutes.

Remove casserole from oven and serve immediately, using a spatula instead of a serving spoon, in order to keep the layering for each portion. Top each serving with a few basil leaves.

# Risotto con Rapini

## RISOTTO WITH *RAPINI*

SERVES 6 TO 8.

1¼ pound *rapini (broccolirab)*, uncleaned
Coarse-grained salt
2 large cloves garlic, peeled

½ cup olive oil
Salt and freshly ground black pepper
A large pinch of hot red pepper flakes

2 cups raw rice, preferably Italian Arborio
About 5 cups chicken broth, preferably homemade

Clean *rapini* very well, discarding the tough stems (should yield about 1 pound of cleaned *rapini*), and soak in a bowl of cold water for ½ hour.

Bring a large pot of cold water to a boil over medium heat. Add coarse salt, then drain the vegetable and add it to pot. Boil for 5 minutes, drain it and cool under cold running water. Coarsely chop *rapini* on a board and cut garlic into small slivers.

Place a heavy medium-sized casserole with ¼ cup of the oil over medium heat. When the oil is warm, add the garlic and sauté for 2 minutes. Add the greens and season with salt, pepper and hot pepper flakes. Mix very well and cook for 5 minutes, stirring every so often with a wooden spoon. Remove half of the sautéed *rapini* to a crockery or glass bowl, cover it and place it in the oven at the lowest temperature.

Add the remaining ¼ cup olive oil to the casserole, then the remaining *rapini*, mix very well and cook for 2 or 3 minutes more. Add the rice to the casserole and sauté for 4 minutes, stirring constantly with a wooden spoon.

Meanwhile, heat the broth over medium heat. Start adding broth, ½ cup at a time, stirring constantly, but do not add more broth until that previously added has been absorbed by the rice. When 4 cups of the broth have been absorbed, *risotto* should be ready, the texture very creamy and the rice *al dente*. Taste for salt and pepper, mix again and serve immediately. Top each serving with some of the reserved *rapini* from the oven.

# Fregola

*Fregola*, or *Succú*, is prepared from coarsely ground semolina, the same used for couscous, but which with water added becomes pasta. The coarse semolina is placed in a large round terra-cotta pot, called *sa scivedda*, sprinkled with salted lukewarm water with or without saffron and dried in the sun in the way that pasta was made in premechanized times. Sardinians and other Italians are adamant that this is not a version of Middle Eastern and North African couscous, but is an ancient indigenous method analagous to the 2,000-year-old Sicilian invention of dried pasta or to the Northern Italian *pasta gratugiata*, in which the flour and water form a ball which is dried and then grated. The dried *fregola* emerges in different sizes: the larger ones are used for pasta, the smaller ones as pastina for broth.

In the *fregola* dishes here, as with all that are made with sauce, the grain is first boiled, then mixed with the sauce and "stewed" in the oven, so the grain is never mushy nor does it fall apart.

FROM SARDINIA

# *Fregola o Succú con i Fagioli*
## *FREGOLA* WITH BEANS

SERVES 6 TO 8.

1 cup dried cannellini or borlotti beans
1 tablespoon olive oil
Coarse-grained salt

FOR THE SAUCE
1 medium-sized red onion, cleaned
2 large cloves garlic, peeled
15 sprigs Italian parsley, leaves only

4 ounces prosciutto or pancetta, in one piece
½ cup olive oil
Salt and freshly ground black pepper
A large pinch of hot red pepper flakes

PLUS
A large pinch of ground saffron,

preferably Sardinian
Coarse-grained salt
1 pound dried saffron *fregola* or freshly prepared *fregola* (see ingredients and Note, page 72)

TO SERVE
Several fresh basil leaves, torn into thirds

Soak the beans in a bowl of cold water overnight. Next morning, drain the beans and put them in a stockpot with 5 quarts of cold water and the oil. Set pot over medium heat and cook the beans for about 45 minutes. Add salt to taste at the very last moment. By that time beans should be cooked but still retain their shape. Drain beans, saving the cooking water, and place them in a crockery or glass bowl, covering with dampened paper towels.

Finely chop onion, garlic and parsley all together. Cut prosciutto or pancetta into tiny pieces. Place a medium-sized casserole, preferably of terra-cotta, with the oil over medium heat. When the oil is warm, add the chopped ingredients and sauté for 5 minutes. Add prosciutto and sauté for 5 minutes more. Add the beans and cook for another 5 minutes. Mix very well and season with salt, pepper and the hot pepper. Remove casserole from heat, cover and let rest until needed.

Place the bean water in a stockpot and set over medium heat. When the water reaches a boil, add the saffron and coarse salt to taste. Add the *fregola* and cook it for about 15 minutes for homemade or longer for dried.

Preheat the oven to 375 degrees. Drain the *fregola*, saving some of the water. Transfer *fregola* to a large oven-proof casserole, then add the beans with all their juices and mix very well. If there is no liquid, add a little of the *fregola* water. Bake, covered, for 10 minutes. Remove from oven, add the basil, mix very well and serve hot.

# Fregola con Patate e Sedano
## FREGOLA WITH POTATOES AND CELERY

SERVES 8.

FOR HOMEMADE *FREGOLA*
- 1 pound couscous, not precooked
- 1 cup cold water
- 1 extra-large egg
  A large pinch of ground saffron, preferably Sardinian
  A pinch of salt

OR
- 1 pound large dried saffron *fregola*, preferably imported from Italy

FOR THE SAUCE
- 2 large cloves garlic, peeled
- 1 medium-sized red onion, cleaned
- 20 large sprigs Italian parsley, leaves only
- 4 large celery stalks
- 3 ounces prosciutto or pancetta, in one piece
- ¼ cup olive oil
- 1¼ pound all-purpose potatoes

Salt and freshly ground black pepper
- 1 to 1½ cups of hot chicken or meat broth, preferably homemade

OPTIONAL
  A large pinch of hot red pepper

TO COOK THE PASTA
  Coarse-grained salt
  A large pinch of ground saffron

TO SERVE
- 30 large fresh basil leaves, left whole

Prepare the fresh *fregola* (see Note).

Finely chop garlic, onion, parsley and celery all together on a board. Cut prosciutto into tiny pieces or coarsely grind it. Heat the oil in a medium-sized casserole over medium heat. When the oil is warm, add the chopped ingredients along with the prosciutto and sauté for 5 minutes, stirring as needed.

Meanwhile, peel the potatoes, cut them into 1-inch cubes and place them in a bowl of cold water to keep them from discoloring. When the sautéed vegetables are ready, drain the potatoes and transfer them to casserole, adding enough cold water to barely cover the potatoes. Season with salt and pepper, reduce heat to low and simmer, covered, for about 15 minutes, adding more water if necessary to keep potatoes covered. After 15 minutes, potatoes should be almost cooked.

Meanwhile, preheat the oven to 375 degrees. Bring a large pot of cold water to a boil. Add coarse salt to taste and the saffron. Add the *fregola* and cook for about 15 minutes for homemade, or longer for dried. If all the juices are absorbed, add 1 to 1½ cups of hot broth. By that time "pasta" should be cooked but still *al dente*. Drain the "pasta" and add it to the potato mixture. With a wooden spoon, mix very well to incorporate all the sauce. Cover and place in the oven for 10 minutes.

Remove "pasta" from oven, uncover pot and sprinkle evenly with the basil leaves. Mix again, transfer everything to a large serving platter and serve hot.

NOTE: *To prepare fresh* fregola, *first preheat the oven to 150 degrees. Place the couscous on a large serving platter and spread it all over. Mix the cold water with the egg, salt and saffron, if using. Drizzle 2 tablespoons of the mixture over the couscous. Start rubbing the grains between the palms of your hands so the water is absorbed uniformly. Transfer the couscous to a jelly-roll pan and bake for 15 minutes. Remove from the oven and let the couscous rest until cool, about 1 hour. Add 2 more tablespoons of the water mixture and repeat the same technique, adding more liquid and rubbing the grain again. Some tiny balls begin to form. Return to the oven for 15 minutes more, remove, let cool and with 2 more tablespoons of the liquid each time, repeat the procedure until all the liquid is used up. At that moment you have formed the* fregola *by attaching grains of couscous together in small balls. If you want to separate the larger ones—to be used boiled with a sauce— from the smaller ones used for broth, place all the* fregola *in a sifter and gently shake it; the small ones will pass through and the larger ones will remain in the sifter.*

Fregola con patate e sedano *with the classic Sardinian serving ladle*

# Fregola ai Gamberi
## SARDINIAN "PASTA" WITH SHRIMP

SERVES 8 TO 10.

1½ pounds unshelled medium-sized shrimp
Coarse-grained salt
1 large lemon

FOR THE TOMATO SAUCE

2 pounds very ripe fresh tomatoes *or* 2 pounds canned tomatoes, preferably imported Italian, undrained
6 large cloves garlic, peeled but left whole
1 cup olive oil

Salt and freshly ground black pepper
½ to 1 teaspoon hot red pepper flakes

PLUS

½ pound couscous (not precooked) prepared as saffron *fregola*, adding the saffron to the ½ cup of cold water and 1 egg (see Note, page 74)
½ pound couscous (not precooked) prepared as *fregola* without saffron (see Note, page 74)

OR

1 pound dried large saffron *fregola*, preferably imported from Italy

TO COOK THE *FREGOLA* (EITHER DRIED OR HOMEMADE)

2 large pinches ground saffron

OPTIONAL

10 large fresh basil leaves

Soak the shrimp in a bowl of cold water for 30 minutes with a little coarse-grained salt and the lemon cut in half and squeezed.

Place a large pot of cold water over medium heat. When the water reaches a boil, add coarse-grained salt to taste, then drain and rinse the shrimp and add them to the pot to cook for 1 minute. Drain shrimp, saving the cooking water, and shell and devein them. Strain the cooking water by passing it through several layers of paper towels or through a coffee filter into a clean stockpot.

Prepare the sauce: If using fresh tomatoes, cut them into pieces. Put fresh or canned tomatoes into a medium-sized saucepan with the garlic and oil and place pan over medium heat; cook for 25 minutes, stirring occasionally with a wooden spoon. Pass contents of pan through a food mill, using the disc with the smallest holes, into a second saucepan. Season with salt, pepper and the red pepper flakes and let simmer for 10 minutes more.

Meanwhile, preheat the oven to 375 degrees. Bring the stockpot of shrimp water back to a boil over medium heat. When the water reaches a boil, add the saffron, then the 1 pound of dried or homemade *fregola*, and cook it for about 15 minutes for homemade, or longer for dried, bearing in mind that it will finish cooking in the oven. As the *fregola* boils, transfer the sauce to a very large oven-proof casserole, add the shrimp and mix well. If basil is used, add it at this point. Drain *fregola*, transfer it to the casserole containing the sauce, mix well again and bake, covered, for 10 minutes. Remove from oven and serve immediately.

## Malloreddus

*Malloreddus* is the dialect name for *Gnocchetti sardi*. They are made by mixing semolina flour with water, eggs and sometimes saffron, then rolling it into a long thin rope which is then divided into 1-inch pieces. Each of these pieces is pressed with the thumb against the bottom of a special basket, called a *ciuliri*, which is made with the stems of dried wheat. They emerge in the classic shape: long, concave and serrated on the outer side. This pasta is popular all over Sardinia and is tossed with different ingredients, depending on the locality.

We present two recipes: *Malloreddus al pomodoro "a stuffai,"* in which the pasta is left to stand in its tomato sauce for some minutes before serving, and *Malloreddus al sugo di pollo,* in a delicious chicken sauce.

FROM SARDINIA

# Malloreddus al Pomodoro "A Stuffai"

## *MALLOREDDUS* IN SCALLION-FLAVORED TOMATO SAUCE

SERVES 4 TO 6.

FOR THE PASTA
- 4 cups very fine semolina flour
- 1½ cups lukewarm water
- A pinch of salt
- A large pinch of ground saffron (optional)

OR
- 1 pound dried *malloreddus*

FOR THE SAUCE
- 10 scallions
- 2 medium-sized cloves garlic, peeled
- 15 sprigs Italian parsley, leaves only
- 2 ounces pancetta, in one piece
- 4 tablespoons olive oil
- 1½ pounds fresh, very ripe tomatoes *or* 1½ pounds drained canned tomatoes,

preferably imported Italian
Salt and freshly ground black pepper

TO COOK THE PASTA
- Coarse-grained salt

TO SERVE
- 20 basil leaves, torn into thirds
- 4 tablespoons freshly grated *Pecorino Sardo*

Prepare the fresh pasta using the ingredients and quantities listed above, placing the saffron in the well with the salt and water (see technique, page 294). Shape the dough into *malloreddus* and let the pasta rest on cotton towels until needed.

Clean the scallions, removing the green part. Coarsely chop scallions, garlic and parsley all together on a board. Cut pancetta into thin pieces. Place a medium-sized skillet with the oil over medium heat. When the oil is warm, add the chopped ingredients and pancetta and sauté for 5 minutes, stirring with a wooden spoon every so often.

Meanwhile, if using fresh tomatoes, pass them through a food mill, using the disc with the smallest holes, into a crockery or glass bowl. Add fresh or canned tomatoes to skillet and cook for 20 minutes, seasoning with salt and pepper and mixing occasionally.

Bring a large pot of cold water to a boil. When the water reaches a boil, add coarse salt to taste, then the *malloreddus* and cook the fresh pasta for 5 to 9 minutes, depending on dryness, or the dried pasta for about 15 minutes or until *al dente.* Drain the pasta and transfer it to a large bowl. Pour the sauce over the pasta, add the basil and mix very well. Cover bowl for 5 minutes before serving. Sprinkle each serving with cheese and a twist of black pepper.

*The sauced Malloreddus, with a ceramic hen, the symbol of Sardinia, and a handwoven rug in typical pattern from the island*

# Malloreddus al Sugo di Pollo

## FRESH SARDINIAN *CAVATELLI* WITH CHICKEN SAUCE

SERVES 6 TO 8.

FOR THE PASTA

4 cups very fine semolina flour

1½ cups lukewarm water

A pinch of salt

A large pinch of ground saffron

OR

1 pound dried *malloreddus*

TO COOK THE PASTA

Coarse-grained salt

FOR THE SAUCE

1 chicken (about 3½ pounds), cut into 16 pieces

2 tablespoons (1 ounce) sweet butter or lard

1 tablespoon olive oil

Salt and freshly ground black pepper

2 large red onions, cleaned

2 pounds very ripe tomatoes *or 2* pounds drained canned tomatoes, preferably imported Italian

2 tablespoons tomato paste

2 large pinches ground saffron

20 basil leaves, fresh or preserved in salt (see page 294)

TO SERVE

Freshly grated aged *Pecorino Sardo* or *Pecorino Romano*

Prepare the fresh pasta with the ingredients and quantities listed above, placing the saffron in the well of the flour with the water and salt (see technique for mixing and kneading, page 294). Shape the dough into *malloreddus*. Let the pasta rest on cotton towels until needed. *Malloreddus* are better if prepared 1 or 2 days in advance.

Prepare the sauce: Wash the chicken carefully and pat it dry with paper towels. Place a medium-sized casserole with the butter and oil over medium heat. When the butter is melted, add the chicken and sauté for 5 minutes, stirring with a wooden spoon. Season with salt and pepper. Meanwhile, finely chop the onions on a board and pass fresh or canned tomatoes through a food mill, using the disc with the smallest holes, into a crockery or glass bowl. Transfer the chicken to a serving platter, using a strainer-skimmer, so all the juices remain in the casserole. Add the onion to the casserole and sauté for 10 minutes or until translucent. Add the tomatoes and tomato paste, mix very well and season with the saffron; simmer for 2 minutes. Return the chicken to the casserole, add the basil and simmer for 30 minutes, stirring every so often with a wooden spoon. Taste for salt and pepper.

Set a pot of cold water over medium heat. When the water reaches a boil, add coarse salt to taste, then the pasta and cook the fresh pasta for 5 to 9 minutes, depending on the dryness, or the dried pasta for about 15 minutes or until *al dente*. Drain the pasta, transfer it to the casserole with the sauce and mix very well for 30 seconds over low heat. Serve with freshly grated *Pecorino*.

## Gnocchi

Sardinia's most typical potato *gnocchi* are *Gnocchi alla sassarese*. Another type of potato *gnocchi* are the remarkable ones from Elba, *Gnocchi di patate al sugo di piccione*, in squab sauce. Unlike the shell-shaped *Gnocchetti sardi*, these potato *gnocchi* are both rolled into the rope and cut but are not shaped.

The main criterion for good *gnocchi* is lightness. This is achieved most easily by cooking the potatoes in salted boiling water, uncovered, so the steam evaporates, then ricing the peeled potatoes while still very hot and letting them, once riced, stand until they are cold. In this way they will absorb much less flour. Adding grated cheese or eggs to the potatoes, as is sometimes done, does make them tougher and gummy. Only seasonings such as salt, saffron, black pepper or nutmeg, depending on the location, should be added. The squab sauce from Elba is interesting, because the sequence of adding the aromatic herbs is highly unusual and the *gnocchi* are served with a tiny piece of the squab itself.

FROM SARDINIA

# Gnocchi di Semolino alla Sarda
## "PILLAS" OR SEMOLINA *GNOCCHI*

### SERVES 8 TO 10.

*Gnocchi di semolino alla sarda*, "pillas" in dialect, is dressed with a meat sauce, which as is typical for Sardinia, is made with several different meats, here pork and beef.

The butter that is used in this recipe is a modern substitute for lard as is the butter used in most of the Sardinian and Sicilian recipes. Lard was traditionally very much used, and butter is for the most part quite foreign to these islands and to Southern Italy in general.

FOR THE *GNOCCHI*
5½ cups whole milk
   A large pinch of ground saffron
¾ pound very fine semolina
   Salt and freshly ground black pepper
   Freshly grated nutmeg to taste
4 tablespoons (2 ounces) sweet butter
2 extra-large egg yolks
1 extra-large egg
¼ cup lukewarm chicken broth, preferably homemade

2 ounces freshly grated aged *Pecorino*
FOR THE SAUCE
¾ pound boneless pork loin, in one piece
¾ pound beef, in one piece
¼ cup olive oil
4 tablespoons (2 ounces) sweet butter
1 cup dry red wine
1 medium-sized red onion, cleaned
2 pounds very ripe tomatoes *or* 2

pounds drained canned tomatoes, preferably imported Italian
2 medium-sized cloves garlic, peeled
5 basil leaves, fresh or preserved in salt (see page 294)
   Salt and freshly ground black pepper
PLUS
8 tablespoons (4 ounces) sweet butter, cut into pats
8 tablespoons freshly grated aged *Pecorino*

Prepare the *gnocchi*: Wet the bottom of a medium-sized casserole with cold water, then pour in the milk and set casserole over medium heat. When the milk reaches a boil, add the saffron, then start adding the semolina, very slowly, continuously stirring with a wooden spoon to prevent lumps from forming. When all the semolina is incorporated, cook for about 10 minutes more, still stirring constantly with the spoon. Season with salt, pepper and nutmeg, then add the butter and cook for 2 minutes more. Meanwhile, line with plastic wrap a 15½-by-10½-inch jelly-roll pan and lightly oil it.

When the semolina is ready, remove casserole from the heat, stir for a few seconds more, then mix the egg yolks and the whole egg with the broth. Add the egg mixture to the semolina along with the grated cheese and stir very well. Transfer mixture to the prepared pan and spread it out evenly, using a spatula moistened with hot water. Let the semolina rest until cold, a minimum of 1 hour. (Semolina may be prepared even one day in advance.)

Prepare the sauce: Remove all the extra fat from the meats. Place a medium-sized casserole with the oil and butter over medium heat. When the butter is melted, add the meat and sauté for 10 minutes, turning it several times. Add the wine and let it evaporate for 10 minutes more.

Meanwhile, coarsely chop the onion. If tomatoes are fresh, cut them into small pieces. Pass fresh or canned tomatoes through a food mill, using the disc with the smallest holes, into a crockery or glass bowl.

Transfer the meat to a chopping board, cut it into thin strips and coarsely grind it in a meat grinder. Return ground meat to the casserole along with the chopped onion and cook for 5 minutes more. Finely chop garlic and basil together. Add tomatoes and the chopped ingredients to the casserole, season with salt and pepper and cook, covered, for 1 hour, mixing occasionally.

When ready, unmold the cooled semolina onto a chopping board and cut it into 3-inch discs. Use 2 or 3 pats of the butter to heavily butter a 13½-by-8¾-inch glass baking dish. Preheat the oven to 375 degrees.

Assemble the dish: Arrange half of the semolina discs in a single layer in the prepared baking dish. Top with half of the sauce, then half of the grated cheese and half of the remaining pats of butter. Repeat same procedure, but top layer should be of sauce, not of cheese. Bake for 25 minutes and serve hot.

# Gnocchi di Patate al Sugo di Piccione
## POTATO GNOCCHI WITH A SQUAB SAUCE

SERVES 8 TO 10.

2 squab, with their innards
1 large red onion, cleaned
2 medium-sized celery stalks
2 medium-sized carrots, scraped
½ cup olive oil
1 cup dry white wine
1 tablespoon tomato paste
1½ pounds fresh tomatoes *or* 1½ pounds drained canned tomatoes, preferably imported Italian

A large pinch of hot red pepper flakes
Salt and freshly ground black pepper to taste
20 sprigs Italian parsley, leaves only
2 large sage leaves, fresh or preserved in salt (see page 294)
2 cups chicken broth, preferably home-made

FOR THE GNOCCHI
3 pounds all-purpose potatoes
Coarse-grained salt
1 cup unbleached all-purpose flour
Salt to taste
Large pinch of grated nutmeg
TO COOK THE GNOCCHI
Coarse-grained salt
TO SERVE
Freshly grated *Parmigiano*

Carefully clean and wash the squab, saving the liver, heart and gizzard. Cut the squab in half, then cut each half into 3 pieces.

Finely chop onion, celery and carrots all together on a board. Heat the oil in a medium-sized casserole over medium heat. When the oil is lukewarm, add the chopped ingredients and sauté for 15 minutes, stirring with a wooden spoon.

Meanwhile, finely chop the livers, hearts and gizzards all together and add to casserole along with the squab pieces; sauté for 10 minutes, turning the squab pieces over twice. Add the wine and let it evaporate for 10 minutes more.

Place the tomato paste in a medium-sized crockery or glass bowl. If fresh tomatoes are used, cut them into small pieces. Pass fresh or canned tomatoes through a food mill, using the disc with the smallest holes, into the bowl with the tomato paste and mix very well. Pour the mixture over the sauteéd squab, season with the hot pepper and salt and black pepper to taste and simmer for 2 minutes. Finely chop parsley and sage all together and add to casserole. Mix very well and let the sauce simmer for 25 minutes, adding 1 cup of the broth as needed.

The squab should be cooked and quite soft by this time. Transfer the squab pieces to an oven-proof china or glass bowl, cover it and place it in the oven just with the pilot on or turned to "warm." Add the remaining cup of broth to casserole with the squab sauce, taste for salt and pepper and reduce for 15 minutes more, stirring every so often with a wooden spoon.

Meanwhile, place potatoes in a stockpot, add coarse salt to taste and enough cold water to cover potatoes completely. Set pot, uncovered, over medium heat and cook until potatoes are soft, about 35 minutes, depending on their size. When ready, peel potatoes, still very hot, and pass them through a potato ricer onto a board. Let the riced potatoes rest until cold.

Bring a large pot of cold water to a boil over medium heat. Knead ¾ cup of the flour into the riced potatoes and season with salt and nutmeg. Cut the potato mixture into several pieces and, using your fingers and the palms of your hands, roll out "ropes" about 1 inch in diameter, incorporating the remaining ¼ cup of flour. Cut each rope into ½-inch pieces.

Transfer the sauce to a very large skillet and reduce until quite thick, over low heat, about 2 minutes. When the water in the stockpot reaches a boil, add coarse salt to taste, then the *gnocchi*, 10 to 15 at time, and when they come to the surface of the water, use a skimmer to transfer them into the sauce in the skillet. Repeat the same procedure until all the *gnocchi* are in the sauce. Serve immediately with freshly grated *Parmigiano* and a small piece of the squab.

NOTE: *1 chicken liver can be substituted for the squab innards.*

# Gnocchi alla Sassarese
## POTATO GNOCCHI

SERVES 8 TO 10.

FOR THE *GNOCCHI*

- 3 pounds all-purpose potatoes
  Coarse-grained salt
- 1 cup unbleached all-purpose flour
  Salt to taste
- 2 large pinches ground saffron, preferably Sardinian

FOR THE SAUCE

- 6 ounces pancetta or prosciutto, in one piece

- 1 large red onion, cleaned
- 15 sprigs Italian parsley, leaves only
- 15 basil leaves, fresh or preserved in salt (see page 294)
- 8 large sage leaves, fresh or preserved in salt (see page 294)
- ½ cup olive oil
- 2 pounds fresh tomatoes or 2 pounds drained canned tomatoes, preferably imported Italian

Salt and freshly ground black pepper
About 1 cup chicken or meat broth, preferably homemade

TO COOK THE *GNOCCHI*

Coarse-grained salt
Large pinch of ground saffron, preferably Sardinian

TO SERVE

Freshly grated *Pecorino Romano*

Place potatoes in a stockpot, add coarse salt to taste and enough cold water to cover potatoes completely. Set pot, uncovered, over medium heat and cook until potatoes are soft, about 40 minutes, depending on their size.

Meanwhile, prepare the sauce: First cut pancetta or prosciutto into small pieces, then use a meat grinder to coarsely grind. Finely chop onion, parsley, basil and sage all together on a board.

Place a medium-sized casserole with the oil over medium-high heat. When the oil is warm, add the ground meat along with the chopped ingredients and sauté for 15 minutes, stirring every so often with a wooden spoon. If fresh tomatoes are used, cut them into pieces, then pass fresh or canned tomatoes through a food mill, using the disc with the smallest holes, into a crockery or glass bowl. Season the sautéed ingredients with salt and pepper and add the broth. Lower heat and simmer for about 15 minutes. Add the tomatoes and cook for 35 minutes, stirring every so often with a wooden spoon.

When potatoes are ready, peel them, still very hot, and pass them through a potato ricer, using the disc with the smallest holes, onto a board. Let the riced potatoes rest until cold.

Bring a large pot of cold water to a boil over medium heat. Knead ¾ cup of the flour into the riced potatoes and season with salt and the saffron. Cut the potato mixture into several pieces and, using your fingers and the palms of your hands, roll out "ropes" about 1 inch in diameter, incorporating the remaining ¼ cup of flour. Cut each rope into ½-inch pieces.

Transfer the sauce to a very large skillet and reduce over low heat, until quite thick, about 5 minutes.

When the water in the stockpot reaches a boil, add coarse salt to taste and the saffron. Add the *gnocchi*, 10 to 15 at a time, and when they come to the surface of the water, use a skimmer to transfer them into the sauce in the skillet. Repeat the same procedure until all the *gnocchi* are in the sauce. Serve hot with freshly grated *Pecorino Romano*.

## Polenta

In both Sardinia and Sicily, polenta is a full dinner by itself, not a first course, like the soft polenta *Batuffoli* from Livorno, or the accompaniment to a main dish, like the famous combination of liver with onions and grilled polenta of Venice.

Our Sicilian polenta contains both *rape* and ground pork. Sometimes the *rape* cooking water rather than broth is used to make the polenta, but the resultant strong taste may not be pleasing to everyone. Making it with broth is also authentic.

*Polenta sarda* has not only sausages or ground pork but a lot of vegetables and aromatic herbs, as well as mozzarella, which is added at the last moment.

FROM SICILY

# *Polenta alla Siciliana*
## POLENTA IN THE SICILIAN STYLE

SERVES 8 TO 10.

1½ pounds *rape* (*broccolirab*)
   Coarse-grained salt to taste
1 large clove garlic, peeled
1½ cups olive oil

1 pound ground pork
   Salt and freshly ground black pepper
½ teaspoon hot red pepper flakes
7 cups cold chicken broth, defatted
½ pound coarse stone-ground yellow

cornmeal, preferably imported Italian
PLUS
8 to 10 teaspoons olive oil

Clean *rape* very well, discarding the tough stems (should yield about 1 pound of cleaned *rape*), and soak it in a bowl of cold water for ½ hour.

Bring a large pot of cold water to a boil, add coarse-grained salt to taste, then drain the *rape* and add it to pot. When the water returns to a boil, cook the greens for 8 minutes. Drain and cool greens under cold running water. Lightly squeeze the *rape* and coarsely chop it on a board, then coarsely chop the garlic separately.

Place a large heavy casserole with the oil over medium heat. When the oil is warm, add the pork and garlic and sauté for 10 minutes, stirring every so often with a wooden spoon. Add the *rape*, salt and pepper to taste and the red pepper flakes. Sauté for 10 minutes more, mixing the greens into the pork. Add the broth to casserole and when it reaches a boil, start pouring the cornmeal in a very slow stream, simultaneously stirring with a wooden spoon. Be sure to pour the cornmeal slowly and steadily and to keep stirring, so that the polenta does not become very lumpy. Stir slowly, without stopping, for 55 minutes from the point when all the cornmeal was added to the pot.

Five minutes before the polenta is ready, taste for salt and pepper. Remove from heat and serve immediately, directly from the casserole, with 1 teaspoonful of oil over each serving.

# Polenta Sarda con Salsicce
## POLENTA WITH SAUSAGES, SARDINIAN STYLE
SERVES 8 TO 10.

4 ounces pancetta, in one piece
1 large celery stalk
2 medium-sized carrots, scraped
1 medium-sized red onion, cleaned
2 small cloves garlic, peeled
10 sprigs Italian parsley, leaves only
3 basil leaves, fresh or preserved in salt (see page 294)
4 tablespoons olive oil
8 ounces ripe tomatoes *or* 8 ounces drained canned tomatoes, preferably imported Italian
Salt and freshly ground black pepper

FOR THE POLENTA
16 cups cold chicken broth, defatted, or cold water
¾ pound coarse stone-ground yellow cornmeal, preferably imported Italian
4 ounces mozzarella, in small pieces

8 ounces Italian sausages with hot pepper but without fennel seeds, skins removed and crumbled *or* 8 ounces of ground pork mixed with salt, black pepper and hot pepper flakes
Salt and freshly ground black pepper

TO SERVE
Freshly grated *Pecorino Romano*

Cut pancetta into tiny pieces. Finely chop celery, carrots, onion, garlic, parsley and basil all together on a board. Place a medium-sized saucepan with the oil over medium heat. When the oil is warm, add the pancetta along with the chopped ingredients and sauté for 5 minutes, stirring every so often with a wooden spoon.

If fresh tomatoes are used, cut them into pieces, then pass fresh or canned tomatoes through a food mill, using the disc with the smallest holes, into a crockery or glass bowl. Add tomatoes to saucepan, season with salt and pepper and mix very well. Keep cooking for 20 minutes more, adding some lukewarm water if the sauce begins to stick. At the end of the 20 minutes, the sauce should be rather thick and homogeneous. Let it rest until needed.

Bring the broth or cold water to a boil in a medium-sized stockpot over medium heat, then pour in the cornmeal in a very slow stream, simultaneously stirring with a wooden spoon. Be sure to pour the cornmeal slowly and steadily and to keep stirring, so that it does not become lumpy. Stir slowly, without stopping, for 25 minutes from the time when all the cornmeal was added to the pot.

Add the prepared sauce to the polenta and keep stirring for 10 minutes more. Add the mozzarella and the sausages to the polenta and keep stirring for 20 minutes more.

Just 5 minutes before ready, taste for salt and pepper. Serve hot with freshly grated *Pecorino Romano* sprinkled over each individual serving.

*Couscous di Carloforte (recipe on following pages)*

# Couscous di Carloforte
## COUSCOUS WITH MIXED MEATS AND FOWL

### SERVES 8 TO 10 AS FIRST COURSE.

Carloforte is a small island off Sardinia, frozen in time. Though this is an island of fishermen, its famous couscous is dressed with a rich meat sauce. Instead of serving the grain along with pieces of meat and vegetables, the combination of pork, beef, lamb and chicken is cooked together, ground and combined in a sauce which is mixed with the cooked grain. Served as a first course (in place of pasta or soup), it is nonetheless the pride of the island, whose inhabitants consider it the most refined of couscous dishes, and many visitors agree. (Sprinkling the couscous with just a little water to help it steam does not change it to a pasta as does the larger amount of water used to make *fregola*.)

FOR THE SAUCE

1 pork chop (about 4 ounces of meat)
8 ounces beef chuck or sirloin
8 ounces lamb shoulder, extra fat removed
2 chicken legs *or* 1 chicken leg with the thigh attached
4 cloves garlic, peeled
2 tablespoons fresh rosemary leaves
6 large fresh sage leaves
Salt and freshly ground black pepper
6 tablespoons olive oil

PLUS

3 celery stalks
15 sprigs Italian parsley, leaves only
1 carrot, scraped
1 small red onion, cleaned
6 tablespoons olive oil
1 cup dry red wine
3 tablespoons tomato paste
5 cups very light broth, completely defatted, preferably homemade
1 whole clove

Salt and freshly ground black pepper

FOR THE COUSCOUS

1 pound couscous, not precooked
A large pinch ground saffron, preferably Sardinian
½ teaspoon fine salt
2 tablespoons olive oil
10 bay leaves
Coarse-grained salt

TO SERVE

5 tablespoons olive oil

Remove bones from any meats that have them, cut the meat into large pieces and save the bones. Finely chop garlic, rosemary and sage all together on a board. Place the meat and the bones in a crockery or glass bowl, then add the chopped ingredients, salt and pepper to taste and the oil. Mix very well and marinate, in the refrigerator, for at least 1 hour before using it, mixing twice more.

Meanwhile, coarsely chop celery, parsley, carrot and onion all together on a board. Place a medium-sized casserole with the oil over medium heat. When the oil is warm, add the chopped ingredients and carefully sauté for about 10 minutes, stirring almost constantly. All the ingredients should be very well sautéed until light golden in color (more than translucent but not at all burned). Add contents of the bowl containing the marinated ingredients to the casserole, mix very well and cook, stirring frequently, for about 15 minutes.

Place couscous in a large bowl (called a *mafaradda*). Sprinkle with the ground saffron and the salt, then drizzle 1 tablespoon of cold water on top. Start rubbing the couscous between the palms of your hands, incorporating all the water. Keep repeating, adding 3 more tablespoons of water, one at a time, and oiling your palms several times, using the 2 tablespoons of oil.

Bring a large pot of cold water to a boil over medium heat. The mouth of the pot should be wide enough that a colander could be inserted inside. When the water reaches a boil and the couscous is ready to be cooked, add salt to the boiling water and line a colander with a thick cheesecloth or cotton towel. On top of the cloth arrange all the bay leaves, then place the prepared couscous over them. Fold the overhanging sides of the cloth over the couscous. Cover colander and insert it in the pot of boiling water. If the space between the colander and the pot is too wide and a lot of steam escapes, quickly make a thick dough using flour and water and with this dough seal the space completely, or seal it by wetting a large towel and tying it all around. Cook the couscous for 1½ hours, mixing it two or three times. Be sure that you always have a lot of water underneath in order to produce a lot of steam to cook this coarse-ground semolina. Keep the finished couscous warm over simmering water as you prepare the sauce.

Continue with the sauce: Add wine to the casserole, raise the heat and cook for 2 to 3 minutes. Dissolve the tomato paste in 1 cup of the broth and add it to the casserole, along with the clove. Lower the heat and cook for 20 minutes more, adding extra broth as needed, about 2 more cups.

When ready, remove all the meats from the casserole, discard the bones and coarsely grind the meats together into a crockery or glass bowl. Return the ground meat to the casserole, season with salt and pepper and cook for 15 minutes more, stirring every so often with a wooden spoon. Add 1 more cup of broth and simmer for 1½ hours, adding the remaining cup of broth as needed. Taste for salt and pepper. For the seasoning, keep in mind that the cooked semolina need not have a strong flavor. After the 1½ hours, the sauce should be rather thick and smooth. Remove the clove and discard.

Transfer the cooked couscous from the colander to a large bowl, keeping or discarding the bay leaves as you prefer. Then add two-thirds of the sauce and mix very well. Cover the bowl and wrap it with towels to keep the couscous warm and to allow it to rest enough to absorb and become integrated with the sauce.

When ready to serve, add the olive oil, and mix very well. Divide the seasoned couscous among individual warmed dishes and top with the remaining sauce.

# SOUPS

Sardinia, more than the other islands—indeed perhaps more than any other region of Italy—specializes in soups. It is in these dishes rather than in independent creations that Sardinia's vegetables are shown to best advantage. In place of separate vegetable dishes more ambitious legume preparations are offered. In the soups, however, the legumes are combined with one or more defining vegetables. In our sampling these include combinations that individually feature spinach, celery or fennel bulbs.

Sicily has some trademark soups, the most interesting and most common of which is based on an ingredient that is rarely available outside of the island—the long leaves and stems of the zucchini plant, called *tenderumi*. Though *tenderumi* are ignored by the rest of the world, the Sicilians have made them their specialty. But I do stress Sicily's vegetable dishes in another chapter, as they too play an important role in this rich repertoire.

Elba and Giglio have their own traditional soups based on the Tuscan tradition, a sampling of which is also included.

*The* tenderumi *is the basis of one of the most common Sicilian soups (see page 88).*

# Minestra o Zuppa di Sedani, Zuppa di Fave and La Favata

A *zuppa* always contains bread in some form. Homemade croutons, small pieces of bread, freshly fried or toasted, may be added at the last moment in place of bread slices. Sardinian soups most often employ pieces of their own flat *carta da musica* bread. Sometimes this bread is broken into large pieces, soaked, made into sandwiches of several layers with cheese in between, pressed together, fried and then added to the soup. The difference between *zuppa* and *minestra* is that the latter uses some short pasta in place of the bread.

I have noticed that the celery in Sardinia is often round rather than concave and so is very meaty and fuller in flavor than the normal celery used elsewhere mostly as an aromatic herb, but the recipe here yields good results.

Fava beans, along with the legumes chick-peas and lentils, are the only bean types that existed in the Mediterranean before Columbus. Fresh favas, which have a short season, as well as dried, shelled or unshelled favas, are used in a variety of soups, appetizers and vegetable courses in Sicily and Sardinia. Elba and the other islands tend to use only fresh favas.

In addition to favas, the Sardinians also include a green vegetable, such as the spinach in the *zuppa di fave.*

*La Favata* for Maundy Thursday is one of the most elaborate holiday preparations in Sardinian cooking. It is not difficult to make, but has many ingredients, mostly a variety of pork meats. Our version is relatively simple because many of the lesser used pork cuts traditionally included are available only when a pig is freshly slaughtered. We use only 3 meats; on the island as many as 10 or 15 might be included. In the winter, when a pig is killed, the farmers all over Italy use all the parts in some preparation, most usually a type of salami.

# Minestra o Zuppa di Sedani
## CELERY SOUP

SERVES 6 TO 8.

8 cups cold water
1 pound celery stalks, cleaned and all
the threads removed
Coarse-grained salt

FOR THE SOUP

2 medium-sized cloves garlic, peeled
2 medium-sized carrots, scraped
1 small red onion, cleaned

10 sprigs Italian parsley, leaves only
5 tablespoons olive oil
4 ounces ground pork
4 cups boiling water
Salt and freshly ground black pepper

PLUS

Several pieces of *carta da musica* (see
page 242), broken into small pieces,

*or* ½ pound of dried short pasta,
such as *chiocciole* (snails), preferably
imported from Italy

TO SERVE

Abundant freshly grated *Pecorino
Romano* or *Parmigiano Reggiano*

Place a medium-sized stockpot with the 8 cups of cold water over medium heat.
Cut the cleaned celery stalks into 8-inch pieces.

When the water reaches a boil, add coarse salt to taste, then the celery and
cook for 10 minutes.

Meanwhile finely chop garlic, carrots, onion and parsley all together on a
board.

Place a second medium-sized stockpot with the olive oil over medium heat.
When the oil is warm, add the chopped ingredients along with the ground pork
and sauté for 10 minutes.

When ready, use a strainer to transfer the celery from the stockpot to a board
and save its cooking water, transferring it to the second stockpot containing the
sautéed chopped vegetables and aromatic herbs. Simmer for 20 minutes.

Cut each piece of celery into three strips. Add the 4 cups of boiling water to
the stockpot and cook for 10 minutes more before adding the celery. Season with
salt and pepper. Add the pasta and cook for 10 to 12 minutes, depending on the
brand.

Let the soup rest, covered, for 10 minutes before serving. Enrich with abundant freshly grated *Pecorino Romano*.

# *Zuppa di Fave*
## FAVA BEAN SOUP

### SERVES 8.

8 ounces dried fava beans with skins

2 large red onions, cleaned and finely sliced

2 large cloves garlic, peeled but left whole

6 tablespoons olive oil

2 ounces pancetta or prosciutto, in one piece

Salt and freshly ground black pepper

3 quarts warm chicken or meat broth, completely defatted, preferably homemade *or* 3 quarts lukewarm water

1½ pounds spinach, already cleaned with large stems removed

PLUS

*Carta da musica* bread (see page 242) *or* 1 cup croutons, lightly toasted or fried

TO SERVE

Freshly ground black pepper

OPTIONAL

Olive oil

Soak the fava beans in a bowl of cold water overnight. Next morning, remove the skins and wash them very well under cold running water.

Place a medium-sized stockpot with the olive oil over medium heat. When the oil is warm, add the onions and the cloves of garlic and sauté until onions become translucent, about 5 minutes, stirring every so often with a wooden spoon. Meanwhile, using an electric meat grinder, coarsely grind pancetta and add it to the stockpot. Cook for 5 more minutes, then add the fava beans. Sauté for 2 or 3 minutes and season with salt and pepper. Pour in the broth and simmer for 1 hour.

Meanwhile place the spinach in a bowl of cold water and soak until needed. When ready, drain the spinach and add it to the stockpot; cook for 20 minutes and taste for salt and pepper.

If you are using *carta da musica* bread, break it into 2-inch pieces, add to the stockpot and cook for 1 minute. If you are using croutons, toasted or fried, divide them among the individual soup bowls and ladle the soup over them. Serve the *zuppa* hot or after 2 or 3 hours at room temperature, with 2 twists of black pepper over each portion. A little oil may be drizzled over each serving of *zuppa*.

The *zuppa* may be prepared 1 day in advance and reheated at the last moment; sometimes fava beans absorb a lot of broth so a little more broth may be needed. The *carta da musica* bread, if used, should be added just before serving. No cheese should be used.

*Fresh shelled fava beans, with skins still on*

# La Favata del "Giovedì Grasso"
## FAVA BEAN SOUP FOR MAUNDY THURSDAY

SERVES 8 TO 10.

1 pound dried fava beans with skins
  Coarse-grained salt
4 ounces pork meat (from the loin)
1 Italian sweet sausage without fennel
  seeds, skinned, *or* 3 ounces pork
1 fennel bulb
2 ounces pancetta or prosciutto

1 medium-sized red onion, cleaned
3 cloves garlic, peeled
10 sprigs Italian parsley, leaves only
5 sage leaves, fresh or preserved in salt
  (see page 294)
10 mint leaves
4 tablespoons olive oil

1 large dried wild fennel stalk (see
  Note)
  Salt and freshly ground black pepper
PLUS
  *Carta da musica* (see page 242) *or*
  slices of country-style bread, toasted
  (1 slice per person)

Soak the fava beans in a bowl of cold water overnight. Next morning, drain the beans and bring a large pot of cold water to a boil over medium heat. Add coarse salt to taste, then the beans and cook for about 45 minutes or until the beans are very soft. Let the beans rest in the cooking water until needed.

Use a meat grinder to grind the pork and sausage coarsely all together. Clean and cut the fennel bulb into small pieces. Soak the fennel in a bowl of cold water until needed. Cut pancetta into tiny pieces, then finely chop onion, garlic, parsley, sage and mint all together on a board.

Set a medium-sized stockpot with the oil over medium heat. When the oil is warm, add pancetta and all the chopped herbs and vegetables and sauté for 5 minutes, stirring with a wooden spoon. Add the ground pork and sausage and cook for 2 minutes more. Add 2 quarts of cold water and bring to a boil.

Meanwhile, drain the fava beans and remove the skins. When the soup reaches a boil, add the dried wild fennel, the drained beans and the cut-up fennel bulb, drained; simmer for 15 minutes. Taste for salt and pepper and cook until the fennel bulb is very soft and the fava beans are almost puréed. Stir so the soup does not stick because of the fava beans.

Discard the wild fennel and taste again for salt and pepper. Cook for about 20 minutes more until the soup is rather thick. Ladle into individual soup dishes over a slice of toasted bread or some Sardinian *carta da musica*, crumbled.

NOTE: *Dried wild fennel stalks are available at gourmet food shops.*

# Minestra di Fagioli

## BEAN SOUP

SERVES 6 TO 8.

½ pound dried cannellini beans
5 fresh sage leaves
2 tablespoons olive oil

FOR THE SOUP

1 medium-sized red onion, cleaned
1 celery stalk
1 medium-sized carrot, scraped
½ cup olive oil

2 tablespoons tomato paste
Salt and freshly ground black pepper
Hot red pepper flakes to taste

PLUS

1 pound all-purpose potatoes, peeled and cut into 1-inch cubes

FOR THE PASTA

1½ cups unbleached all-purpose flour

3 tablespoons semolina flour
2 extra-large eggs
A pinch of salt

OR

¾ pound dried tagliatelle, preferably imported Italian

TO SERVE

Freshly grated *Pecorino Romano*

Soak the beans overnight in a bowl of cold water. Next morning, place a medium-sized pot with 2½ quarts of cold water over medium heat. When the water reaches a boil, rinse the beans and add them to the pot, along with the sage and olive oil, and simmer for 45 minutes. By that time beans should be cooked but still retain their shape. Add coarse salt to taste and simmer for 2 minutes more.

Drain the beans, saving the water but discarding the sage leaves, and place the beans in a crockery or glass bowl, covered with paper towels dampened with cold water, until needed.

Meanwhile, coarsely chop onion, celery and carrot all together on a board. Set a medium-sized stockpot with the oil over medium heat. When the oil is warm, put in the chopped ingredients and sauté for 3 or 4 minutes, mixing every so often with a wooden spoon. Add tomato paste and season with salt, pepper and hot pepper. When tomato paste is dissolved, add the cut-up potatoes and mix well so that potatoes will absorb some of the sauce. Then pour in the bean water and simmer for 30 minutes. (The classic recipe uses the bean water, but the soup will be much more flavorful using a chicken or vegetable broth instead.)

If using fresh pasta, prepare it with the ingredients and quantities listed above, placing the semolina flour in the well of the unbleached flour (see page 294). Prepare tagliatelle according to directions, but the thickness should be about 1/16 inch; on a hand pasta machine, take it to the next to last setting, and the length should be about 6 inches. Let the pasta rest on cotton towels until needed.

When the soup is ready, cook the pasta, fresh or dried, in the soup itself and when the pasta is almost ready, add the reserved beans. Taste for seasoning and simmer until the pasta is ready. If dried pasta is used, cooking time for *al dente* is longer than that for fresh pasta.

Serve hot immediately with freshly grated *Pecorino Romano* or a few hours later at room temperature. At room temperature, drizzle a little oil over each serving.

## Ceci
### CHICK-PEAS

In the *minestra* from Sardinia, the chick-peas are left whole, cooked with sage and olive oil and then combined with chopped sautéed fennel bulb. A combination of several different short dried pastas, types not specified, perhaps leftovers, is added. Sicily has a similar *minestra*, but in place of fennel bulb, it is flavored with wild fennel.

*Crema* soups are *passati*, that is, made from puréed vegetables, not only the chick-peas but also the aromatic vegetables used to flavor the beans. This use of the word "cream" in Italian does not imply the addition of any cream and is nothing like the "cream of" type soup with which we are familiar. The dried wild *porcini* are soaked and then cut into pieces before being added. Some of the rich mushroom water also is added.

FROM SARDINIA
# Minestra di Ceci e Finocchi
## CHICK-PEA AND FENNEL SOUP

### SERVES 8.

½ pound dried chick-peas
5 sage leaves
2 tablespoons olive oil
   Coarse-grained salt

FOR THE SOUP
2 fennel bulbs, cleaned and cut into 1½-inch pieces (about 1 pound)
1 large red onion, cleaned
2 cloves garlic, peeled
5 tablespoons olive oil
2 tablespoons tomato paste
   Salt and freshly ground black pepper

PLUS
8 ounces of dried pasta of different cuts, such as elbows mixed with ditalini, or similar combinations

TO SERVE
   Freshly ground black pepper

Soak the chick-peas in a bowl of cold water overnight. Next morning, drain the peas and rinse under cold running water. Place a stockpot with at least 5 quarts of cold water over medium heat. Add the chick-peas, sage and oil to the pot and cook for about 1 hour. Add coarse salt to taste and cook for 5 minutes more. Drain the chick-peas, discard the sage leaves and save the cooking water. Let the peas rest, covered, in a crockery or glass bowl until needed.

Put the fennel in a bowl with cold water until needed. Coarsely chop onion and finely chop the garlic on a board. Place a stockpot with the oil over medium heat. When the oil is warm, add the chopped ingredients and sauté for 5 minutes, stirring with a wooden spoon. Add the tomato paste and mix very well. Drain the fennel, add it to the pot and season with salt and pepper. Pour in 6 cups of the bean cooking water and simmer for 30 minutes. Taste for salt and pepper, then add pasta and chick-peas at the same time and cook for 10 minutes more. Cover stockpot and let the soup rest for at least 15 minutes before serving.

This soup may also be prepared in the morning and set aside to rest, covered, until dinnertime when it is eaten at room temperature. Serve with freshly ground black pepper.

# Crema di Ceci ai Funghi

## CHICK-PEA SOUP WITH MUSHROOMS

SERVES 8.

2 cups dried chick-peas
3 quarts cold water
1 large carrot, scraped and cut into large pieces
1 medium-sized red onion, cleaned and cut into fourths
1 large clove garlic, peeled
1 bay leaf, left whole
2 tablespoons olive oil

2 ounces pancetta or prosciutto, in one piece
Coarse-grained salt

PLUS

1 ounce dried *porcini* mushrooms
15 sprigs Italian parsley, leaves only
1 small clove garlic, peeled
2 tablespoons olive oil
Salt and freshly ground black pepper

1 cup of the strained mushroom soaking water *or* 1 cup chicken broth, preferably homemade

OPTIONAL

1 tablespoon tomato paste dissolved in the strained mushroom soaking water

TO SERVE

Italian parsley leaves
A few drops of olive oil

Soak the chick-peas in a large bowl of cold water overnight. Next morning, drain and rinse the peas and place them in a medium-sized stockpot. Add the 3 quarts of cold water, carrot, onion, garlic and bay leaf, then the olive oil and the pancetta. Set pot over medium heat and boil the peas for at least 50 minutes or until soft. Meanwhile, soak the mushrooms in a bowl of lukewarm water for ½ hour.

When chick-peas are soft, add coarse salt to taste and cook for 5 minutes more. Discard the bay leaf and pancetta and pass all the contents of the stockpot through a food mill, using the disc with smallest holes, into a clean medium-sized stockpot. Set stockpot over medium heat and reduce for 10 minutes more.

Meanwhile, finely chop the parsley and garlic all together on a board. Clean the soaked mushrooms very well, removing all the sand attached to the stems, and coarsely chop them. Clean the soaking water by passing it through paper towels several times or through a coffee filter. Save 1 cup of this water for this recipe and freeze the remaining water to use later as a flavor enhancer when you prepare a meat sauce.

Place the 2 tablespoons of olive oil in a small saucepan and set pan over low heat. When the oil is warm, add the chopped ingredients and very lightly sauté for 2 minutes. Add the mushrooms and sauté for 2 minutes more. Pour the cup of mushroom soaking water into the pan, season with salt and black pepper and simmer for 15 minutes.

Pour the contents of the saucepan into the stockpot containing the puréed chick-peas, mix very well and let simmer over low heat for at least 15 minutes more, stirring every so often with a wooden spoon to prevent the "cream" from sticking to the bottom of the stockpot.

Serve hot or at room temperature, sprinkling over each serving the parsley leaves and if desired, a few drops of olive oil. This "cream" may even be prepared the day before and reheated at the last moment before serving.

# Zuppa di Funghi
## MUSHROOM SOUP

### SERVES 8 TO 10.

The island of Elba is just off Tuscany and though it has distinctly local dishes, its style is basically Tuscan, joining a few ingredients in a simple, flavorful combination. This variation of the many versions of Tuscan wild mushroom *zuppa* is specific to Elba.

1½ ounces dried *porcini* mushrooms

3 ounces prosciutto

15 sprigs Italian parsley, leaves only

1 medium-sized clove garlic, peeled

¼ cup olive oil
Salt and freshly ground black pepper to taste

PLUS

2 quarts defatted chicken broth, preferably homemade

1¾ pounds all-purpose potatoes, peeled and cut into 2-inch cubes

TO SERVE

16 heaping tablespoons croutons

2 cups vegetable oil (½ sunflower oil, ½ corn oil)

1 very large clove garlic, peeled
Salt and freshly ground black pepper

8 large fresh basil leaves

8 sprigs Italian parsley, leaves only

Soak the mushrooms in a bowl with 1 quart of lukewarm water for ½ hour.

Meanwhile finely grind prosciutto and finely chop parsley and garlic together on a board.

Place a medium-sized stockpot with the broth over medium heat. When the broth reaches a boil, add the potatoes and simmer for about 35 minutes, by which time potatoes should be almost liquified. Pass contents of stockpot through a food mill, using the disc with smallest holes, into a crockery or glass bowl and let rest until needed.

Drain the mushrooms and carefully clean them, removing all the sand attached to the stems. Strain the soaking water by passing it several times through a strainer lined with paper towels.

Heat the olive oil in a medium-sized stockpot over low heat. When the oil is warm, add the ground prosciutto and the chopped ingredients and sauté for 5 minutes, stirring every so often with a wooden spoon.

Meanwhile, coarsely chop the mushrooms. Add the mushrooms to the pot, stir very well and season with salt and pepper. Cook for 2 minutes, then add the mushroom water, a little at a time, and cook for 15 minutes more. Pour in all the broth containing the riced potatoes, bring to a boil and simmer for 20 minutes, stirring every so often with a wooden spoon and seasoning with salt and pepper.

Meanwhile, prepare the croutons: Heat the vegetable oil in a skillet over medium heat. Add the whole clove of garlic and sauté for 20 seconds. Add the croutons and fry until golden. Transfer them to a serving platter lined with paper towels to absorb excess fat and sprinkle with salt and pepper to taste. Discard the clove of garlic.

When the broth becomes smooth and rather thick, immediately ladle it into individual soup bowls. Top each serving with some of the croutons, then some parsley and basil leaves, and serve immediately.

Porcini *mushrooms*

This soup may be prepared in advance and reheated at the very last moment. If the mushroom flavor is not full-bodied, with a rich aroma, enhance the mushroom flavor by adding a small quantity of the reserved mushroom water to the broth.

# Minestra di Fregola e Arselle
## CLAM SOUP WITH *FREGOLA*

### SERVES 6.

This *minestra* is prepared along the central western coast of Sardinia where the *arselle*, which are smaller than "Manila" clams, are found. The sight of the fishermen pulling nets full of these tiny clams onto the beach at Tharros, with its impressive Phoenician, Carthaginian and Roman ruins, is striking. The sautéed clams are added to hot chicken broth, and the small saffron *fregola* are added at the end. The soup is thin, like broth, and contains just a small amount of clams and *fregola*. In Italy, the combination of chicken broth and meat with seafood is found only in Sardinia. This soup is less frequently made now, so I was amazed to discover how delicious and briny it is.

¾ pound of the very smallest clams you can find
Coarse-grained salt
TO COOK THE CLAMS
2 medium-sized cloves garlic, peeled
10 sprigs Italian parsley
3 tablespoons olive oil

Salt and freshly ground black pepper
½ cup dry white wine
FOR THE SOUP
2 medium-sized cloves garlic, peeled
15 sprigs Italian parsley, leaves only
4 tablespoons olive oil
8 cups completely defatted chicken broth, preferably homemade

Salt and freshly ground black pepper
PLUS
Coarse-grained salt
8 ounces small saffron *fregola* (see Note, page 72)
TO SERVE
Fresh basil leaves

Be sure clams are very fresh and still alive. Place them in a bowl of cold water with a little salt added and let rest in the refrigerator until needed.

Meanwhile, finely chop garlic and parsley for the clams together on a board. Place a skillet with the oil for the clams over low heat. When the oil is warm, add the chopped ingredients and sauté for 2 minutes. First drain the clams and rinse them very well under cold running water. Add the clams to the skillet and cook them, covered, for 2 minutes. Then raise the heat and uncover. Add the wine and season with salt and pepper. Cover and cook for 4 or 5 minutes more, shaking skillet several times.

Then transfer clams to a plate, discarding the ones that have not opened. Lift out the clams and discard the shells. Strain the juices from the skillet directly into the stockpot, discarding what remains in the strainer. Let stockpot simmer for 15 minutes more.

Meanwhile, coarsely chop the garlic and parsley for the soup on a board. Place a medium-sized stockpot with the oil for the soup over medium heat. When the oil in the stockpot is warm, add the chopped ingredients and sauté for 2 minutes. Pour the broth into the stockpot and let simmer for 25 minutes.

*Harvesting the tiny clams just off the coast of the sparkling sea of Sardinia*

Meanwhile, bring a large pot of cold water to a boil, add coarse salt to taste, then the *fregola* and cook for about 15 minutes for the very small *fregola* or longer for the larger type. When you try it, it should be cooked but still have a bite. Throughout Italy, pasta served with broth or even in minestroni is always cooked completely, but *fregola*, even for broth, is cooked like a sauced pasta, that is, still with a bite.

Three or four minutes before the *fregola* is ready, add the clams to the broth. When ready, strain the *fregola*, add it to the broth and simmer for 1 minute, seasoning with salt and pepper. Serve hot with basil leaves. Occasionally servings are garnished with a slice of tomato.

# Gran Minestrone

## "GRAND" MINESTRONE

SERVES 6 TO 8.

We end with the *Gran minestrone del Giglio*. This small jewel of an island, smaller than Elba, off the Tuscan coast is known for the variety of its fish. Lobster is so plentiful that the natives consider it a "cheap" food; Gigliese consider this elaborate minestrone more of a treat.

Farro (spelt or emmer), an ancient soft wheat known to the Romans, is still used in the Etruscan areas of Italy, mainly Tuscany. It is difficult though not impossible to separate the bran from the seed, which in our health-conscious days would be considered a blessing. Therefore it has most often been used as a whole grain, more rarely ground as flour. Depending on where it is grown, the soaking and cooking time of farro varies. Most dishes based on farro are soups.

Fava beans, another component, are often available only dried with the skins still on and must be soaked overnight before they are soft enough to be shelled.

1  medium-sized carrot, scraped
2  large celery stalks
2  medium-sized cloves of garlic, peeled
4  ounces Savoy cabbage leaves, cleaned and large veins removed
8  ounces skinned dried fava beans (see Note)

8  ounces farro (spelt or emmer, types of soft wheat berry) (see Note)
4  tablespoons olive oil
8  ounces very ripe tomatoes *or* 8 ounces drained canned tomatoes, preferably imported Italian
3½ quarts cold chicken or meat broth, preferably homemade and complete-

ly defatted *or* 3½ quarts cold water
Salt and freshly ground black pepper

TO SERVE

6  to 8 teaspoons olive oil
Freshly ground black pepper

OPTIONAL

About 1 cup of toasted or lightly fried *crostini* (croutons)

Finely chop carrot, celery and garlic all together on a board. Cut the cabbage into thin strips and soak it in a bowl of cold water. Meanwhile, soak the fava beans and the farro together in a bowl of cold water for 15 minutes.

Place a medium-sized stockpot with the oil over medium heat. When the oil is warm, add the chopped ingredients and sauté for 2 minutes, stirring constantly with a wooden spoon.

If fresh tomatoes are used, cut them into pieces. Pass fresh or canned tomatoes through a food mill, using the disc with smallest holes, directly into the stockpot. Drain the cabbage and add it to the pot; mix very well.

Drain the fava beans mixed with the farro and add them to the stockpot along with the cold broth or water; simmer for 1½ hours, adding salt and pepper to taste after 1 hour. By that time fava beans should be completely dissolved and the farro cooked.

Let the minestrone rest for 10 minutes before serving it with a teaspoon of oil drizzled over each serving along with a twist of black pepper. If using croutons, sprinkle them still warm over each serving, and the minestrone becomes a *zuppa*.

You may prepare this minestrone in the morning, let it rest in the stockpot

*The old-time glassed-in kitchen cabinet, here from Giglio, with postcards and other mementos.*
*The Gran minestrone is in the old-fashioned soup bowls.*

and serve at room temperature in the evening. This is the normal way of serving
it during the summer.

NOTES: *If shelled dried fava beans are not available, use the unshelled ones, soaking overnight in*
*cold water and shelling them before using.*

    *If farro is not extremely fresh and does not soften somewhat after 1 hour of soaking, soak*
*overnight in cold water before using it.*

# MAIN COURSES

POULTRY ◆ MEAT ◆ GAME

*I*n Sicily, Sardinia and the other islands, the diet is so strongly based on grains, vegetables and, in some areas, fish, that though a wide variety of meats and game is available, the meals including meat are often rather special, not everyday fare or taken for granted. Swordfish and tuna, with their dense meatlike textures, are quite frequent.

When meat is part of a meal, it still frequently may be one of the types which belong to the past in most of Italy and elsewhere, such as *castrato* (castrated male sheep), goat or kid. We don't include recipes for these more difficult to obtain meats, but for the variety of meats and game that we do, remember that they usually form part of a rather special meal.

# FROM SICILY
# *Pollo e Carciofi al Tegame*
## CHICKEN STEWED WITH ARTICHOKES

### SERVES 8.

Almost every region of Italy has its own version of chicken with artichokes, the variations consisting mainly in the particular combination of spices and herbs used. The flavor of chicken is a perfect foil for the more forceful taste of other ingredients. Artichokes especially can produce many different flavors, depending on the seasoning and method of cooking. In central Italy dishes of chicken and artichokes are sautéed with white wine and lemon juice. In other regions capers or flavorings such as thyme, hot pepper or saffron are added. The Sicilian version is the most complex, with the addition of many ingredients typical of the island and one that is not—tarragon.

1 chicken (about 3½ pounds)
½ cup dry white wine
  Salt and freshly ground black pepper
½ tablespoon red wine vinegar

FOR THE TOMATO SAUCE

1 large red onion, cleaned
2 medium-sized cloves garlic, peeled
10 basil leaves, fresh or preserved in salt (see page 294)
½ cup olive oil

2 pounds ripe tomatoes, blanched and seeded (see Note, page 40), *or* 2 pounds drained canned tomatoes, preferably imported Italian
  Salt and freshly ground black pepper

FOR THE ARTICHOKES

4 large artichokes
1 lemon
3 cloves garlic, peeled
1 heaping tablespoon fresh tarragon leaves

½ cup olive oil
3 ounces prosciutto or pancetta, in one piece
  Salt and freshly ground black pepper
1 cup lukewarm chicken or meat broth, preferably homemade

PLUS

2 cloves garlic, peeled
10 sprigs Italian parsley, leaves only

Cut the chicken into eighths, wash very carefully and dry with paper towels.

Prepare the tomato sauce: Coarsely chop the onion, garlic and basil all together on a board. Heat the oil in a medium-sized casserole over medium heat. When the oil is warm, add the chopped ingredients and sauté for 5 minutes, stirring every so often with a wooden spoon.

Preheat the oven to 375 degrees. If the tomatoes are fresh, cut them into large pieces. Add fresh or canned tomatoes to the casserole, season with salt and pepper and simmer for 15 minutes.

Meanwhile, clean the artichokes (see Note, page 190). Cut artichokes into fourths or eighths, depending on their size, and put them in a bowl of cold water with the lemon cut in half and squeezed. Cut prosciutto into tiny pieces and finely chop garlic and tarragon together on a board.

When tomato sauce has simmered for 15 minutes, add the chicken pieces, preferably in a single layer, and cook for 2 minutes on each side. Use a pair of tongs to transfer the chicken pieces to a baking dish and place the dish in the preheated oven for about 35 minutes, adding the wine a little at a time as needed, seasoning with salt and pepper and adding the vinegar when the chicken is almost cooked.

Meanwhile, keep reducing the tomato sauce until it is quite thick, about 15 minutes more. Let sauce rest, then skim off all the fat.

Cook the artichokes: Chop garlic and tarragon together on a board. Heat the oil in a large casserole over medium heat. When the oil is warm, add prosciutto and the chopped ingredients and sauté for 5 minutes. Drain artichokes and add them to casserole. Season with salt and pepper and sauté for 5 minutes. Add ½ cup of the broth, cover casserole and cook until artichokes are cooked but still retain their shape, adding more broth if needed. The cooking time will depend on the size of the artichokes.

Meanwhile, finely chop garlic and parsley together.

When the tomato sauce, chicken and artichokes are all ready, assemble the dish: Transfer the chicken pieces, without their juices, to the casserole containing the tomato sauce and cook for a few seconds, mixing very well, then transfer the contents of this casserole to the casserole holding the artichokes. Sprinkle with the chopped parsley and garlic, mix well and cook for a few seconds more. Transfer everything to a very large serving platter and serve hot.

*The ridged tomatoes most often used throughout Italy when making sauces of fresh tomatoes*

# Pollo o Coniglio al Guazzetto
## SAVORY CHICKEN OR RABBIT

### SERVES 4 TO 6.

On the mainland, the term *al guazzetto* is most often used to refer to "stews," usually of fish such as squid, cuttlefish or octopus, which require a long cooking time in their own juices, together with aromatic vegetables and herbs. In Sardinia, it is difficult to understand what dishes called by this name have in common, except that most of them contain capers, which are added early in the cooking, not at the last moment before serving, which is more typical.

1 (3½-pound) chicken or rabbit, cleaned and cut into 8 pieces
5 tablespoons olive oil
Salt and freshly ground black pepper

PLUS
15 sprigs Italian parsley, leaves only
3 medium-sized cloves garlic, peeled
8 tablespoons capers in wine vinegar, drained
1 medium-sized red onion, cleaned

Pinch of ground saffron
½ cup lukewarm water
¼ cup red wine vinegar
Salt to taste

TO SERVE
Italian parsley leaves

Remove the extra fat from the chicken pieces. Place a heavy medium-sized casserole with the oil over medium heat; the casserole should be large enough to hold all the chicken in a single layer. When the oil is warm, add the chicken, raise the heat to medium-high and sauté until the pieces are lightly golden all over, 4 to 5 minutes. Season with salt and pepper.

Finely chop parsley, garlic, 4 tablespoons of the capers and the onion all together on a board. Dissolve the saffron in the water. When the chicken is golden, add the chopped ingredients to the casserole along with the remaining 4 tablespoons of capers, left whole. Turn the chicken pieces over, then after 1 minute pour in the vinegar and the saffron water. Cover the casserole and cook for about 20 minutes, turning the chicken over 3 times and adding a little lukewarm water if needed. The sauce should be rather thick. Taste for salt.

Transfer the chicken to a large warmed serving platter, pour the sauce over the chicken and sprinkle with parsley leaves. Serve hot.

*A fowl wrapped in myrtle branches*

# Gallina al Mirto

*A gallina is almost completely wrapped in the branches of leaves, which are not, as you might assume, bay leaves, but rather myrtle (mirto). In Sardinia, these pungent leaves are often added to a meat stew or used in the unusual way shown in the photo. Either before or after being poached in salted water the bird is wrapped in the branches and then left overnight, nowadays in the refrigerator, to absorb the flavor. Before it is served the meat is drizzled with just a little oil or, more traditionally, with some melted lard and sprinkled with black pepper. A rabbit may also be prepared in the same manner.*

*Myrtle leaves and/or berries are used to prepare a famous Sardinian liqueur called mirto. Very strong and dry, it is both for drinking and for seasoning cakes. The wreaths made to crown Roman poets and emperors were more often made of myrtle than of bay.*

# Daino o Coniglio ai Carciofi alla Siciliana

## VENISON OR RABBIT WITH ARTICHOKES, SICILIAN STYLE

### SERVES 4.

1 pound of boneless venison fillet (½ inch thick) *or* 1 small rabbit, cut into 6 pieces, *or* 1 pound boneless chuck steak

3 lemons

FOR THE SAUCE

6 large artichokes

1 lemon

3 tablespoons olive oil

¼ cup unbleached all-purpose flour
Salt and freshly ground black pepper

1 cup dry white wine

2 to 2½ cups meat broth, preferably homemade

4 large cloves garlic, peeled

PLUS

2 whole anchovies is salt, boned and cleaned

(see Note, page 30), *or* 4 anchovy fillets in oil, drained

1 cup meat broth, preferably homemade

20 sprigs Italian parsley, leaves only, coarsely chopped

2 large cloves garlic, peeled, finely chopped

If you are using venison or chuck steak, you have to marinate the meat in a crockery or glass bowl with the juices of the 3 lemons overnight. If using rabbit, 4 hours is long enough to marinate it.

Meanwhile, soak the artichokes in a bowl of cold water with the lemon, cut in half and squeezed, for ½ hour. Then clean the artichokes (see Note, page 190). Cut the artichokes into quarters and return them to the acidulated water.

Heat the olive oil in a medium-sized casserole over medium heat. When the oil is warm, lightly flour the meat on both sides and add it to the casserole. Sauté the meat for 1 minute on each side, then drain the artichokes and add them to the casserole. Season with salt and pepper and cover casserole. Cook for 15 minutes, without mixing. Add the wine, but do not mix, cover again and cook for 10 minutes more. Start adding broth, ½ cup at a time, turning the meat twice and lightly turning the artichokes. The entire period of cooking should be about 1 hour. After the first cup of broth, add the 4 cloves of garlic, whole, and they will dissolve by the time the meat is ready.

Use a slotted spoon to transfer the meat and all the artichoke pieces but 4 to a warmed serving platter, and cover it to keep the meat warm. Add the anchovy fillets; mix very well. Cook for 30 seconds, then add the cup of broth and use a wooden spoon to mash the artichokes in the casserole until they are completely dissolved. Add the parsley and garlic, mix very well, then pour all the sauce over the meat and the artichokes on the serving platter. Serve hot.

NOTE: *If rabbit is used, not only is it marinated for 4 hours only, but it is cooked for a much shorter time as well, no longer than 1 hour, because the meat is much more tender.*

# Pollo con le Melanzane

## CHICKEN AND EGGPLANT, SICILIAN STYLE

SERVES 4 TO 6.

1 chicken (about 3½ pounds)
2 tablespoons olive oil
   Salt and freshly ground black pepper
1 pound cleaned eggplant, peeled and cut into 1-inch cubes
   Coarse-grained salt
3 large cloves garlic, peeled
3 fresh sage leaves
2 celery stalks

2 ounces pancetta, in one piece
5 tablespoons olive oil
4 tablespoons red wine vinegar or dry Marsala wine
1½ pounds ripe tomatoes *or* 1½ pounds drained canned tomatoes, preferably imported Italian
3 tablespoons tomato paste

FOR THE EGGPLANT
2 cups vegetable oil (½ sunflower oil, ½ corn oil)
   About 1 cup unbleached all-purpose flour

PLUS
15 sprigs Italian parsley, leaves only, coarsely chopped
1 clove garlic, peeled and finely chopped

Cut the chicken into 10 pieces and place it in a crockery or glass bowl. Add the oil, season with salt and pepper and let marinate for ½ hour, turning the chicken once.

Place the eggplant in a bowl of cold water, add 2 teaspoons of coarse salt and let rest until needed.

Coarsely chop garlic, sage, celery and pancetta all together on a board. Heat the olive oil in a large skillet over medium heat. When the oil is warm, add the chopped ingredients and sauté for 2 minutes. Put the chicken pieces with any unabsorbed marinade into the skillet and sauté until lightly golden all over, 3 to 4 minutes. Season with salt and pepper, then add the wine vinegar and let it evaporate for 2 minutes on higher heat. If fresh tomatoes are used, cut them into large pieces. Add fresh or canned tomatoes to the skillet along with the tomato paste, lower heat and cook for at least 15 minutes, stirring every so often with a wooden spoon and adding a little water if needed. By that time the chicken should be cooked and very juicy and should have formed a very rich sauce.

Meanwhile, drain the eggplant cubes and pat them dry with paper towels. Heat the vegetable oil in a skillet over high heat. When the oil is hot (about 400 degrees), dredge the eggplant lightly in flour and fry them until golden all over, 30 seconds on each side.

Line a serving platter with paper towels to absorb excess oil. When cooked, transfer eggplant to the towel-lined serving platter.

When the chicken is ready, add fried eggplant to the skillet along with the parsley and garlic; mix very well. Transfer everything to a fresh large serving platter and serve hot.

*Galletto alla Cacciatora* • *Rotolo di Pollo in Salsa Piccante*

The following two chicken dishes are quite spicy. Elba's "hunter's style" chicken contains onions, hot green peppers (used on the Tuscan coast as well as in Naples), red pepper flakes and sage (often used with game), resulting in a lusty outdoor flavor. In the Sardinian one, air-dried tomatoes are combined with capers and wine vinegar. In Italy, especially Sardinia, air-dried tomatoes, the original version of the now trendy "sun-dried" tomatoes, are ground and added to a sauce or stuffing to enrich the taste. They are even added to tomato sauce to intensify its flavor, but are not eaten whole.

FROM ELBA

# *Galletto alla Cacciatora*
## ROOSTER OR CHICKEN WITH HOT GREEN PEPPERS

SERVES 4 TO 6.

1 chicken (about 3½ pounds)
2 large red onions, cleaned
½ cup olive oil
1 cup dry white wine
2 Italian hot green peppers*

10 sage leaves, fresh or preserved in salt (see page 294)
3 small very ripe tomatoes, blanched and seeded (see Note, page 40), *or* 3 canned tomatoes, drained and seeded

Salt and freshly ground black pepper
A large pinch of hot red pepper flakes

TO SERVE
Fresh sage leaves

Cut the chicken down the breast and flatten it. Carefully wash the chicken and dry it with paper towels.

Coarsely chop the onions on a board. Place a medium-sized heavy skillet with the oil and the onions over medium heat and sauté for 15 minutes, stirring every so often with a wooden spoon. Arrange the chicken over the onions and sauté for 15 minutes on 1 side, shaking the skillet several times to keep the fowl from sticking to the bottom. Turn the chicken over and sauté for 5 minutes. Add the wine and cook for 5 minutes more.

Clean the Italian peppers, removing the seeds and the inner membranes, and cut the peppers into thin strips. Add the peppers, the whole sage leaves and the tomatoes, cut into large pieces, to the chicken. Season with salt, pepper and the hot pepper flakes. Cook for 2 or 3 minutes on the same side, then turn over the whole chicken with all the peppers, tomatoes and the seasoning and sauté for 10 minutes more. By that time the chicken should be cooked, otherwise turn it again and finish cooking it. Cut chicken into fourths, arrange the pieces in a serving dish and pour the sauce over the meat. Serve with fresh sage leaves.

* It is often more convenient to obtain the long, thin green hot peppers at Korean or Chinese markets; these are very similar to the Italian ones and more commonly available.

# Rotolo di Pollo in Salsa Piccante
## BONED AND ROLLED-UP CHICKEN IN PIQUANT SAUCE

SERVES 6 TO 8.

1 chicken (about 3½ pounds), cleaned
2 small cloves garlic, peeled
15 sprigs Italian parsley, leaves only
4 ounces pancetta or fat prosciutto, in one piece
Salt and freshly ground black pepper to taste

TO BAKE

4 tablespoons olive oil

Salt and freshly ground black pepper
½ cup dry white wine

FOR THE SAUCE

1 ounce air-dried tomatoes (not the ones preserved in oil)
4 tablespoons capers in wine vinegar, drained
3 cloves garlic, peeled
20 sprigs Italian parsley, leaves only

¼ cup olive oil
½ cup red wine vinegar or ¼ cup if very strong vinegar
1 cup cold water
Salt and freshly ground black pepper

TO SERVE

10 sprigs Italian parsley, leaves only
4 tablespoons capers in wine vinegar, drained

Bone the chicken as for galantine, leaving all the meat attached to the skin (see page 295). Place the boned chicken with the skin facing down on a board. Make several slits in the meaty parts, using a sharp knife, to distribute the meat itself uniformly.

Finely chop garlic and parsley together on a board and cut pancetta into thin strips. Mix the chopped ingredients with salt and pepper to taste, then sprinkle the mixture evenly over the chicken. Arrange the pancetta all over the chicken, placing the strips lengthwise. Roll up the chicken, starting from one side, being sure to tuck in boned legs and wings. Tie the rolled-up chicken like a salami (see page 295).

Preheat the oven to 400 degrees and pour the olive oil into a metal baking dish. Place the chicken in the dish, season with salt and pepper and bake for 30 minutes, turning the chicken twice and seasoning the second side. Pour the wine over the chicken and bake for 25 minutes more, turning and basting the bird 3 times.

Meanwhile, prepare the sauce: Finely grind air-dried tomatoes, capers, garlic and parsley all together in a food processor or blender. Set a medium-sized casserole with the oil over medium heat. When the oil is warm, add the ground ingredients and sauté for 5 minutes, stirring every so often with a wooden spoon. Add the vinegar and evaporate it for 5 minutes. Add the water and reduce for 15 minutes more or until the sauce is reduced by one-third. Season with salt and pepper to taste. Be careful, though, for sometimes tomatoes have some salt added. (The sauce can be prepared in advance and reheated at the last moment when the chicken is ready.)

Transfer the cooked chicken to a serving platter and let cool for 15 minutes before cutting it into 8 slices. Discard the thread. Arrange the chicken slices in a row, the pieces overlapping, on a large serving platter. Pour the reheated, very warm sauce over the chicken and cover the platter for 5 minutes before serving. Serve with parsley leaves mixed with capers.

# Gallo Vecchio alla Palermitana

## CHICKEN IN SICILIAN BREAD CRUMB SAUCE

SERVES 4.

In Italian cooking there are still strict distinctions among types of chicken. This recipe calls for an old rooster, with its lean, dense and flavorful meat, so that the unusual bread-crumb-based sauce will not overpower the flavor of the meat. The bread crumbs, used in many old recipes, form a highly seasoned sauce here. The rooster, once cooked, is traditionally presented on a bed of mixed greens and aromatic herbs—a "modern" presentation that clearly has been around for a long time.

FOR THE BROTH

- 1 medium-sized red onion, peeled
- 2 medium-sized stalks celery
- 2 medium-sized carrots, scraped
- 5 sprigs Italian parsley
  Coarse-grained salt
- 1 chicken (about 3½ pounds)

FOR THE BREAD CRUMBS

- 20 sprigs Italian parsley, leaves only
- 3 large cloves garlic, peeled

- 1 cup unseasoned very fine bread crumbs, lightly toasted, preferably homemade
- ½ teaspoon dried Italian oregano
  Salt and freshly ground black pepper

FOR THE SAUCE

- 2 medium-sized cloves garlic, peeled
  Juice of 4 large lemons
- ½ teaspoon dried Italian oregano
- 10 tablespoons olive oil
  Salt and freshly ground black pepper

THE SALAD

- 1 large bunch curly endive
- 2 medium-sized fennel bulbs
- 12 radishes
- 20 green olives in brine

SALAD DRESSING

- 6 to 8 tablespoons olive oil
- 4 tablespoons red wine vinegar
  Salt and freshly ground black pepper to taste

Place a large cast-iron pan inside the oven and preheat it to 400 degrees.

Bring a medium-sized stockpot of cold water to a boil over medium heat. When the water reaches a boil, add all the vegetables and coarse-grained salt to taste, lower heat and simmer for 10 minutes.

Meanwhile, clean and wash the chicken very well, removing the extra fat from the cavity. Open the chicken like a *braciola* by cutting it all along the breast and flattening it. Dry it with paper towels. Add chicken to boiling broth and simmer for 2 minutes.

Meanwhile, prepare the bread crumbs: Finely chop parsley and garlic together on a board. Place the bread crumbs in a small bowl and add the chopped ingredients, oregano and salt and pepper to taste. Mix very well to completely integrate the chopped ingredients. Carefully transfer the chicken from the stockpot to a board. Mound bread crumbs over the chicken and press as much of them as possible onto the chicken surface. Turn the bird over several times, repeating this procedure, trying to thoroughly coat the chicken with as much of the bread crumbs as possible.

Prepare the sauce: Finely chop the garlic on a board and transfer it to a small crockery or glass bowl. Add the lemon juice, oregano, olive oil and salt and pepper to taste and mix very well with a spoon. Pour 1 tablespoon of the sauce into the hot iron pan, then place the chicken flat, skin side down, in the pan and cover it with all the remaining bread crumbs. Pour 6 tablespoons of the sauce over the chicken and bake for 15 minutes. Pour 4 more tablespoons of the sauce over the chicken and cook for 10 minutes. Using a large spatula, turn the chicken over, pour the remaining sauce over it and bake for the final 25 minutes.

Meanwhile, prepare the salad: Wash and clean the endive, cut it into 2-inch pieces and put them in a bowl of cold water. Discard the tough outer leaves of the fennel, cut the tender part into half-inch pieces and add to the bowl with the endive, along with the radishes, cleaned and left whole.

Just before the chicken is ready, drain the salad and transfer it to a bowl. Add the olives and toss it with the oil, vinegar and salt and pepper to taste. Make a bed of the prepared salad on a large serving dish. Transfer the chicken with all the bread crumbs from the pan onto the large dish and serve with some of the salad, cutting the chicken with poultry shears. Chicken and salad are to be eaten together.

# Galletto al Vino e Limone

## CHICKEN IN CASSEROLE, ENNA STYLE

SERVES 4 TO 6.

In this dish the rooster must be young; without the right type of chicken the dish could suffer. Although this highly integrated sauce hides nothing and the enveloped chicken pieces are remarkably flavored, they must retain their own taste.

1 chicken (about 3½ pounds), preferably free-range
1 large red onion, cleaned
¼ cup olive oil
1 cup chicken broth, preferably homemade, completely defatted
Abundant salt and freshly ground black pepper

½ cup dry white wine
½ cup not very strong red wine vinegar
2 tablespoons lemon juice
10 sprigs Italian parsley, leaves only
5 large basil leaves, fresh or preserved in salt (see page 294)
10 large bay leaves

PLUS
2 large tomatoes, diced
½ tablespoon olive oil
Pinch of salt
Freshly ground black pepper

TO SERVE
Fresh basil and parsley leaves

Clean and wash the chicken and remove all the extra fat. Cut it in half, then cut each half in 3 pieces. Coarsely chop the onion on a board. Place a medium-sized skillet, large enough to hold the chicken pieces in one layer, with the oil over medium heat. When the oil is warm, add the onion and sauté for 2 minutes. Meanwhile, finely chop the parsley and basil together on a board.

When the onion is ready, remove skillet from the heat, arrange the chicken over the onion, then pour over the broth, seasoned very well with salt and pepper. The amount of salt and pepper should be more than usual, because the seasoning is done only at this step. Add the wine, vinegar and lemon juice and sprinkle with the finely chopped parsley and basil. Top everything with the whole bay leaves. Set skillet over low heat, cover, and cook for 1 hour, checking every 20 minutes, without stirring, to see if more liquid is needed. If the chicken is not a free-range one, the cooking time will be much shorter.

Meanwhile, mix the tomatoes with the oil and season with salt and pepper. Refrigerate until needed.

When the chicken is cooked completely, the liquid should have become a rather thick sauce. If the sauce is not thick enough, transfer chicken to a serving dish and cover it, then reduce the sauce, removing all the fat from the top, uncovered, over high heat for 5 to 10 minutes.

When sauce is ready, discard the bay leaves. Pour sauce over chicken and let rest for a few minutes before serving. Serve with the fresh basil and parsley leaves sprinkled over and some of the diced tomatoes all around the meat.

# Sardinian Market

In central Sardinia, the lion's share of the meat market is taken by meat such as lamb, goat and horsemeat, and by fowl. Many stands sell horsemeat, which is now quite expensive, because it is still strongly believed that this meat and its broth give strength to the elderly and to very young people.

# Cosciotto di Pollo Ripieno
## BONED, STUFFED CHICKEN LEGS

SERVES 8.

The humble attached leg and thigh of the chicken are completely boned to form a unique casing for many aromatic herbs and spices. The result is very tasty small salamis to be sliced for a formal dinner or buffet.

4 large chicken thighs with legs attached

FOR THE STUFFING

6 tablespoons unseasoned very fine bread crumbs, lightly toasted, preferably homemade

1 cup lukewarm chicken or beef broth, preferably homemade

4 tablespoons capers in wine vinegar, drained

1 medium-sized clove garlic, peeled

2 ounces pitted green olives in brine, drained

10 sprigs Italian parsley, leaves only

4 large basil leaves, fresh or preserved in salt (see page 294)

Salt and freshly ground black pepper

A large pinch of oregano

4 tablespoons olive oil

2 tablespoons pine nuts (*pignoli*)

OPTIONAL

16 thin slices of prosciutto or pancetta to wrap the stuffed *cosciotti*

TO COOK

2 medium-sized carrots, scraped

4 celery stalks

6 tablespoons olive oil

Salt and freshly ground black pepper

1¾ cups dry white wine

TO SERVE

Fresh basil leaves

Italian parsley leaves

Remove bones from leg and thigh, leaving the two attached; be careful not to break the skin. Remove the tough tendons from the legs.

Prepare the stuffing: Soak the bread crumbs in the broth for 15 minutes. Meanwhile, finely chop capers, garlic, olives, parsley and basil all together on a board. Drain the bread crumbs and combine them with the chopped ingredients in a crockery or glass bowl. Season with salt, pepper and oregano and pour in the oil. Mix very well with a wooden spoon. Add the pine nuts and mix again.

Sew up the small opening at the end of each chicken leg. Then sew the larger opening, leaving a small hole to insert the stuffing. Using a pastry bag, fill the pocket with the prepared stuffing. Do not overstuff, or the skin will break. Finally, sew up the remaining small hole. Wrap each thigh with the prosciutto or pancetta slices, if using. I prefer the taste without prosciutto wrapping, though the wrapping protects the skin from breaking. Tie the wrapped or unwrapped *cosciotto* like a salami (see page 295) and prick with a needle in several places.

When all the *cosciotti* are ready, finely chop carrots and celery on a board. Place a medium-sized skillet with the oil over low heat. When the oil is warm, add the chopped carrots and celery and sauté 5 minutes, stirring every so often with a wooden spoon. Arrange the prepared *cosciotti* in the skillet and sauté them, still over low heat, for 15 minutes, turning them over 4 or 5 times. Season with salt and pepper. Pour in ¾ cup of the wine, cover the skillet and cook for 35 minutes, turning the meat over 4 times and adding the remaining wine as needed. The chicken should be cooked and a thick sauce formed. Remove skillet from the heat, transfer the chicken to a serving dish, cover and let rest at least ½ hour.

Meanwhile, pass the sauce through a food mill, using the disc with the smallest holes, into a bowl, then return the sauce to the skillet and cook for 5 minutes, adding a little broth or water if needed. A very smooth sauce should result.

To serve, untie the meat and discard the prosciutto slices, if used. Remove the thread from the chicken and slice *cosciotti* like a salami, into slices about 1 inch thick. Serve the meat sprinkled with the basil and parsley leaves and some of the reheated sauce on the side.

# Festival

In Macomer, a small town not far from Nuoro, every year the days of June 12, 13 and 14 are dedicated to honoring the saints Antonio da Padova and San Pantaleo. The people in the procession, wearing their local costumes, move, barefoot most of the time, from the church in the city dedicated to San Pantaleo to the one outside dedicated to Saint Antonio. The gunshots announce the arrival of the procession, alerting the residents to stop working and join the celebration.

Macomer is a very well-known center for the production of sheep's milk cheese.

*Triple concentrated tomato paste, sold loose*

MAIN COURSES

# *Falsomagro*

## STUFFED BEEF SIRLOIN

SERVES 8 TO 10.

This most famous of all Sicilian meat dishes, which originated in Palermo, is not served in restaurants all over the island. There are so many variations in its stuffings that the original recipe has probably been lost. The name means literally "fake lean" and probably refers to the very lean beef slices that hide a very rich and exuberant stuffing. The technique is similar to that of the *Cima* of the frugal Genoese, who also hide a rich stuffing inside what seems to be simple boiled veal shoulder.

The slow cooking of this dish yields a luxuriant sauce, which is often saved to dress pasta. Using a meat preparation and its sauce in separate dishes or courses is typical of the Naples region also.

2 pounds beef sirloin, in one piece, butterflied

FOR THE STUFFING

4 extra-large hard-boiled eggs

4 ounces prosciutto, in one piece

4 ounces pancetta, in one piece

8 ounces *Caciocavallo* or *Provolone* or Fontina

4 ounces fresh shelled peas, *or 4* ounces frozen "petite" peas

Coarse-grained salt

15 sprigs Italian parsley, leaves only

1 medium-sized clove garlic, peeled

2 scallions

8 ounces sweet Italian sausages with or without fennel seeds

8 ounces ground beef

1 extra-large egg

2 ounces freshly grated *Pecorino* or *Sardo*

2 tablespoons olive oil

Freshly ground black pepper to taste

TO COOK THE *FALSOMAGRO*

8 ounces Italian sweet sausages with or without fennel seeds

4 tablespoons olive oil

Salt and freshly ground black pepper

1 cup dry red wine

5 tablespoons tomato paste

1½ cups chicken or beef broth

Place the meat on a board and open it out like a large *braciola*. Place the hard-boiled eggs in a row lengthwise down the center of the meat. Cut the prosciutto and pancetta into thin strips almost the length of the meat. Cut the cheese into ½-inch cubes. Arrange the strips of pancetta and prosciutto lengthwise alongside the eggs on both sides, then make 2 outer rows with the cheese.

Blanch the peas in a small casserole of water with coarse-grained salt added for 2 minutes. Finely chop parsley, garlic and scallions together on a board. Remove skin from the sausages and put them in a crockery or glass bowl. Add to the bowl the chopped ingredients, ground beef, peas, egg, grated cheese and olive oil. Season with pepper and mix all the ingredients together. Spread this *farcia* over the eggs, meat strips and cheese. Roll up the *braciola*, starting from either the left or right end, and tie like a salami (see page 295).

To cook the *falsomagro*, remove the skin from the sausages, then heat the oil in a large oval casserole over medium heat. When the oil is warm add the sausages and sauté for 2 minutes. Then add the *falsomagro* and sauté for 10 minutes, turning it frequently. Season with salt and pepper. Add the wine and let it evaporate for 10 minutes. Dissolve the tomato paste in the broth. Add ½ cup of the broth, cover the casserole and cook over low heat for 2 hours, adding the remaining broth as needed and turning the meat several times. Let the *falsomagro* rest in the casserole, covered, at least 1 hour before slicing.

Serve it at room temperature with the sauce reheated.

# Cotolette di Vitello o Maiale alla Sarda

## VEAL CUTLETS OR PORK CHOPS, SARDINIAN STYLE

### SERVES 6.

The breading for this veal cutlet contains oregano as well as saffron mixed with bread crumbs. Though saffron was used mostly for color in the Renaissance, even a pinch imparts a very distinctive flavor if it is not masked by a lot of other spices. When served, the cutlet is topped with diced uncooked tomatoes, celery and herbs—another traditional combination which has re-emerged as a seemingly new "healthful" dish in our time.

6 veal cutlets *or* 6 boneless pork chops
3 extra-large eggs, lightly beaten
Pinch of salt
1 cup unseasoned very fine bread crumbs, lightly toasted, preferably homemade
2 medium-sized cloves garlic, peeled
15 sprigs Italian parsley, leaves only
Salt and freshly ground black pepper

Pinch of dried Italian oregano
Pinch of ground saffron, preferably Sardinian

FOR THE VEGETABLES
1½ pounds fresh tomatoes, ripe but not overripe
1 medium-sized red onion, cleaned
4 white inner celery stalks, cleaned and cut into small pieces

18 large fresh basil leaves
18 fresh mint leaves
Salt and freshly ground black pepper
3 tablespoons olive oil
1 tablespoon lemon juice

PLUS
1 quart vegetable oil for frying (½ corn oil, ½ sunflower oil)

Soak the cutlets or chops in the eggs, adding a little salt, for 30 minutes.

Place the bread crumbs in a small bowl, then finely chop garlic and parsley together on a board. Add chopped ingredients to the bread crumbs, along with salt and pepper to taste, and mix well with a wooden spoon. Set aside.

Carefully wash tomatoes, cut them into cubes of less than ½ inch and place them in a crockery or glass bowl. Coarsely chop the onion and add to tomatoes, along with the celery, 6 of the basil leaves, torn into thirds, all the mint leaves, salt and pepper to taste, the oil and the lemon juice. Mix well and refrigerate, covered, until needed.

When meat is ready, add the oregano and saffron to the bread crumb mixture, mix well, then spread out the mixture on a piece of aluminum foil.

Heat the vegetable oil in a large skillet over medium heat. When the oil is hot (about 375 degrees), remove meat from the eggs and bread each cutlet or pork chop thoroughly on both sides. Line a serving dish with paper towels. Fry the cutlets or chops until lightly golden on both sides, less than 1 minute on each side for cutlets or 1 full minute on each side for chops. As they are cooked, transfer them to the towel-lined dish to drain. Top each cutlet or chop with some of the tomato mixture and 2 of the remaining basil leaves and serve.

*A cutlet, and behind it, zucchini fried Sardinian style (coated with semolina)*

# *Bistecca di Enna*

## SICILIAN BEEFSTEAK, ENNA STYLE

SERVES 4.

2 T-bone steaks, each about ½ inch thick (about 1¾ pounds total)

FOR THE MARINADE

Salt and freshly ground black pepper

15 whole black peppercorns

6 tablespoons freshly squeezed lemon juice

10 tablespoons olive oil

4 large cloves garlic, peeled and left whole

3 large bay leaves

2 large lemon slices

2 teaspoons dried oregano *or* a few sprigs fresh

TO COOK

About ¾ cup unseasoned very fine

bread crumbs, lightly toasted, preferably homemade

Salt and freshly ground black pepper to taste

2 large pinches dried oregano

TO SERVE

3 bunches *rucola* (arugula)

Lemon wedges

Trim the extra fat from the steaks. Place the meat in a crockery or glass bowl, season with salt and pepper to taste, then add the lemon juice, olive oil, garlic, bay leaves, lemon slices and oregano. Let the meat marinate, covered, in the refrigerator, for at least 2 hours before cooking, turning the meat several times.

The steaks are to be cooked either on a grill over an open fire or under the broiler in the oven. Prepare the fire in advance so you will have hot ash to cook over or preheat the broiler.

First, spread out the bread crumbs on a piece of aluminum foil and season with salt, pepper and oregano, then place the meat on top. The steaks should have absorbed most of the lemon juice and olive oil, but if some liquid remains, drizzle it over the meat.

When ready to cook, take some of the bread crumbs from the foil and pat them first on the top side of the meat, then on the bottom. Repeat this procedure on both sides several times until a crust of bread crumbs is formed. Gently transfer the meat to the grill over the hot ash or under the oven broiler. Cook the steaks to desired degree of doneness—7 to 8 minutes on each side for medium-rare, reversing the meat 4 times during its cooking time. The bread crumbs should be darker than golden.

Meanwhile, clean and coarsely cut the arugula and arrange it on a serving dish. The classic greens used in Sicily are wild field greens, which are rather bitter. The substitution of arugula gives the closest taste to these wild field greens. When the meat is ready, transfer it onto the bed of arugula and serve hot with lemon wedges.

# Polpette "Infilzate"
## SKEWERED VEAL MEATBALLS

SERVES 4.

This dish consists of veal meatballs cooked on skewers, and it is the type of skewer used that makes the dish distinctive. Even if cooked on the usual bamboo or metal skewers, the lemon-oregano sauce will produce a very pleasant result. But if you can use skewers made from branches of the bay or orange tree, as the Sicilians do, the result is truly extraordinary.

1¼ pounds ground veal shoulder
2 small cloves garlic, peeled
15 sprigs Italian parsley, leaves only
3 ounces freshly grated *Pecorino Romano*, preferably imported Italian
2 extra-large eggs
  Salt and freshly ground black pepper
  Pinch of dried oregano

PLUS

9 (½-inch-thick) slices of long, thin Italian bread
16 bay leaves
  About 2 tablespoons olive oil mixed with 2 tablespoons lemon juice

FOR THE SAUCE

15 sprigs Italian parsley, leaves only

2 very small cloves garlic, peeled
½ cup olive oil
¼ cup lukewarm water
2 tablespoons lemon juice
½ teaspoon dried oregano
  Salt and freshly ground black pepper

TO SERVE

  Italian parsley leaves

Place the meat in a crockery or glass bowl. Finely chop garlic and parsley together on a board. Add the chopped ingredients along with the cheese and the eggs to the bowl and season with salt, pepper and the oregano. Mix very well with a wooden spoon.

Preheat the oven to 400 degrees or prepare the fire for the grill with enough wood or charcoal to leave quite a lot of hot ash.

Divide the meat mixture into 8 portions and shape them into round balls. Thread a slice of bread onto a skewer, then a bay leaf, then, gently, one of the meat balls. Keep repeating this order until all the ingredients are used up. The opposite end of the skewer will finish with a bay leaf and a slice of bread. It is better to spread the ingredients out over 2 skewers instead of one so they are easier to turn over.

Gently transfer the skewer(s) to a very well-oiled hot grill or onto an oiled baking dish. Drizzle the 2 tablespoons of oil/lemon juice over the skewer and grill or bake for about 6 minutes on each side, adding more oil if necessary.

Meanwhile, prepare the sauce: Place parsley, garlic and the oil in a blender or food processor and blend until a very soft emulsion forms. Add the lukewarm water, lemon juice, salt and pepper to taste and the oregano and blend again. Transfer the sauce to a saucepan and place the pan in a water bath. Keep the sauce warm, stirring constantly with a wooden spoon, but do not let it reach a boil.

When the meat is ready, unthread the contents of the skewer onto individual plates. Each serving will have a *crostino* bread slice and a *polpetta*. Spoon some of the sauce to one side on each plate and sprinkle each portion with parsley leaves. Serve hot.

*One of the skewers before they are divided into servings*

# Ossobuco ai Carciofi
## OSSOBUCO WITH ARTICHOKE SAUCE

SERVES 6.

Originally this dish was made with the leftover, "poorer" parts of the veal or lamb, which required a very long cooking time. The resultant stew was too soft, with the mushy artichokes completely incorporated into the meat. I have sampled the original version, which is no longer used, and must concur that though the taste was very good, the texture was unacceptable. This is an updated version, in which a different cut of veal is combined with exactly the same ingredients to produce a far more enjoyable result.

FOR THE SAUCE
- 6 large artichokes
- 2 lemons
- 20 sprigs Italian parsley, leaves only
- 4 large cloves garlic, peeled
- ½ cup olive oil
- Salt and freshly ground black pepper
- 1 cup chicken broth, preferably home-made

TO COOK THE *OSSIBUCHI*
- 6 large veal *ossibuchi* (about 2 inches thick)
- ½ cup olive oil
- About 1 cup unbleached all-purpose flour
- Salt and freshly ground black pepper
- Freshly grated nutmeg
- 1 cup dry white wine
- About 2 cups chicken broth, preferably homemade

FOR THE *GREMOLADA*
- 20 sprigs Italian parsley, leaves only
- 1 medium-sized clove garlic, peeled
- Grated peel of 1 large lemon
- Salt and freshly ground black pepper

Soak the artichokes in a bowl of cold water with one of the lemons, cut in half and squeezed, for ½ hour. Clean the artichokes (see Note, page 190). Cut 3 artichokes lengthwise into eighths and the other three into small pieces. Put the artichokes in 2 clean bowls, both containing cold water, and in each bowl half of the remaining lemon, squeezed, and set aside until needed.

Finely chop parsley and garlic together on a board. Place a medium-sized casserole with the oil over medium heat. When the oil is warm, add the chopped aromatic herbs and sauté for 2 minutes. Drain the small pieces of artichoke and add them to the casserole; sauté for 5 minutes, stirring every so often with a wooden spoon. Season with salt and pepper. Add ½ cup of the broth, cover the casserole and cook for 15 minutes, incorporating the remaining ½ cup of the broth after 10 minutes.

Meanwhile, tie each *ossobuco* with a string, so that the meat remains attached to the bone. Place a medium-sized oven-proof casserole with the oil over medium heat. When the oil is warm, add the *ossibuchi*, lightly floured on the cut sides, and sauté the meat for 1 minute on each side. Season with salt, pepper and nutmeg. Add the wine and let it evaporate for 15 minutes.

When ready, ladle all the cooked artichokes and their juices over the meat, then pour in the 2 cups of broth. The liquid should almost reach the top of the meat. Season with more salt and pepper, cover casserole and place it in the cold oven. Heat the oven to 400 degrees and bake for 1 hour, turning the meat once and adding more broth if needed. By that time the meat should be cooked and very soft.

*One of Sardinia's* nauraghi, *mysterious structures, probably fortresses, which continued to be used during the Carthaginian and Roman occupation*

Transfer the *ossibuchi* to a serving dish and cover the dish to keep them warm. Pass the sauce from the casserole through a food mill, using the disc with the smallest holes, into a medium-sized saucepan. Place pan over medium heat, taste for salt and pepper and reduce for 15 minutes or until the sauce has a thicker consistency. Drain the artichoke eighths and add them to the pan containing the strained sauce. Mix very well and cook for about 15 minutes or until the artichokes are soft.

Meanwhile, prepare the *gremolada*: Finely chop the parsley and garlic together on a board. Transfer the chopped ingredients to a crockery or glass bowl, add the grated lemon peel and season with salt and pepper; mix very well.

When ready to serve, remove the strings from the meat, place *ossibuchi* in a large casserole and pour the sauce over; reheat for a few minutes.

Remove strings and arrange *ossibuchi* on individual plates. Top with sauce and some *gremolada* and serve with artichoke pieces on the side.

# Ossobuco al Limone con Fagioli

## LEMON-FLAVORED *OSSOBUCO* WITH CANNELLINI BEANS

### SERVES 6.

The combination of meat or poultry with beans in a single dish is a favorite with the bean-eating Tuscans, and this lemony version is particular to Elba, which belongs to the region.

**FOR THE BEANS**
- 1 pound dried cannellini beans
- 1 tablespoon olive oil
- 4 sage leaves, fresh or preserved in salt (see page 294)
- 3 ounces prosciutto or pancetta, in one piece
  Coarse-grained salt

**FOR THE SAUCE**
- 2 medium-sized carrots, scraped
- 1 medium-sized red onion, cleaned
- 2 celery stalks
- 10 sprigs Italian parsley, leaves only
- 4 sage leaves, fresh or preserved in salt (see page 294)

- ½ tablespoon rosemary leaves, fresh or preserved in salt or dried and blanched (see page 294)
- ½ cup olive oil
  Salt and freshly ground black pepper

**TO COOK THE *OSSIBUCHI***
- 6 large veal *ossobuchi* (about 2 inches thick)
- ½ cup olive oil
  About 1 cup unbleached all-purpose flour
  Salt and freshly ground black pepper
  Grated peel of 1 lemon (see page 294)
  Juice of ½ lemon
- 1 cup dry white wine

- 1 to 2 cups chicken broth, preferably homemade

**FOR THE *GREMOLADA***
  Grated peel of 1 large lemon (see page 294)
- 10 sage leaves, fresh or preserved in salt (see page 294)
- 15 sprigs Italian parsley, leaves only
- ½ tablespoon rosemary leaves, fresh or preserved in salt or dried and blanched (see page 294)
- ¼ cup olive oil
- 1 teaspoon lemon juice
  Salt and freshly ground black pepper to taste

Soak the beans overnight in a bowl of cold water. Next morning, set a pot with 6 cups of cold water, the oil, sage and prosciutto over medium heat. Drain the beans and add them to the pot; boil for 45 minutes, by which time beans should be almost cooked. Add coarse salt to taste and cook for 2 or 3 minutes more. Drain the beans, place them in a crockery or glass bowl covered with a piece of paper towel dampened in cold water and let stand until needed.

Coarsely chop carrots, onion, celery, parsley, sage and rosemary all together on a board. Heat the oil in a medium-sized casserole over medium heat. When the oil is warm, add the chopped ingredients and sauté for 10 minutes, stirring with a wooden spoon every so often. Season with salt and pepper.

Meanwhile, tie each *ossibuco* with string, so that the meat remains attached to the bone. Place a medium-sized oven-proof casserole with the oil over medium heat. When the oil is warm, add the *ossobuchi*, lightly floured on the cut sides, and sauté for 1 minute on each side. Season with salt and pepper.

When both the *ossibuchi* and the chopped vegetables are ready, ladle all the vegetables and their juices over the meat. Scatter the grated lemon peel and pour the lemon juice over.

Preheat the oven to 375 degrees. Sauté the *ossibuchi* for 2 minutes more, turning them over once. Add the wine and cook for 5 minutes more. Add enough broth to reach the top of the *ossibuchi*, cover casserole and place it in the preheated oven for 1 hour or more, until the meat is cooked and soft, adding more broth as needed.

Transfer the *ossibuchi* to a serving dish and cover the dish to keep the meat warm. Pass the sauce from the casserole through a food mill, using the disc with the smallest holes, into a medium-sized saucepan. Place pan over medium heat, taste for salt and pepper and reduce for 10 minutes or until sauce has a thicker consistency.

Meanwhile, prepare the *gremolada*: Finely chop lemon peel, sage, parsley and rosemary all together on a board. Transfer chopped ingredients to a crockery or glass bowl, add the oil and the lemon juice and season with salt and pepper; mix very well.

When ready to serve, heat the beans in half the sauce over low heat and taste for salt and pepper. Remove strings and arrange *ossibuchi* on individual plates. Top with some sauce and a little *gremolada* and serve with some of the beans on the side.

*The yellow broom flowers, so common in all of Tuscany, are part of the Elba landscape.*

# Polpettone alla Siciliana
## MEAT LOAF, SICILIAN STYLE

SERVES 6 TO 8.

*Castrato*, castrated lamb, is the meat used in the original Sicilian recipe but it is almost unavailable now. I use turkey meat instead, with excellent results.

1 pound all-purpose potatoes
  Coarse-grained salt
1 pound of turkey breast or veal
3 large cloves garlic, peeled and cut into slivers
20 sprigs Italian parsley, leaves only
3 heaping tablespoons capers in wine vinegar, drained

2 whole anchovies, preserved in salt, cleaned and boned (see Note, page 30), or 4 anchovy fillets, packed in oil, drained
  Salt and freshly ground black pepper
  A large pinch of dried oregano
  About ½ cup unbleached all-purpose flour

TO COOK THE *POLPETTONE*
⅓ cup olive oil
1 cup dry white wine
1½ pounds very ripe tomatoes *or* 1½ pounds drained canned tomatoes, preferably imported Italian
  Salt and freshly ground black pepper

Boil the potatoes with the skins on in salted water until very soft, about 35 minutes. Meanwhile, cut the turkey into medium-sized pieces. When potatoes are ready, remove the skins, cut potatoes into pieces and let rest until cold, about ½ hour. Coarsely grind the turkey breast with a meat grinder, using the disc with medium-sized holes, into a crockery or glass bowl. Change the disc to the one with the smallest holes to grind the potatoes, garlic, parsley, capers and anchovies into the bowl with the turkey meat. Season with salt, pepper and oregano, then add 3 tablespoons of the flour and mix everything together, using a wooden spoon.

Sprinkle the remaining flour on a board, turn out the contents of the bowl onto the board and roll it out in the shape of a long loaf, about 3 inches high. Be sure the flour coats the loaf completely.

Heat the oil in a skillet over medium heat. When the oil is rather hot (about 375 degrees), gently transfer the meat loaf to the skillet. Since no eggs or cheese are used as a binder, the loaf is very fragile, and you must handle it very carefully so it does not fall apart. Sauté for 2 minutes, then use two metal spatulas to turn the meat loaf over and sauté for 2 minutes more on the opposite side. Add the wine, tightly cover the skillet and cook for 15 minutes, shifting the loaf a little every so often to let some of the wine get underneath the meat.

If using fresh tomatoes, cut them into pieces. Pass fresh or canned tomatoes through a food mill, using the disc with the smallest holes, into a crockery or glass bowl. Add the puréed tomatoes to the skillet, placing some of the tomato on top of the loaf. Season tomatoes with salt and pepper, then cover the skillet again and simmer for about 20 minutes, basting the meat loaf with the tomato sauce.

Remove the skillet from the heat and let rest, covered, for at least ½ hour before carefully transferring the meat loaf to a serving platter. Pour all the sauce over the meat and let rest for about 15 minutes before slicing the loaf. Top each slice with some of the sauce and serve. This dish may be eaten cold with just the sauce reheated at the very last moment.

*A bunch of fresh oregano*

# Involtini alla Siciliana
## INVOLTINI SICILIAN STYLE

SERVES 6.

In Sicily, as you move from one small town or village to another, from small to large city, you will find a different type of *involtini* specific to each. The stuffing, the wrapping and even the way of cooking will vary. The "bundles" are threaded on a skewer and baked or even deep-fried. When grilled over charcoal, they are usually called *salsiccini*, but they are still basically *involtini*.

I have included a few variations of the stuffing in the recipe, but there are many, many more. Again, I prefer to use Fontina cheese instead of *Caciocavallo*, an authentic substitution, because the latter is very strong and tends to overpower the other flavors.

6 veal scaloppine (about 1 pound), pounded
2 tablespoons (1 ounce) sweet butter, at room temperature

FOR THE STUFFING
15 sprigs Italian parsley, leaves only
2 medium-sized cloves garlic, peeled
3 tablespoons unseasoned very fine bread crumbs, lightly toasted, preferably homemade
3 ounces Bologna or Italian salami
½ pound Fontina or *Caciocavallo* (see headnote)
1 extra-large egg
Salt and freshly ground black pepper to taste

VARIATIONS FOR THE STUFFING
1) To be added to the stuffing
  2 tablespoons pine nuts (*pignoli*)
  2 tablespoons raisins
2) To be added to the stuffing; omit bread crumbs, cheese and 3 ounces Bologna
  4 ounces boiled ham
  3 ounces Italian salami
  4 ounces Italian Bologna
3) Add both 1) and 2) to the remaining ingredeints of the stuffing

TO COOK THE *INVOLTINI*
  2 medium-sized red or white onions, cleaned, sliced in half lengthwise with each half cut into quarters
  About ¾ cup unseasoned very fine bread crumbs, lightly toasted, preferably homemade
  Salt and freshly ground black pepper
  2 extra-large eggs
24 large bay leaves
  2 tablespoons olive oil

TO SERVE
  1 large lemon cut into wedges

Be sure scaloppine are pounded evenly. Melt the butter and let rest until cool. Meanwhile, coarsely grind parsley, garlic, bread crumbs, Bologna or salami and Fontina or *Caciocavallo* all together, using a meat grinder. Add the whole egg to the ground ingredients and season with salt and pepper.

Use a brush to lightly butter 1 side of each *scaloppina*. Place 1/6 of the stuffing on each and roll them up to form 6 bundles. Make sure the stuffing is completely enclosed.

Soak the onions in a bowl of cold water for a few minutes. Season the bread crumbs with salt and pepper and lightly beat the eggs with a little salt.

Preheat the oven to 375 degrees and have hot ash on the hearth ready. The *involtini* are first grilled on skewers over hot ash and then placed in the oven. If you do not have a cooking hearth or open-air barbecue, use the broiler of the oven. If you don't have a broiler, then use just the oven, still preheated to 375 degrees, for both stages.

Dip each *involtino* in the beaten egg, then roll it in the seasoned bread crumbs. Holding 2 metal skewers together (the double skewers will keep the *involtini* from moving as you turn them over), thread 2 pieces of the onion, then 2 bay leaves, the *involtino* and 2 more bay leaves. Keep adding the ingredients in the same order, ending with 2 pieces of onion.

*The* involtini *may be sliced and served on a bed of greens, in the classic Sicilian manner.* Gallo vecchio alla palermitana *has the traditional mixed greens as well. The greens are meant to be eaten together with the meat. This is not a new discovery of "nouvelle cuisine."*

Place the double skewer over the grill, drizzle with 1 tablespoon of the oil and grill for 2 minutes. Turn the *spiedino* over, drizzle with the remaining tablespoon of oil and grill for 2 minutes more. Transfer the skewers with the meat to a baking pan and bake for 15 minutes, turning the meat once. Remove from the oven, transfer the meat and onions onto a serving dish and serve hot with the lemon wedges.

The tiles under the plate of Involtini alla siciliana *on the preceding page are the same as those that pave the Great Stairway of Caltagirone, the most famous in Sicily. Caltagirone's ceramics are among the highest quality in all of Italy and their ceramic school is celebrated.*

# Polpette al Marsala

## MARSALA-FLAVORED MEATBALLS

### SERVES 6 TO 8.

3 ounces crustless white bread
1 cup milk
1 ounce blanched almonds
1 ounce unblanched almonds
1 medium-sized red onion, cleaned (see Note)
3 large cloves garlic, peeled
15 sprigs Italian parsley, leaves only
1 pound pork meat, from the loin, *or* 1 pound beef sirloin
2 extra-large eggs
1 extra-large egg yolk
  Salt and freshly ground black pepper

4 tablespoons dry Marsala
3 ounces Fontina or *Caciocavallo*, cut into very small pieces

TO COOK THE *POLPETTE*

1 cup unseasoned very fine bread crumbs, lightly toasted, preferably homemade (see Note)
1½ cups vegetable oil (½ sunflower oil, ½ corn oil)
¼ cup olive oil

TO SERVE

  Salt
  Lemon wedges

OPTIONAL FOR SERVING

1) Tomato sauce prepared with fresh or canned tomatoes cooked with garlic lightly sautéed in olive oil and seasoned with salt and black pepper.

2) The fried meatballs may be placed in a lightly oiled glass baking dish with 1 teaspoon of dry Marsala poured over each *polpetta*, then baked in an oven preheated to 375 degrees for 10 minutes.

In a small bowl, soak the bread in the milk for ½ hour. Finely grind blanched and unblanched almonds together with the onion, garlic and parsley and place them in a crockery or glass bowl. Coarsely grind the meat and add it to the bowl.

Transfer the bread with all the milk to a small saucepan and set it over low heat. Simmer about 10 minutes, stirring every so often, until a paste forms. Let rest until cool, about ½ hour.

Add the bread "paste" along with the eggs and egg yolk to the bowl and mix very well. Season with salt and pepper, then add the Marsala and the cheese. Stir very well to incorporate all the ingredients. The mixture should be quite smooth and a little loose.

Heat the vegetable oil and olive oil in a skillet over medium heat. Line a serving platter with paper towels. Place the bread crumbs on a plate. Using about 1½ tablespoons of the mixture, form a long rather than round shape, about 1 inch thick. Generously bread all over and fry in the hot oil until golden on all sides, less than 30 seconds on each side. Tranfer the *polpette* to the towel-lined serving platter to absorb excess oil. When all the *polpette* are on the dish, remove the paper from under them, sprinkle with a little salt and serve hot with lemon wedges.

NOTES: *Fifteen scallions, all the green part removed, may be substituted for the onion.*

*You may fry the* polpette *with flour instead of bread crumbs or with no coating at all. Two rarer variations are to dip the* polpette *in lightly salted beaten eggs before coating them with bread crumbs or to first flour them and then dip them in the eggs, omitting bread crumbs.*

# Polpettone di Agnello e Carciofi in Crosta

## LAMB/ARTICHOKE LOAF IN CRUST

### SERVES 6 TO 8.

Wrapping meat, vegetables and cheese in dough is a strong Sicilian tradition, which may have originated in the old *guastelle*, mainly from Ragusa, where bread dough, the size of either whole breads or rolls, is wrapped around meat, most popularly spleen, or different types of cheese. Eventually, the bread dough evolved into *briosce*, a pastry stuffed with meat and vegetables. Included among these dishes are *arancine*, in which rice takes the place of the yeast dough as the wrapper.

3 large artichokes
1 large lemon
15 sprigs Italian parsley, leaves only
2 medium-sized cloves garlic, peeled
6 tablespoons olive oil
Salt and freshly ground black pepper
1½ pounds ground lamb shoulder
2 extra-large eggs
½ cup freshly grated *Pecorino Romano*

FOR THE CRUST
THE SPONGE

1 ounce fresh compressed yeast *or* 2 packages active dry yeast
½ cup lukewarm water, or warm water if using dry yeast
¾ cup plus 1 tablespoon unbleached all-purpose flour
Pinch of salt
Pinch of freshly ground pepper

THE DOUGH

6 tablespoons (3 ounces) sweet butter
5 extra-large egg yolks
½ cup lukewarm water
2½ cups unbleached all-purpose flour
Salt and freshly ground black pepper
Freshly grated nutmeg to taste

TO BAKE

Olive oil to coat the baking dish
1 extra-large egg

Soak the artichokes in a bowl of cold water with the lemon, cut in half and squeezed, for ½ hour.

Clean the artichokes (see Note, page 190) and cut them into small pieces. You will have about 18 ounces of cleaned artichokes.

Finely chop parsley and garlic together on a board. Place a medium-sized casserole with the oil over medium heat. When the oil is warm, add the chopped ingredients and sauté for 1 minute. Add the artichokes, cook for 2 minutes, then add salt and pepper to taste and 1 cup of cold water. Cover casserole and cook, adding more water as needed, until artichokes are very soft and no liquid remains in casserole. If artichokes are not extremely fresh, you may need as much as 3 cups of water to cook them. Transfer contents of casserole to a crockery or glass bowl and let cool for about ½ hour.

Meanwhile, prepare the sponge for the crust: Dissolve the yeast in the lukewarm or warm water. Place the ¾ cup of flour in a bowl and make a well in it. Then add the dissolved yeast and salt and pepper to the well. Mix together the ingredients in the well, then incorporate all the flour. Sprinkle the remaining tablespoon of flour over the sponge, cover the bowl with a towel and let rest in a warm place away from drafts until the sponge has doubled in size (about 1 hour).

(Signs that the sponge has doubled in size are the disappearance of the tablespoon of flour or the formation of large cracks on top.)

Melt the butter in a large metal bowl over a pot of hot water, remove it from the heat and let the butter cool for 5 minutes before using it. When ready, start adding the egg yolks, one at a time, to the cooled butter, mixing with a wooden spoon in a rotary motion. When all the egg yolks are in, add the sponge and the lukewarm water. Mix again very well with a wooden spoon, then start incorporating the flour, a little at a time, stirring constantly until all but ½ cup of the flour is incorporated. Sprinkle salt, pepper and nutmeg over the dough, then mix in ¼ cup more of the flour. At that point the dough should be very smooth and elastic. Cover bowl with a cotton towel until the dough has doubled in size (about 1 hour).

Preheat the oven to 375 degrees and lightly oil a baking dish. Sprinkle the remaining ¼ cup flour on a board. Transfer the dough to the board and knead it for 1 minute, incorporating a little of the flour. With a rolling pin, roll out the dough in a rectangular shape, about ¾ inch thick.

Finish the stuffing: Add the ground lamb, eggs and cheese to the cooled artichokes. Mix very well with a wooden spoon. Taste for salt and pepper. Place the stuffing in the center of the layer of dough and shape it into a long meat loaf. Wrap the dough all around. Transfer the wrapped loaf to the oiled baking dish, placing it with the seam facing down. Lightly oil the dough all over and tightly enclose it in plastic wrap so the *polpettone* keeps its shape while rising and cover it with a cotton towel. Let the wrapped meat rest until doubled in size (about 30 minutes).

When ready, brush the dough with the egg, lightly beaten, and bake for about 40 minutes. Remove from the oven, transfer to a long serving dish and cut into 12 slices. Serve hot, or at room temperature after about 1 hour.

# Sheep Shearing

One does not expect to have three incredible experiences in a day. It would seem to be too much, but when it happened to me, it became a day to remember.

The day was planned around sheep shearing, which I had never before attended. Very early in the morning, at a time when you are usually just thinking about rising, I found myself high on a mountaintop with a cup of warm milk just milked from the sheep. I continued this highly unusual continental breakfast with freshly made goat and sheep ricotta. Then pieces of *carta da musica* bread, used as a receptacle for melting fresh cheese, were placed over a wood fire, and the "bitter" honey from the flowers of the strawberry tree was drizzled over the cheese. The fantastic air, the wind gently blowing in different directions on the mountaintop brought the perfumes from all the different trees and bushes and increased my appetite. After this feast, when I thought I would relax, a glass of wine appeared. The word "no" to a glass of wine does not exist among shepherds. And so you drink what is really the proper finale, even though it is only 9 a.m.

And then the show starts. There were many sheep where I grew up in Chianti, but I avoided the shearing because I had the feeling it might be a bit cruel. I was completely wrong. The animals seem to understand that it must be done and they remain quiet while the incredible hands of the shepherds, wielding a kind of scissors resembling a medieval instrument of torture, remove the entire coat in a few seconds, with not even the tiniest cut on the animal. Amazed by the shearers' skill, I was watching the scene very carefully, but my peripheral vision was focused on something else: the lamb roasting on a very primitive spit. This lamb, along with different types of salamis made by the shepherds (as was everything else we ate) and wild greens gathered nearby from the mountainside by very expert hands, would comprise our "simple" lunch, which started at noon. Afterward, I was barely able to move, but the naked sheep roamed out toward the other mountains, looking very happy to be so much lighter.

# Agnello con Fregola

## LAMB WITH SARDINIAN "PASTA"

SERVES 8 TO 10.

2 pounds boneless lamb shoulder, cleaned and cut into 1½-inch cubes

½ cup olive oil

2 ounces air-dried tomatoes (see headnote, page 112)

1 large red onion, cleaned

10 sprigs Italian parsley, leaves only

5 basil leaves, fresh or preserved in salt (see page 294)

About 1 cup chicken or meat broth, preferably homemade

Salt and freshly ground black pepper

PLUS

1 pound dried *fregola* (see Note, page 72)

4 to 5 cups chicken or meat broth, preferably homemade

TO SERVE

15 sprigs Italian parsley, leaves only

Be sure the lamb has been cleaned and all the extra fat removed. Heat the oil in a heavy medium-sized casserole over medium heat. When the oil is warm, add the lamb and lightly sauté for 5 minutes, stirring every so often with a wooden spoon.

Meanwhile, use a food processor or blender to finely grind the dried tomatoes and then finely chop the onion, parsley and basil all together on a board. Add the ground tomatoes and the chopped ingredients to the casserole containing the lamb and sauté for 10 minutes, stirring with a wooden spoon. Add ½ cup of the broth, lower the heat and simmer, covered, until lamb is very soft, 45 minutes to 1 hour, adding the remaining broth as needed.

When the meat is ready, taste for salt and pepper and mix again. Use a slotted spoon to transfer the meat to a bowl, then cover the bowl to keep the meat from becoming dry.

Bring the broth to a boil over medium heat and preheat the oven to 375 degrees. Add the *fregola* to the casserole containing all the juices and enough boiling broth to cover the *fregola* completely. Simmer for about 20 minutes or more, depending on the dryness of the pasta, adding more broth if needed. *Fregola* should be completely cooked, but still retain its shape.

Arrange all the lamb over the *fregola*, cover casserole and bake for 15 minutes. Remove from oven, transfer contents of casserole to a large warm serving dish, sprinkle with the parsley and serve hot.

# *Agnello alla Sarda*
## LAMB WITH SAFFRON, SARDINIAN STYLE

SERVES 6.

4 large artichokes
1 lemon
30 sprigs Italian parsley, leaves only
3 large cloves garlic, peeled

¼ cup olive oil
2 pounds boned lamb shoulder, fat removed, cut into 2-inch pieces
1 cup dry white wine

Salt and freshly ground black pepper
About 1 cup chicken or meat broth, preferably homemade
A large pinch of ground saffron

Soak the artichokes in a bowl of cold water with the lemon, cut in half and squeezed, for ½ hour. Clean the artichokes (see Note, page 190) and cut them into eighths. Let the artichokes rest in the acidulated water until needed.

Coarsely chop parsley and finely chop garlic on a board. Heat the oil in a medium-sized casserole over medium heat. When the oil is warm, add half of the parsley and half of the garlic and sauté for 2 minutes. Add the meat and sauté over higher heat for 5 minutes, stirring constantly with a wooden spoon. Add the wine and season with salt and pepper. Lower the heat, cover casserole and cook for about 30 minutes, adding some broth as needed. By that time the lamb should be almost cooked.

Drain artichokes and add them to the casserole, over the lamb, without mixing. Sprinkle with a little salt and pepper. Cover again and cook for 10 minutes.

Meanwhile, bring to a boil 1 cup of cold water, add the saffron and be sure the saffron is completely dissolved. Mix the lamb and artichokes, add the water with the saffron, cover again and cook until the artichokes are almost completely cooked, about 10 minutes.

Use a slotted spoon to transfer lamb and artichokes to a serving dish. Cover dish to keep food warm. Reduce the sauce in the casserole to a quite thick consistency. If a lot of fat has risen to the top, remove it. Return meat and artichokes to the casserole, add the remaining parsley and garlic and mix very well. Transfer contents of casserole to a large serving platter and serve hot.

*Mount Etna*

*Catania is at the base of this active, smoking volcano.*

# Salsicce con le Verdure
## SAUSAGES WITH MIXED VEGETABLES

SERVES 6.

½ cup dried chick-peas or shelled and
  skinned fava beans
1 tablespoon olive oil
  Salt and freshly ground black pepper
3 large artichokes
1 lemon
1 pound fresh peas *or* 1 pound "petite"
  frozen peas

FOR THE SAUCE
1 large red onion
15 sprigs Italian parsley, leaves only
1 clove garlic, peeled
½ cup olive oil
  Salt and freshly ground black pepper

PLUS
6 Italian sweet sausages without fennel
  seeds
4 tablespoons olive oil
  About 1 cup chicken or beef broth,
  preferably homemade
  Salt and freshly ground black pepper

Soak the chick-peas in a bowl of cold water overnight. Next morning, drain them
and place them in a medium-sized casserole with 8 cups of boiling water and the
oil over medium heat. Cook for 45 minutes or until they are almost ready but not
yet completely cooked and soft. Season with salt and pepper.

Soak the artichokes in a bowl of cold water with the lemon, cut in half and
squeezed, for half an hour. Clean the artichokes (see Note, page 190), cut them
into fourths and remove choke. Return the artichokes to the acidulated water
until needed.

Finely chop the onion, parsley and garlic all together on a board. Heat the oil
in a large casserole over medium heat. When the oil is warm, add the chopped
ingredients and sauté for 5 minutes. Drain the artichokes and add them to the
casserole along with the fresh or frozen peas (not defrosted). If artichokes are
oversized and hard, add them 15 to 20 minutes before the peas, adding some lukewarm water as needed. Cook for 5 minutes, stirring every so often with a wooden
spoon. Season with salt and pepper. Drain the chick-peas, discard the poaching
water and add them to the casserole. Cover casserole and cook, adding lukewarm
water as needed, about 20 minutes.

Meanwhile, prick the sausages with a fork and heat the 4 tablespoons of oil
in a medium-sized skillet over medium heat. When the oil is warm, add the
sausages and cook them until no pinkness remains, adding the broth as needed
and salt and pepper to taste. When ready, transfer the sausages to a serving dish
and cover the dish with aluminum foil to keep them warm.

By this time, the vegetables should be almost ready; add the pan juices from
the sausages to the vegetables. Mix very well and taste for salt and pepper.
Artichokes, peas and chick-peas should be soft, but still retain their shape.
Arrange the vegetables all around the sausages and serve hot.

# Pane Frattau

## *FRATTAU* BREAD

### SERVES 4.

4 "sheets" *carta da musica* bread (page 242)

4 cups chicken or vegetable broth, preferably homemade

FOR THE SAUCE

1½ pounds fresh tomatoes or drained canned tomatoes, preferably imported

Italian

4 tablespoons olive oil

1 small clove garlic, peeled and cut into slivers

Salt and freshly ground black pepper

5 large fresh basil leaves

PLUS

Coarse-grained salt

1 tablespoon red wine vinegar

4 extra-large eggs

TO SERVE

Freshly grated *Pecorino Sardo* or *Pecorino Romano*

Cut the fresh tomatoes into pieces, then place fresh or canned tomatoes in a medium-sized saucepan with the olive oil, garlic, salt and pepper to taste and the basil leaves; simmer for 15 minutes.

Pass contents of pan through a food mill, using the disc with the smallest holes, into a crockery or glass bowl. Return the strained sauce to the saucepan and reduce for 5 minutes. Taste for salt and pepper.

Set the *carta da musica* bread, 1 sheet at a time, on a large serving platter, pour 1 cup of the broth over it and let soak for 5 minutes. Carefully transfer each bread sheet onto an individual dish.

Pour ¼ of the still very warm tomato sauce over each sheet and spread it out with a ladle. Fold the overhanging pieces of the bread inward to reproduce the shape of the dish itself. Follow this procedure with all 4 sheets of bread.

Place a medium-sized saucepan with 3 cups of cold water over medium heat. When the water reaches a boil, add salt to taste and the wine vinegar. Break 1 egg in the water and carefully, using a small spoon, fold the white over the egg yolk; simmer for 3 minutes. Using a slotted spoon, transfer the *uovo in camicia* (poached egg) onto the bread and tomato sauce of one of the dishes. Repeat the same procedure with the other 3 eggs. Sprinkle abundant grated cheese over the 4 portions and serve.

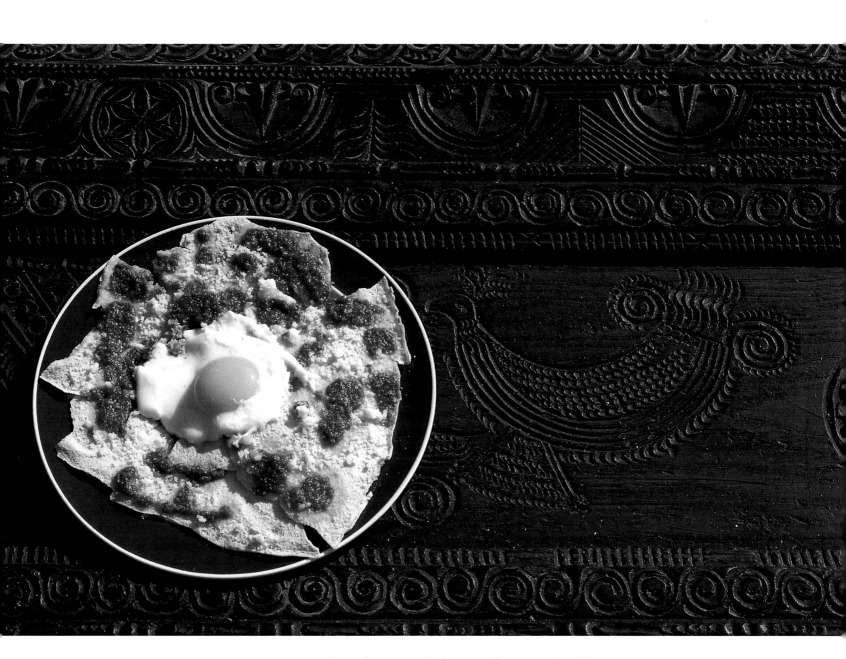

Pane Frattau. *Notice the exquisite Sardinian wood carving on the table.*

# Quaglie alla Stemperata
## QUAIL WITH *STEMPERATA* SAUCE

SERVES 4.

*Stemperata* means "diluted," in reference to the large amount of cold water used to dilute the wine vinegar that forms the liquid in which the ingredients of this dish are cooked. In addition, it is also used to refer to the large quantity of olives which give the dish its character. *Stemperata* sauce is used often with a variety of game meats and fowl, like the quail of this dish, all of which combine very well with it.

FOR THE SAUCE (*SUGO ALLA STEMPERATA*)
- 6 large cloves garlic, peeled
- 6 tablespoons olive oil
- 2 large carrots, scraped
- 3 large celery stalks
- 25 large green olives in brine, drained and pitted
- 3 tablespoons capers in wine vinegar, drained
- 10 large fresh mint leaves
- ½ cup red wine vinegar
- 1½ cups cold water, or more if carrots are not completely cooked
- Salt and freshly ground black pepper

TO COOK THE QUAIL
- 4 quail
- 4 slices pancetta or prosciutto
- Salt and freshly ground black pepper
- 2 tablespoons olive oil

TO SERVE
- Several green olives in brine, pitted but left whole
- Several fresh mint sprigs

Coarsely chop the garlic, then put it in a medium-sized skillet with the oil over medium heat and sauté for 4 minutes or until garlic is golden.

Meanwhile, coarsely chop carrots, celery and olives all together on a board. When ready, add chopped ingredients to the skillet along with the capers and mint leaves, torn into thirds, and sauté for 10 minutes, stirring every so often with a wooden spoon. Add the vinegar and cook for 10 minutes more. Then start adding the cold water, ½ cup at a time, until all the water is used up and the sauce is homogeneous and rather thick. Taste for salt and pepper, remembering that olives in brine give off a lot of salt.

Clean and wash the quail very well and dry them with paper towels. Wrap each quail in a slice of pancetta and sprinkle the cavity of the bird with a little salt and pepper.

Heat the oil in a medium-sized casserole over medium heat. When the oil is warm, add the quail and cook them, turning them several times, until cooked on all sides, about 20 minutes.

Remove pancetta slices from the quail and place birds in the prepared sauce. Let quail cook in the sauce for 2 minutes, with some sauce spooned over them so they absorb the flavors completely.

Transfer everything to a serving dish. Place the whole olives strategically, arrange the mint sprigs around the plate and serve hot. This dish is equally good served at room temperature.

*A display of some of the many varieties of prepared olives*

*In Sicily olives are not only a condiment but are prepared as the main ingredient of dishes.*

# FISH

Sicily's waters yield the full range of Mediterranean seafood. And the Sicilians are among those islanders who consume and enjoy a great deal of it. Some island-dwellers do not take advantage of what their waters offer, but Sicily's many fishermen keep its fish markets stocked with a wide variety. From many dishes ranging from very simple to complex, we have chosen the ones based on fish easily available outside of Sicily that we consider especially interesting.

In contrast, Sardinia does not share the Sicilian enthusiasm for fish. This may be explained in part by its different history. In ancient times, when its coastal settlements were subjected to cruel sea raids by the barbarian and Saracen pirates, the population moved inland, up the hills toward the center of the island. The seaport of Cagliari is a good example of this pattern. The oldest remaining parts of the town, which were built by the Pisan occupiers, are a bit inland, high on a hill. The town was not resettled on the seacoast until more recently. Other evidence supporting this theory are the ruins of the ancient Phoenician and Carthaginian temples also found on the beaches.

The result of this history is that Sardinia, though an island, is more celebrated for the wonderful meat from its mountainous interior than for its fish. Of course, Cagliari, Oristano and Alghero have developed their share of great fish dishes.

Our first five recipes are for dishes based on shrimp from Sicily, Sardinia and Elba. We begin with three from Sicily.

# Crostoni di Gamberi alla Menta

## CROSTONI OF SHRIMP WITH MINT SAUCE

### SERVES 4 TO 6.

In *Crostoni di gamberi alla menta*, the lightly fried shrimp are arranged over large slices of country-style bread and covered with an unusual sauce containing capers and anchovies and flavored with fresh mint.

1 pound shelled and deveined medium-sized shrimp
Coarse-grained salt
1 lemon
Salt
About 1 cup unbleached all-purpose flour

TO FRY
¾ quart vegetable oil (½ corn oil, ½ sunflower oil)
6 tablespoons olive oil

FOR THE SAUCE
2 ounces of crumb from a loaf of bread several days old
½ cup very light red wine vinegar
1 small clove garlic, peeled
2 heaping tablespoons capers in vinegar, drained
1 whole anchovy, preserved in salt, boned and cleaned (see Note, page 30) *or* 2 anchovy fillets, packed in oil, drained
15 large sprigs Italian parsley, leaves only
20 large fresh mint leaves

½ tablespoon granulated sugar
Salt and freshly ground black pepper
6 to 8 tablespoons olive oil, depending on the consistency of the sauce

PLUS
4 to 6 slices of country bread (about 4-by-4 inches and ½-inch thick), lightly toasted
About ¼ cup chicken broth

TO SERVE
Large sprigs Italian parsley, leaves only
Fresh mint leaves

Soak the shrimp in a bowl of cold water with a little coarse salt added and the lemon, cut in half and squeezed, for ½ hour.

Meanwhile, prepare the sauce: Soak the bread in the vinegar for 15 minutes. Squeeze out the bread and discard the vinegar. Place the bread, garlic, capers, anchovy fillets, parsley and mint in a blender or food processor and blend all the ingredients together. Season with the sugar and salt and pepper to taste. Add the olive oil and blend again until a very smooth paste forms. Transfer the mint sauce to a crockery or glass bowl, cover and refrigerate until needed.

Drain the shrimp and rinse them under cold running water, then pat them dry with paper towels. Heat the vegetable oil with the olive oil in a medium-sized skillet over medium heat. When the oil is hot (about 375 degrees), quickly place the shrimp in a large colander, sprinkle them first with some salt, then all the flour. Shake the colander vigorously so excess flour is removed. Place the shrimp in the hot oil, raise the heat and cook for 1 minute, turning the shrimp over 3 or 4 times with a metal skimmer. Heat the chicken broth.

Line a serving dish with paper towels and a second serving dish with the toasted, still lukewarm, slices of bread. Sprinkle each slice with a few drops of the broth. Transfer the shrimp onto the paper-lined dish to absorb excess fat, then transfer and arrange them over the bread slices. Spoon the mint sauce over the shrimp, sprinkle with the parsley and mint leaves and serve. This dish may also be served at room temperature.

# Gamberetti al Sugo
## SHRIMP IN TOMATO/CAPER SAUCE

SERVES 6.

*Gamberetti al sugo* includes in its tomato sauce so many of the wonderful aromas that characterize Sicilian food: the combination of raisins, pine nuts, capers and bay leaves. The tomato does not dominate but melds into a complex flavor.

2 pounds medium-sized shrimp, uncleaned
Coarse-grained salt
1 lemon

FOR THE SAUCE

1 medium-sized red onion, cleaned
2 medium-sized cloves garlic, peeled

1 large celery stalk
1 small carrot, scraped
½ cup olive oil
1 pound very ripe tomatoes *or* 1 pound drained canned tomatoes, preferably imported Italian
Salt and freshly ground black pepper

PLUS

4 tablespoons raisins
4 tablespoons pine nuts (*pignoli*)
6 tablespoons capers, preserved in wine vinegar, drained
8 bay leaves

TO SERVE

Fresh basil and parsley leaves

Soak the shrimp in a bowl of cold water, with a little coarse salt added and the lemon, cut in half and squeezed, for ½ hour.

Bring a medium-sized pot of cold water to a boil over medium heat. Add coarse salt to taste, then drain the shrimp, rinse them under cold running water, add them to pot and cook for 1 minute. Remove shrimp, then shell and devein them and let stand until needed.

Prepare the sauce: Finely chop onion, garlic, celery and carrot all together on a board. Place a medium-sized skillet with the oil over medium heat. When the oil is warm, add the chopped ingredients and sauté for 10 minutes, stirring every so often with a wooden spoon.

If fresh tomatoes are used, cut them into pieces. Pass fresh or canned tomatoes through a food mill, using the disc with the smallest holes, into a crockery or glass bowl. Add tomatoes to pan and cook for 15 minutes, stirring every so often with a wooden spoon. Season with salt and pepper.

Meanwhile, soak the raisins in a small bowl of lukewarm water for 10 minutes and preheat the oven to 375 degrees. Drain the raisins and add them along with the pine nuts and capers to the skillet to cook for 10 minutes more.

Transfer contents of skillet to a medium-sized terra-cotta or glass baking dish. Arrange all the shrimp over the sauce, then distribute the bay leaves over the shrimp. Bake, covered, for 10 minutes. Remove shrimp from oven, discard the bay leaves, mix very well and serve sprinkled with basil and parsley leaves.

# FISH MARKET IN MAZZARA DEL VALLO

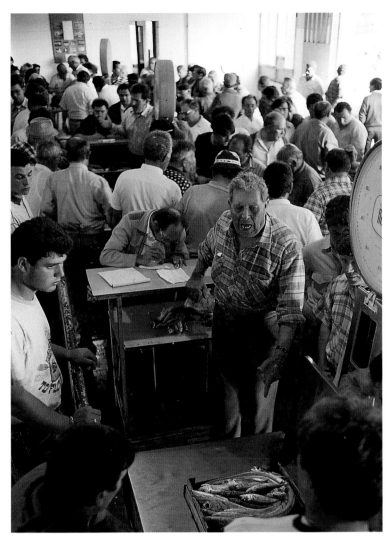

Mazara del Vallo, in the province of Trapani, is a very active fishing port and an important agricultural center close to Selinunte, site of one of the most famous ruins of an ancient Greek city.

From Mazara del Vallo to Selinunte, the landscape is a panorama of classic island beauty, with a wonderful blue sea and very flat fields irrigated by a rustic but very efficient system. Besides the ubiquitous wild fennel and the finocchiella, there is also a very aromatic type of wild parsley, which is what gave Selinunte its name, because this parsley is called selinon in Greek.

In the late afternoon, when the sun is not so strong, there is a long line of different-sized fishing boats returning after a long day of fishing. Just looking at the faces of the fishermen, you understand their catch. If somebody was really unlucky and got very few fish or not very commercial ones, you will hear them crying: Solo scarpe vecchie . . . (only old shoes). But the lucky ones quickly unload the wooden boxes full of different types of fish, go directly inside the fish market and immediately begin the bidding on their "property." Fifteen or twenty fishermen all trying to get the best price for their catches, which most of the time are of the same quality, creates a very animated scene. In that moment you see the skill these fishermen have developed in selling, not only in the shortest time, but especially for the highest price.

# Spiedini di Gamberi alla Siracusana

## GRILLED SHRIMP, SYRACUSE STYLE

### SERVES 6.

In *Spiedini di gamberi alla siracusana*, shrimp are skewered with pieces of yellow and red peppers and then cooked, preferably over hot ash, as done in Siracusa. The hot dish is served with an uncooked, fresh sauce that includes diced tomato, garlic and basil—all ingredients of the local pesto of Syracuse.

24 medium-sized shrimp, shelled and
    deveined
    Coarse-grained salt
1 lemon
1 yellow bell pepper
1 red bell pepper
4 tablespoons olive oil

About 1 cup unseasoned very fine bread crumbs, lightly toasted, preferably homemade
Salt and freshly ground black pepper

FOR THE SAUCE
1 large very ripe tomato (about 8 ounces)
10 sprigs Italian parsley, leaves only

2 medium-sized cloves garlic, peeled
10 large fresh basil leaves
½ cup olive oil
Salt and freshly ground black pepper to taste

TO SERVE
Fresh basil leaves

Soak the shrimp in a bowl of cold water with coarse salt added and the lemon, cut in half and squeezed, for ½ hour.

Clean the peppers, discarding the stems and inner membranes, and cut them into 2-inch squares.

The shrimp and peppers are to be cooked on skewers over abundant hot ash or in the oven. Prepare the fire or when ready preheat the oven to 400 degrees.

Meanwhile, prepare the sauce: Cut the tomato into tiny pieces, with the skin and seeds, and put into a crockery or glass bowl. Coarsely chop parsley and finely chop garlic on a board. Tear the basil leaves into thirds. Add all the aromatic herbs to the bowl with the tomato, then add the olive oil and season with salt and pepper. Mix very well and refrigerate until needed.

When ready, drain shrimp and rinse under cold running water. Thread individual skewers, starting with a piece of pepper, then a shrimp. Each skewer will have 5 pieces of pepper and 4 shrimp. When all the skewers are ready, drizzle with the 4 tablespoons of olive oil, then coat the peppers and shrimp with bread crumbs. Place skewers on a grill with hot ash underneath or in a baking dish placed in the preheated oven. Grill for 2 minutes on each side, seasoning with salt and pepper. Serve immediately with basil leaves and the sauce on the side.

OPPOSITE:
*Mending the fishing nets*

# Gamberi con Piselli

## SHRIMP WITH PEAS

### SERVES 6 TO 8.

From Sardinia, we have *Gamberi con piselli*, shrimp stewed with fresh scallions and peas, and flavored with Sardinia's beloved saffron.

2 pounds medium-sized shrimp, not shelled
Coarse-grained salt
1 lemon

FOR THE SAUCE

15 scallions
2 medium-sized cloves garlic, peeled

15 sprigs Italian parsley, leaves only
½ cup olive oil
1 pound very ripe tomatoes, blanched (see Note, page 40), seeded and cut into small pieces, *or* 1 pound drained canned tomatoes, preferably imported Italian, seeded

Salt and freshly ground black pepper
A large pinch of ground saffron, preferably Sardinian
1½ pounds shelled fresh peas *or* 1½ pounds frozen "petite" peas

TO SERVE

10 sprigs Italian parsley, leaves only

Soak the shrimp in a bowl of cold water with a little coarse salt added and the lemon, cut in half and squeezed, for ½ hour.

Meanwhile, clean the scallions, discarding the green part, and carefully wash them. Finely chop scallions, garlic and parsley all together on a board. Shell and devein the shrimp and wash them under cold running water.

Heat the oil in a medium-sized casserole over low heat. When the oil is warm, add the chopped ingredients and sauté for 10 minutes, stirring every so often with a wooden spoon. Add tomatoes and cook for about 15 minutes. Season with salt and pepper and the saffron, then add the shrimp and cook for 2 minutes. Transfer shrimp to a bowl, trying not to take any of the sauce, and cover bowl to keep shrimp warm.

Add peas to casserole containing tomato sauce, mix very well and cook until they are quite soft, 15 to 25 minutes, adding a little water if needed. Taste for salt and pepper. When the peas are ready, return shrimp to casserole, mix very well, then transfer everything to a large serving platter. Sprinkle evenly with the parsley leaves and serve hot.

# Patate e Gamberi alla Marcianese

## SHRIMP AND POTATOES BAKED WITH TOMATOES

SERVES 6 TO 8.

Marciana Marina, a tiny port in Elba, is known for its *Patate e gamberi alla marcianese*, a shrimp stew that is baked in the oven with potatoes, fresh tomatoes and a large quantity of fresh basil.

2 pounds cleaned medium-sized shrimp
Coarse-grained salt
1 lemon
2 pounds very ripe slicing tomatoes
¼ cup olive oil

FOR THE POTATOES
2 pounds all-purpose potatoes
1 cup vegetable oil (½ sunflower oil, ½ corn oil)
½ cup olive oil
PLUS
Salt and freshly ground black pepper

Hot red pepper flakes
40 large basil leaves, fresh or preserved in salt (see page 294)
TO BAKE
¼ cup olive oil
TO SERVE
Fresh basil leaves

Devein the shrimp and soak them in a bowl of cold water with coarse salt added and the lemon, cut in half and squeezed, for ½ hour.

Cut tomatoes into ½-inch slices and heat the oil in a medium-sized skillet over medium heat. When the oil is warm, start adding the tomatoes, a few at a time, and sauté for 1 minute on each side. Transfer the sautéed tomatoes to a large serving dish. When all the tomato slices are cooked and in the serving dish, pour over all the juices from the skillet. Let tomatoes rest and cool completely.

Meanwhile, peel potatoes and slice them to the same thickness as the tomatoes. Place potatoes in a bowl of cold water as you heat the vegetable and olive oil in a fryer. When the oil is hot (about 375 degrees), drain potatoes, dry them with paper towels and fry them until lightly golden all over, about 10 minutes. Transfer to a serving dish lined with paper towels to drain completely.

Preheat the oven to 375 degrees. Heavily oil a large round oven-proof casserole, preferably of terra-cotta. Arrange half of the potatoes in a single layer on the bottom of the casserole and sprinkle with salt and pepper. Then top the potatoes with a layer of half of the sautéed tomatoes and their juices. Season with salt, pepper and hot pepper flakes; then top the tomatoes with a layer of half of the basil leaves. Drain the shrimp and rinse them very well under cold running water. Arrange all the shrimp over the basil, season with salt and pepper and drizzle with 2 tablespoons of the oil. Repeat the layering but in this order: basil, potatoes and the top layer of tomatoes, seasoning each layer the same as its corresponding lower layer. Pour the remaining olive oil over the top and bake, covered, for 40 minutes, by which time the shrimp should be cooked.

Remove the casserole from the oven and let rest for a few minutes before serving. Use a large serving spoon to spoon out each serving, going all the way through the different layers. Serve topped with basil leaves.

# THE GRAND TONNARA

*T*una and swordfish have an importance in Sicily and to some extent in Sardinia unparalleled by any other fish or meat. They are plentiful, wonderfully fresh and always available. The density of the flesh of these fish makes them as substantial as meat.

Tuna, actually a symbol of Sicily, has endless preparations. Over many centuries the fishing of it has become a ritual usually reserved for the Sicilians, but if one is lucky enough to take part in it, it is an experience never to be forgotten. I spent three days in Trapani in hopes of participating in the expedition, plus two more days waiting for the tuna to "enter" into the stream that would carry them to the Grand Tonnara.

The great tuna fishing festival that takes place off the coast of Marsala in western Sicily in the month of May is not only a fishing expedition but an ancient and picturesque rite. The expedition takes advantage of the passage of large schools of immense tuna at that time of year.

We went out on a boat to accompany the expedition from the island of Favignana, just off the coast at Marsala, home of the famous wine.

Imagine our surprise when we saw the crew of giant long-haired blond fishermen, so unlike the popular image of Sicilians. We learned that Viking raiders of the Middle Ages had settled on this beautiful little island, probably so much more appealing than their frosty homeland, and that they had remained there all these centuries. These men, their descendants, needed all their stamina for the gathering of the huge fish.

The fishing itself is done in a ritualistic way, undoubtedly unchanged since medieval times. The large nets are moved back and forth in rhythm while the men chant a centuries-old traditional song that is chanted only on this occasion, and then with all their force they hoist their rich cargo onto the deck. We remained at sea for many hours, as the fishing must take place far from the shore in the deep waters where the tuna pass.

The tuna come from the deep ocean, pass along the Iberian coast and into the Mediterranean, then down to Sicily to reproduce. Along the way they meet the knowledgeable fishermen of Iberia and Sicily. The Sicilians build a small underwater "city" of nets with its own doors, galleries and corridors all leading to the *corpu* (the "death chamber"), where the catch takes place. The crew (*tunnaroti*) are led by the *rais*, from the Latin *rex* meaning "king," who is in charge of all details of the catch. It is when the *rais* gives the signal that the fish have entered their waters that the *tunnaroti* begin their ancient chanting. The song they sing is the same one that the Spanish sailors chant along their coast.

Four Sicilian tuna recipes and one from Sardinia follow.

Very early in the morning the boats are getting into position surrounding the "city" of nets.

As the fish move toward the *corpu*, the nets are tightened section by section, to a rhythmic chant that ensures that they are pulled evenly. The chant is led by the *rais* and answered by the chorus of the *tunnaroti*, much like the responsorial Gregorian chant.

All the boats have come together in a closed square around the *corpu*. The bottom of the net enclosed within is pulled up, a job requiring great force as the net contains all the huge fish.

The chanting stops and one hears individual groups of three men counting 1, 2, 3. The leader of the group obeys the signal to harpoon a tuna; the other two catch hold of the fins and with great effort lift the giant fish onto the boat.

The tuna are trapped on the boat. One can't help feeling some sadness in that moment for these great defeated creatures.

*A novice tuna fisherman—the author—carefully watching the proceedings of the Tonnara*

# *Tonno all'Agro*

## FRESH TUNA IN SAVORY VINEGAR SAUCE

SERVES 6.

Sardinia's *Tonno all'agro* recalls a classic Genoese seasoning, preserved anchovies combined with dried *porcini* mushrooms. This could reflect a direct influence, as the Genoese fleet was an important presence on the island in medieval times.

2 pounds tuna, in one piece
½ cup red wine vinegar
3 whole anchovies, preserved in salt, boned and cleaned (see Note, page 30) *or* 6 anchovy fillets, packed in oil, drained
1 ounce dried *porcini* mushrooms
2 small red onions, cleaned
2 medium-sized carrots, scraped
2 celery stalks

A few fresh thyme leaves *or* a pinch of dried thyme plus 1 sprig fresh thyme *or* ½ teaspoon dried thyme
½ cup olive oil
2 tablespoons (1 ounce) sweet butter
5 bay leaves
About ½ cup unbleached all-purpose flour
½ pound very ripe tomatoes *or* ½ pound drained canned tomatoes,

preferably imported Italian
Salt and freshly ground black pepper
1 cup white wine
1 lemon

TO SERVE
10 sprigs Italian parsley, leaves only, left whole
2 tablespoons fresh thyme leaves or additional parsley

Clean the tuna, removing the skin, and cut it into 6 slices. Place tuna in a bowl with 6 cups of cold water and the vinegar. Let fish soak for ½ hour.

Soak the mushrooms in 2 cups of lukewarm water for ½ hour. Finely chop onions, carrots and celery all together on a board.

When ready, drain the fish and dry it with paper towels. Top each tuna slice with 1 anchovy fillet cut into 4 pieces each. Season with the few fresh thyme leaves or a small pinch of dried thyme. Roll up each slice and tie it like an *involtino*.

Clean the mushrooms, removing all the sand attached to the stems, and coarsely chop them on a board.

Place a medium-sized skillet with the oil and butter over medium heat. When the butter is melted, add the chopped ingredients, except the mushrooms, the bay leaves and the thyme. Sauté for 10 minutes, stirring every so often with a wooden spoon, then lightly flour the fish and add to the skillet. Cook for 5 minutes, turning it several times.

Pass the tomatoes through a food mill, using the disc with the smallest holes, into a crockery bowl. Season the fish with salt and pepper, add tomatoes and cook for 5 minutes more, by which time the fish should be completely cooked. Transfer the fish to a serving platter and cover platter to keep the fish warm.

Add the mushrooms to the skillet and cook for 2 minutes, then pour in the wine and simmer until a rather thick sauce forms, about 20 minutes. Squeeze lemon and add juice to skillet. Taste for salt and pepper.

Return fish to skillet for less than 1 minute to warm it up, then transfer tuna and all the sauce to a serving platter. Sprinkle with parsley and thyme and serve hot, first removing the thread from the fish *involtini*.

# Tonno al Forno

## BAKED TUNA STEAKS

SERVES 4 TO 6.

For this, a kind of sandwich is made of the tuna steak between layers of a mixture of grated onion and potato. The fish does not overcook after 40 minutes of baking because the layers of onion and potato are thick enough to insulate the fish from most of the heat. The tuna emerges perfectly cooked. This technique is very trendy now, but it has long been used in southern Italy.

2 tuna steaks no thicker than ½ inch (about 1½ pounds total)
6 tablespoons lemon juice
  Coarse-grained salt
½ cup olive oil

5 tablespoons capers in wine vinegar, drained
2 medium-sized cloves garlic, peeled
15 sprigs Italian parsley, leaves only
1 pound all-purpose potatoes
½ pound cleaned red onion

Salt and freshly ground black pepper
TO BAKE THE FISH
2 tablespoons olive oil
TO SERVE
Fresh basil leaves

Clean the tuna very well, then soak it in a bowl of cold water with 2 tablespoons of the lemon juice and coarse salt for ½ hour.

Meanwhile, pour the remaining 4 tablespoons of the lemon juice and the ½ cup of olive oil in a medium-sized crockery or glass bowl. Finely chop capers, garlic and parsley all together on a board, then add them to the bowl containing the lemon juice/oil mixture.

Peel the potatoes and use a hand grater to coarsely grate them directly into the same bowl with the other ingredients. Repeat the same procedure with the onion. Season with salt and pepper and mix very well with a wooden spoon.

Preheat the oven to 400 degrees.

Drain the tuna, rinse it under cold running water and dry it with paper towels. With the 2 tablespoons of oil, coat a glass or terra-cotta baking dish. Sprinkle half of the aromatic herb/vegetable mixture from the bowl over the bottom of the dish. Place the tuna steaks on top, then cover the fish with the remainder of the mixture. Bake for 40 minutes, by which time the fish should be cooked but still quite juicy. Serve directly from the baking dish sprinkled with fresh basil leaves, torn into thirds.

# *Tonno al Cartoccio*

## TUNA COOKED IN A PAPER BAG

### SERVES 4 TO 6.

Just off Messina, in Sicily, is the tiny island of Lipari, one of the Eolie chain. It is famous for its incredibly large capers, and one of its typical dishes is *Tonno al cartoccio*, tuna made with capers.

2 tuna steaks no thicker than ½ inch (about 1½ pounds total)
Coarse-grained salt

1 lemon

2 heaping tablespoons large capers in wine vinegar, drained

15 large sprigs Italian parsley, leaves only

2 basil leaves, fresh or preserved in salt (see page 294)

1 medium-sized clove garlic, peeled

3 tablespoons olive oil
Salt and freshly ground black pepper to taste

PLUS

1 large tomato (about 6 ounces), ripe but not overripe

2 tablespoons olive oil
Salt and freshly ground black pepper

TO SERVE

Parsley and basil leaves, left whole

Soak the tuna in a bowl of cold water with 2 teaspoons of coarse salt added and the lemon, cut in half and squeezed, for ½ hour.

Meanwhile, finely chop capers, parsley, basil and garlic all together on a board. Transfer chopped ingredients to a small crockery or glass bowl, add the oil and season with salt and pepper; mix well.

Drain the tuna, rinse it under cold running water and dry it with paper towels. Spread only 1 side of the tuna with the caper paste.

Preheat the oven to 400 degrees.

Finely slice the tomato without removing skin or seeds. Heat the oil in a large skillet over medium heat and barely sauté the tomato for 2 minutes. Season with salt and pepper. Transfer contents of skillet to a crockery or glass bowl and let rest until needed.

Prepare 2 pieces of parchment paper or aluminum foil large enough to enclose the individual steaks. If using aluminum foil, lightly oil the shiny side before placing the tuna on it. Transfer the tuna steaks to the parchment or foil. Ladle the tomatoes with their juices over the steaks. Fold over the parchment or foil to resemble a bag and bake for about 15 minutes.

Open the "bags," pour some of the juices over the fish and sprinkle with fresh basil and parsley leaves. Serve hot.

# Tonno o Pesce Spada alla Griglia

## GRILLED TUNA OR SWORDFISH, SICILIAN STYLE

SERVES 4 TO 6.

For *Tonno o pesce spada alla griglia* the fish is left in a very aromatic Sicilian marinade, the same one used in Enna for beefsteak, before cooking.

Use 2 tuna or swordfish steaks, each one no thicker than ½ inch (about 1½ pounds total), using all the ingredients and quantities and following the same procedure as those for *Bistecca di Enna* (see page 127).

# Timballi di Tonno

## FRESH TUNA TIMBALES

SERVES 6.

For *Timballi di tonno*, a mold is lined with fried eggplant slices and filled with fresh fish mixed with aromatic herbs and freshly grated *Pecorino*. Unlike other Italians who rarely combine fish and cheese, Sicilians are not so strict.

1½ small thin eggplants, but not baby ones
Coarse-grained salt
1 quart vegetable oil (½ sunflower oil, ½ corn oil)
¼ cup olive oil
1½ cups unbleached all-purpose flour
FOR THE STUFFING
1 pound fresh tuna, in one piece
1 tablespoon coarse-grained salt
1 lemon
10 large sprigs Italian parsley, leaves only

2 medium-sized cloves garlic, peeled
4 tablespoons olive oil
Salt and freshly ground black pepper
PLUS
2 whole anchovies, preserved in salt, boned and cleaned (see Note, page 30) *or* 4 anchovy fillets, preserved in oil, drained and cut into thirds
10 large black olives preserved in brine, pitted and cut into small pieces
4 tablespoons freshly grated *Pecorino* or *Parmigiano*

3 extra-large eggs
FOR THE SAUCE
2 pounds ripe tomatoes *or* 2 pounds drained canned tomatoes, preferably imported Italian
1 large clove garlic, peeled
4 tablespoons olive oil
Salt and freshly ground black pepper
4 tablespoons capers in wine vinegar, drained
TO SERVE
Fresh parsley and basil leaves

Peel the eggplants, removing the stems, and cut them lengthwise into slices less than ¼ inch thick. Place the slices in a bowl of cold water with the coarse-grained salt and let them soak for ½ hour.

Meanwhile, prepare the stuffing: Place the tuna in a bowl of cold water with the tablespoon of salt and the lemon, cut in half and squeezed, and let soak for ½ hour to remove the blood.

Drain the eggplant slices and rinse them many times under cold running water to be sure all the salt is removed. Dry them with paper towels. Heat the vegetable oil together with the olive oil in a large skillet over high heat. When hot (400 degrees), lightly flour the eggplant slices and fry them a few at a time, a few seconds on each side until lightly golden. Transfer the eggplant as it is cooked to a serving dish lined with paper towels to absorb the excess oil. Let the eggplant rest on the paper towels until needed.

Remove tuna from the water, wash it well, pat dry with paper towels and cut it into ½-inch cubes. Coarsely chop the parsley and finely chop the garlic on a board. Set a medium-sized casserole with the oil over medium heat. When the oil is warm, add the chopped ingredients and sauté for 2 or 3 minutes. Add the tuna, season with salt and pepper and cook, mixing every so often with a wooden spoon, for 15 minutes more, breaking up the pieces of tuna a bit more, but not too much. Transfer the fish with its juices to a crockery or glass bowl. Add the anchovies, mix well and let rest until cool (about ½ hour).

As the fish is cooling, prepare the tomato sauce: If using fresh tomatoes, cut them into large pieces. Put tomatoes in a medium-sized saucepan with the whole clove of garlic and olive oil. Place the pan over low heat and let simmer for 25 minutes, stirring every so often. Pass the contents through a food mill, using the disc with the smallest holes, into a second saucepan. Season with salt and pepper and let simmer for 20 minutes more, adding the capers 2 minutes before removing from the heat. Let the sauce stand until needed.

When the fish is cool, add the olives, cheese and eggs and mix very well with a wooden spoon.

Preheat the oven to 375 degrees and start preparing a *bagno Maria* (water bath) by first placing a towel or several layers of paper towels on the bottom of a roasting pan (the water will be added later). Lightly oil 6 custard cups. Line each cup with the fried eggplant slices, letting the longer pieces hang over the edges. Fill each cup with ⅙ of the stuffing, then fold in the tops of the eggplant slices over the stuffing. Place the prepared cups in the roasting pan, then add enough lukewarm water to reach up to three-quarters of the height of the cups. Bake for 35 minutes.

Meanwhile, reheat the tomato sauce. When ready, remove the custard cups from the water and let rest for a few minutes before unmolding onto individual plates. Serve, surrounded by some of the tomato sauce and sprinkled with some parsley and basil leaves.

# Involtini di Pesce Spada
## (Braciole di pesce spada)
## STUFFED SWORDFISH

SERVES 4.

The preparation of the very popular *Involtini di pesce spada* differs from one region of Sicily to the other. In this version from Palermo, the stuffing of the swordfish includes Fontina, a much more delicately flavored cheese than the *Caciocavallo* which is used in Messina on the opposite side of the island. All versions are flavored with fresh bay leaves, which are placed between the *involtini* on the skewers. Whatever the stuffing, the *involtini* may be served with fresh basil or parsley leaves or with *Salmoriglio* sauce (see page 13).

2 large slices swordfish (about 1¼ pounds total or about 1 pound when cleaned and skinned)
1 lemon
   Coarse-grained salt
4 ounces Fontina
4 cloves garlic, peeled
10 sprigs Italian parsley, leaves only
4 basil leaves

2 tablespoons pine nuts (*pignoli*)
1 tablespoon raisins
   Reserved trimmings of the fish (about 1 ounce)
2 extra-large eggs
   Salt and freshly ground black pepper
TO BAKE
   About ½ cup unseasoned very fine

bread crumbs, lightly toasted, preferably homemade (optional)
2 fresh tomatoes, cut into ½-inch-thick slices
   Several bay leaves
1 tablespoon olive oil
TO SERVE
   Fresh basil leaves

Divide the 2 slices of fish in half to make 4 fish *braciole*. Trim the slices, discarding the skin, and reserve the trimmings. The fish should weigh about 1 pound. Soak the fish for ½ hour in a bowl of cold water with a little coarse salt added and the lemon, cut in half and squeezed.

Prepare a wood fire or preheat the oven to 400 degrees or light your broiler.

Grind all the trimmings of the fish together with the Fontina, garlic, parsley, basil, pine nuts and raisins in an electric meat grinder directly into a crockery or glass bowl. Add the eggs and salt and pepper to taste to the bowl; mix very well.

Divide the stuffing in fourths, one for each slice of fish; roll up the *involtini*. If you desire, coat the *involtini* with bread crumbs, seasoned with salt and pepper. Skewer the *involtini*, alternating slices of tomatoes, bay leaves and the *involtini*. Drizzle with the oil and when the wood is covered with plenty of hot ash put the skewers on the grill or under the broiler or in the preheated oven. Cook for about 10 minutes on each side.

If you decide not to coat the *involtini* with bread crumbs, cooking time will shorten by 2 or 3 minutes per side.

Remove everything from the skewer and divide it into 4 portions. Arrange each *involtino* on an individual plate with slices of cooked tomatoes. Serve hot.

## VARIATION
In the Messina area, the stuffing is prepared with the trimmings of the fish chopped together with unseasoned lightly toasted bread crumbs, garlic, capers and basil, with or without cheese. The cheese used is generally *Caciocavallo*, but I prefer the much lighter flavored Fontina. The *involtini* are coated with bread crumbs and baked for 20 minutes in a 400-degree oven.

*The* Involtini *are facing Piazza Pretoria in Palermo with its famous fountain by the Florentine F. Camilliani about 1575.*
*The nude statuary of the fountain was old stuff for Florence, but in Palermo it was known as "Fountain of Shame."*

2 large cloves garlic, cleaned

2 tablespoons unseasoned very fine
  bread crumbs, lightly toasted, preferably homemade

2 tablespoons capers in wine vinegar,
  drained

4 fresh basil leaves

4 ounces *Caciocavallo* or Fontina cheese

Salt and freshly ground black pepper

2 extra-large eggs

TO BAKE AND TO SERVE, SEE ABOVE.

FISH

# Pesce alla Griglia alla Sarda
## WHOLE GRILLED FISH, SARDINIAN STYLE

SERVES 4.

*Pesce alla griglia alla sarda* exemplifies the islanders' fondness for simplicity. A real Sardinian, especially one from the southern part of the island, adores fish very simply grilled over charcoal. But the preferred method is to place a fresh-caught fish, without cleaning or scaling it, directly on the grill. Once the fish is perfectly cooked, it is carefully skinned and cleaned and then filleted. The seasoning is extremely simple: the fish is soaked in salted water either just before being placed on the grill or after the cleaned fish are filleted. I admit that, not being Sardinian, I do add a few drops of olive oil and a twist of fresh black pepper in the restaurant, even though my Sardinian neighbors give me a contemptuous glance. Needless to say, a wood fire is the preferred method, but the fish also can be broiled.

1 whole fish (about 2 pounds) with head, tail and all the scales left on
Enough cold water to completely cover the fish, placed in a large roasting pan
1 tablespoon coarse-grained salt for every 5 cups of water used to cover the fish

1 large lemon divided in half and squeezed for every 5 cups of water used to cover the fish

OPTIONAL
2 large cloves garlic, peeled and left whole

2 medium-sized dried wild fennel stalks

TO SERVE
Olive oil
Freshly ground black pepper

Carefully wash the fish under cold running water. Leave head, tail and all the scales on. Place the fish in a large glass roasting pan, then add enough cold water to cover and coarse salt as prescribed above. If garlic and wild fennel stalks are used, add them now. Let the fish marinate for 1 hour in a cool place or in the refrigerator.

Prepare a wood fire. The wood should be covered with white ash before the fish goes on the grill. Alternatively, preheat the broiler.

When ready, place the fish directly on a grill over the ash or under the broiler and cook it for 5 to 10 minutes on each side, depending on its size. The scales of the fish must become quite dark in color and almost burned.

Transfer the cooked fish to a board and use a fork and a spoon to remove all the skin. The skin with all the scales attached will come off very easily because the heat detaches the flesh naturally from the skin. Remove the head and the tail and fillet the fish. Serve the whole fillet or part of the fillet with just two drops of olive oil and a half twist of black pepper. In Sardinia most of the time not even the oil and pepper are used.

## VARIATION
The grilled fish is soaked for a few minutes in the same marinade as above but with warm rather than cold water, then cleaned, filleted and served.

# Zuppa di Pesce all'Aragosta

## FISH SOUP WITH LOBSTER

SERVES 6.

For *Zuppa di pesce all'aragosta*, unshelled pieces of lobster are served in their thick sauce, accompanied by bread or *focaccine* toasted and rubbed with garlic.

20 sprigs Italian parsley, leaves only
4 large cloves garlic, peeled
½ cup olive oil
2 pounds very ripe tomatoes, blanched (see Note, page 40) and seeded

Salt and freshly ground black pepper
PLUS
2 medium-sized lobsters, parboiled and cut into large pieces with the shell on

TO SERVE
Several slices of country-style bread or small individual *focaccine*, toasted and rubbed with garlic

Finely chop parsley and garlic together on a board. Heat the oil in a medium-sized casserole over medium heat. When the oil is warm, add the chopped ingredients and sauté for 1 minute. Cut the tomatoes into large pieces and add them to the casserole. Lower the heat, season with salt and pepper and simmer for at least 45 minutes, stirring every so often with a wooden spoon. If the sauce becomes too thick, add about ½ cup cold water.

Add the lobster pieces, mix very well, cover and stew for about 10 minutes.

Divide lobster, shell intact, and sauce among individual bowls and serve hot with *focaccine* still warm from the oven. Sometimes this dish is sprinkled with an abundant amount of fresh basil leaves, cut into thin strips.

*A fishing scene in the ancient Roman mosaics at Piazza Armerina*

# Merluzzo alla Palermitana

## WHITING, PALERMO STYLE

### SERVES 6.

*Merluzzo* is as popular in Sicily as it is throughout the rest of Italy. The light taste of the fresh little whitings is usually enhanced by strong seasonings, as it is here by rosemary and anchovies, in this Palermo version.

3 whole whitings (about 3 pounds) *or* 6 whiting fillets (about 1½ pounds)
Coarse-grained salt
1 large lemon
4 whole anchovies, preserved in salt, boned and cleaned (see Note, page 30) *or* 8 anchovy fillets, packed in oil, drained

4 tablespoons olive oil
15 sprigs Italian parsley, leaves only
1 medium-sized clove garlic, peeled (optional)
4 large sprigs fresh rosemary
2 tablespoons unseasoned very fine bread crumbs, lightly toasted, preferably homemade

Salt and freshly ground black pepper to taste
TO BAKE
2 tablespoons olive oil
1 large lemon, cut into very thin slices
TO SERVE
Juice of 1 large lemon

Open the fish and remove the central bone. You may leave the head and tail on, leaving the fish whole, or remove the head and tail and cut the fish into 2 fillets. Soak the fish in a bowl of cold water, with a little coarse salt added and the lemon, cut in half and squeezed, for ½ hour.

Heat the oil in a small saucepan over low heat. When the oil is lukewarm, add the anchovies and mash them with a fork. Be sure the oil does not become too hot, otherwise the anchovies will crumble and become too strong. Transfer the anchovy sauce to a crockery or glass bowl and let cool for a few minutes.

Finely chop the parsley, with or without the garlic, on a board and preheat the oven to 400 degrees.

Lightly oil a glass baking dish and place the opened whole fish or 1 of the fish fillets in it. Arrange half of the anchovy sauce over 1 side of the whole fish or 1 of the fish fillets. Then place a rosemary sprig over the sauce and sprinkle it with a little salt and black pepper. Use less salt if the anchovies were preserved in salt rather than in oil. Fold over the other side of the whole fish to close it or fit another fish fillet on top of the first to reconstitute a whole fish. Then pour over the remaining anchovy sauce. Sprinkle the chopped parsley, or parsley/garlic, over the anchovy sauce, then lightly sprinkle with the bread crumbs. Season with salt and pepper. Arrange the lemon slices over the fish and circle it with the remaining rosemary sprigs. Bake for 35 to 40 minutes.

Remove fish from oven and discard the lemon slices. Carefully transfer the fish to a warmed serving platter, squeeze the lemon all over and serve hot.

# Pesce alla Vernaccia

## FISH COOKED IN VERNACCIA WINE

### SERVES 4.

*Pesce alla Vernaccia* is simply sautéed and finished with the very characteristic dry Sardinian Vernaccia wine.

1 (2-pound) red snapper or other non-oily fish, completely scaled and cleaned, but with head and tail left on
1 lemon

Coarse-grained salt
1 cup unseasoned very fine bread crumbs, lightly toasted, preferably homemade
Grated peel of 1 large lemon (see page 294)

½ cup olive oil
Salt to taste
1 cup Vernaccia di Oristano (see Note) or dry sherry

TO SERVE
Large black Greek olives, left whole

Soak the fish in a bowl of cold water with the lemon, cut in half and squeezed, and a little coarse salt for ½ hour.

Combine the bread crumbs with the lemon peel. Drain and rinse the fish under cold running water, but do not pat it dry. Coat the fish with the bread-crumb mixture, making sure the fish is completely coated.

Set a large skillet with the oil over medium heat. When the oil is very warm, add the fish, season with salt and sauté for 1 minute. A very light golden crust will form. Carefully turn the fish, sprinkle with salt and sauté for 1 minute more. Pour in the Vernaccia or sherry, lower the heat to medium and slowly cook until the fish is completely done, about 20 minutes, depending on the thickness of the fish. The flat fish, though not as flat as sole or flounder, should be thin enough so the wine can almost cover the whole fish when it is added. Otherwise, at a certain point, the fish will have to be turned again to be sure the other side is completely done.

Add the olives and cook for 1 minute more, then transfer everything—fish, sauce and olives—to a large serving platter. The fish is never filleted before cooking because it would lose a lot of its flavor.

NOTE: *A great Sardinian dessert wine,* Vernaccia di Oristano *is produced in the province of Caliari. Its taste proceeds from pleasant, almost aromatic, to strong and full-bodied, with the complex taste of bitter almonds. It is often compared to sherry as a cooking wine, but I disagree. When it is used in cooking, its alchobol evaporates, leaving an incomparable taste which is not the same as that achieved with sherry. Simple fish dishes finished with this wine are transformed into something so marvelous and classical, they need few other ingredients.*

*Vernaccia di Oristano is also extremly pleasant as an aperitif, an after-dinner drink or an accompaniment to dessert.*

### OPPOSITE:

*The setting is the ruins of the Phoenician city of Tharros, which passed to Carthage then to Rome. The ruins show one of the clearest examples of the Roman sewage system. There is great beauty in the suggestive ruins set against the blue sea, often full of herons.*

# *Aragosta alla Catalana*
## MARINATED LOBSTER SALAD

SERVES 6.

I have never seen this recipe in a cookbook, but in Alghero we ate it everywhere, and the Sardinian cook in a favorite restaurant of mine on the Tuscan coast also makes it. There are several local variations of the dish. Sometimes the marinade contains large pieces of lemon or radish and one version is made with a bit of anchovy. The dish was photographed against the dome of a church of Alghero, San Gaetano, patron saint of the city. The remarkable dome is made of ceramic tiles of many different colors.

FOR THE DRESSING
½ cup very good olive oil
3 tablespoons fresh lemon juice
1 medium-sized clove garlic, peeled
Salt and freshly ground black pepper to taste

FOR THE SALAD
1 pound of boiled lobster meat *or* the meat of 2 (1¼-pound) boiled lobsters, cut into pieces
1 cup coarsely diced celery, taken from the white inner stalks
¾ pound fresh tomatoes, ripe but not overripe, cleaned and diced with skin and seeds
1 medium-sized red onion, cleaned and diced (to yield about 1 ounce)
20 large fresh basil leaves
25 large fresh mint leaves
PLUS
Arugula (*rucola*) or Boston lettuce or red radicchio or a mixture thereof to line serving dish.
Additional diced tomatoes and onions

Combine the olive oil, lemon juice and the garlic in a blender or food processor and blend very well. The garlic will be completely puréed and will form a smooth emulsion with the oil and lemon juice. Season with salt and pepper and blend again.

Place the lobster pieces in a crockery or glass bowl, top with the celery, then the tomatoes and finally the onion. Pour the dressing over the vegetables and top with all the basil and mint leaves. Do not mix. Cover the bowl with plastic wrap and refrigerate for at least 1 hour.

Mix salad very well, cover again and refrigerate for ½ hour more.

Prepare a large serving dish, arranging all the greens in a layer along with the extra tomatoes and onions, and top with the lobster mixture. Drizzle with the dressing and serve.

This lobster dish may be used as an appetizer as well, in which case the amount of vegetable and aromatic herbs would be the same but the amount of lobster would be reduced by half. Sometimes a few medium-sized shrimp, boiled, shelled and left whole, are added to the lobster mixture.

# Couscous alla Trapanese
## COUSCOUS, OLD TRAPANI STYLE

SERVES 8.

Unlike Sardinian couscous, the Sicilian *Couscous alla trapanese* is a main course. Its unusual feature is that fish and chicken are combined in the same dish, a duo sometimes found in Spain but not in Italy. It has become very difficult to find authentic preparations of this dish because today Italians often omit the chicken.

Nowadays people rebel as much at the amount of work and time required to make real couscous as they do to make real polenta. Certainly precooked versions of these grains save time but it is important to understand that in using these precooked versions, the real flavor and texture of the dish are sacrificed.

FOR THE SAUCE

- 1 large red onion, cleaned and coarsely chopped
- ½ cup olive oil
- 1½ pounds of blanched and seeded tomatoes (see Note, page 40), cut into large pieces
  About 2 pounds fish heads and tails, wrapped in cheesecloth
  Salt and freshly ground black pepper
  A large pinch of hot red pepper flakes
- 20 sprigs Italian parsley, leaves only
- 6 large cloves garlic, peeled
- 10 very large fresh basil leaves, left whole
- 4 tablespoons tomato paste
- 3 cups completely defatted chicken broth, preferably homemade

FOR THE FISH AND CHICKEN

- 6 medium-sized *calamari* (about 1½ pounds), cleaned and cut into ½-inch rings
- 2 pounds of different types of non-oily fish, cut into large pieces, with bone (Langoustine, the small lobsters, are optional.)
- 1 large lemon
  Coarse-grained salt
- 1 chicken (about 3 pounds), cut into 10 pieces, with all the extra fat removed

FOR THE COUSCOUS (NOT PRECOOKED)

- 1 pound couscous
  Salt to taste
- ½ cup lukewarm water
  A large pinch of ground saffron
- 2 tablespoons olive oil

- 5 large bay leaves

FOR THE BROTH

- 4 quarts very light chicken broth, preferably homemade
- 4 bay leaves
  A large pinch of ground saffron
- 4 medium-sized carrots, scraped and cut into large pieces

FOR PRECOOKED COUSCOUS

Follow the procedure printed on the box, adding oil, not butter, as well as the bay leaves and ground saffron listed above.

TO SERVE

- 3 or 4 langoustine for decoration (optional)
- 15 sprigs Italian parsley, leaves only, coarsely chopped

Soak the chopped onion pieces in a bowl of cold water for ½ hour. Soak the *calamari* and fish pieces in a large bowl of cold water with the lemon, cut in half and squeezed, and a little coarse salt for ½ hour.

If you are making your own couscous, place the (not precooked) grain in a large bowl. Add salt to the water along with the saffron and start adding the water by tablespoonfuls while constantly rubbing the grains between the palms of your hands. Do not add extra water until the previous tablespoonful has been completely absorbed by the grain and uniformly distributed. When all the water is used up, oil your palms and again rub the grains. Keep repeating until all the oil is used up.

Place the 4 quarts of broth along with the bay leaves, saffron and carrots in a stockpot and bring to a boil over medium heat. Line a colander with a thick cheesecloth then mix the prepared couscous with the bay leaves and put it in the prepared colander. Fold the cheesecloth over the top and insert the colander in the stockpot containing the boiling

broth. Tightly cover the colander with a lid or with aluminum foil. If you have a lot of space between the stockpot and the colander, you can seal it by wrapping a kitchen towel dampened in cold water all around or you can make a dough with flour and water, and attach it all around the opening in order to keep the steam from coming out. (The dough method is Sicilian and probably older than the cloth method.) Let simmer for 1 hour.

Meanwhile, heat the oil in a large casserole over medium heat. When the oil is warm, drain the onions and add them to the casserole; sauté for 5 minutes, stirring constantly. Add the tomatoes and cook for 15 minutes, stirring every so often with a wooden spoon. Add the fish heads and tails with their cheesecloth wrapping and cook for 15 minutes, turning the "bags" over 2 or 3 times. Season with salt, pepper and the hot pepper flakes.

Finely chop parsley and garlic together on a board. Add the chopped ingredients along with the whole basil leaves to the casserole, mix very well and cook for 5 minutes more. Dissolve the tomato paste in the broth and pour it into casserole. Lower heat and simmer for 1 hour. The liquid should be reduced by half. Remove and discard the cheesecloth with all its fish bones.

Taste the sauce for seasoning. Start adding the fish that require at least 35 minutes of cooking time, such as calamari, to the broth. Add the other fish and chicken pieces that take less time as appropriate. The chicken will not take more than 20 minutes to cook. Open the cheesecloth, mix the couscous very well to be sure no lumps have formed, then close it again and cook for 1 hour more.

When the sauce is ready and the fish and chicken are cooked, transfer the couscous to a large serving platter. Pour all the sauce over the couscous, arrange all the fish and chicken, with or without langoustine, on top and sprinkle with parsley. Serve hot.

# VEGETABLES

*M*ost of the vegetables used throughout Italy exist in traditional island recipes. The Sicilian ones, especially, are usually elaborate preparations, often with many ingredients added to the main vegetable to create complex flavors. Such preparations acquire the importance of a main rather than a side dish, even when they are served with meat or fish. Among the vegetables most stressed—perhaps more than they are on the mainland—are eggplant, zucchini, peppers, cauliflower, broccoli and artichokes. And, after Tuscany, the islands offer the greatest variety of dishes using beans, especially the ancient Mediterranean ones, favas, chick-peas and lentils, along with the more recently imported cannellini from the New World.

# Asparagi in Salsa
## ASPARAGUS WITH SAUTÉED ONIONS

SERVES 4.

The asparagus used most commonly both in Sicily and Sardinia are very thin wild ones. They are thinner even than the more familiar cultivated pencil asparagus, and are quite dark in color and with a much more intense flavor. The best known cultivated green asparagus come from the area of Pescia, in Tuscany, while the white ones are native to Bassano, in the Veneto, in Northern Italy. The sauces made with wild asparagus are more pungent, complex and aromatic than those of their better known domestic relatives, which when appropriately poached and dressed with a few drops of uncooked olive oil reveal their milder flavor.

1 pound asparagus, thinnest available
1 medium-sized red onion, cleaned
5 tablespoons olive oil

10 sprigs Italian parsley, leaves only
10 large basil leaves, fresh or preserved in salt (see page 294)

Salt and freshly ground black pepper
TO SERVE
Fresh basil leaves

Remove the white part of the asparagus and cut the remaining green part into 2 pieces, stem and tip. Soak the two different parts in separate bowls of cold water for ½ hour.

Finely chop the onion on a board. Place a medium-sized casserole with the oil over low heat. The size of the casserole should be large enough so the asparagus can be spread out in no more than 2 layers. When the oil is warm, add the chopped onion and gently sauté for 10 minutes, stirring every so often with a wooden spoon.

Coarsely chop parsley and basil together on the board. When the onion is ready, drain the 2 bowls of asparagus. Add the stems to the casserole first, then the tips over them, and sauté for 2 minutes. Add 1 cup of cold water and sprinkle with the prepared parsley and basil. Season with salt and pepper, raise the heat to medium and cover casserole. Cook for 1 minute. If the asparagus are quite thin, by that time they should be ready, cooked but still with a bite; otherwise, add a little more cold water and cook for a few minutes more. Mix very well, and taste for salt and pepper. Cook on high flame for 30 seconds, mixing vigorously, then transfer the contents of casserole to a serving dish. Sprinkle the asparagus with whole basil leaves and serve hot.

# Carciofi
## ARTICHOKES

Italy has many varieties of artichoke, which have different seasons. The species also vary in size, and most artichoke dishes are associated with a particular size of the vegetable as well as with its season.

The tiny artichokes are generally preserved in oil or in a specially concocted aromatic brine. Among the famous dishes associated with the medium-sized ones is *Carciofi alla romana*, with its pungent taste of wild mint, or *mentuccia*, as the Romans call it. Medium-sized and larger artichokes are stuffed. And the Roman artichokes are also used for the celebrated *Carciofi alla giudia*, which are flattened and fried.

Sardinians use the vegetable a lot and have their own prized dishes, but they do not go as far as the Romans in treating the cooking of artichokes as a rite. (In the Campo de'Fiori market of Rome you find stand after stand full of artichokes arranged as huge bouquets of flowers, and the owners, mostly women, proudly declaiming the beauty and delicious flavor of their own as opposed to those of their competitors.)

FROM SARDINIA

# *Carciofi Verdi*
## "GREEN" ARTICHOKES

### SERVES 3 TO 6.

3 large artichokes
1 lemon
15 large sprigs Italian parsley, leaves only

3 large basil leaves
3 large cloves garlic, peeled
5 tablespoons olive oil
Salt and freshly ground black pepper

PLUS
2 extra-large eggs
A pinch of salt
TO SERVE
Lemon slices

Soak the artichokes in a bowl of cold water, with the lemon cut in half and squeezed, for ½ an hour. Clean the artichokes, removing the choke and the tough leaves (see Note, page 190). Cut them first into quarters, then cut each quarter in half. Return the artichoke pieces to the acidulated water until needed.

Finely chop parsley, basil and garlic all together on a board. Set a skillet with the oil over medium heat. When the oil is warm, add the chopped ingredients and sauté for 1 minute, then drain the artichokes, add them to the skillet and cook for 2 minutes, gently mixing them. Season with salt and pepper, add ¾ cup of lukewarm water, cover skillet and cook for 10 minutes more, turning the pieces twice and adding more water if needed. Artichokes should be almost cooked and quite soft but still retain their shape.

Lightly beat the eggs with a pinch of salt and pour them over the artichokes. Mix very well, still on the heat, making sure the eggs are coating the artichokes before transferring the contents of the skillet to a warm serving platter. Serve immediately with lemon wedges.

# Carciofi al Forno
## BAKED ARTICHOKES

SERVES 4 TO 8.

4 large artichokes
2 lemons
   Coarse-grained salt
1 tablespoon unbleached all-purpose flour
20 sprigs Italian parsley, leaves only

2 cloves garlic, peeled
¼ cup unseasoned very fine bread crumbs, lightly toasted, preferably homemade
   Salt and freshly ground black pepper

¼ cup olive oil
   About ½ cup very light chicken broth, preferably homemade
¼ cup freshly grated *Pecorino Romano*
15 fresh mint leaves

Soak the artichokes in a bowl of cold water, with one of the lemons cut in half and squeezed, for ½ hour. Clean the artichokes, removing the tough leaves and the choke, and cut them into quarters (see Note). Return the cleaned artichokes to the acidulated water until needed.

Bring a medium-sized stockpot of cold water to a boil over medium heat. Add coarse salt to taste, the remaining lemon cut in half and the tablespoon of flour dissolved in 1 cup of cold water. Drain artichokes and add them to the stockpot; cook for at least 5 minutes. The time varies a lot depending on the artichokes; they are ready when they are no longer hard but still have a bite. Transfer artichokes onto paper towels and cover them with additional paper towels moistened with cold water.

Preheat the oven to 375 degrees.

Finely chop parsley and garlic together on board. Mix the chopped ingredients with the bread crumbs in a small bowl, adding a pinch of salt and black pepper.

Lightly oil a glass baking dish and mix the remaining oil with the broth. Make a layer of the artichoke quarters with the inside part facing up. Sprinkle the artichokes evenly with herbed bread crumbs, then the grated cheese and finally the mint leaves. Drizzle with the olive oil and bake, covered, for 20 minutes. Remove from oven and serve directly from the baking dish.

NOTE: *To clean artichokes, trim off all of the darker outer ring of the stem. The inner core is the best part because it has the real taste of the artichoke. Remove as many rows of the outer leaves as necessary to arrive at those tender inner rows where you can clearly see the separation between the green at the top and the light yellow at the bottom. Then remove the top green part. Press your thumb on the bottom of each leaf, the white part, to hold it in place, and with the other hand, tear off the top green part. As each new row is uncovered the tender yellow part of the leaves will be bigger.*

*When you reach the rows in which only the very tips of the leaves are green, cut off all the tips together with a knife.*

*It is best to cut the artichoke into quarters lengthwise, in order to remove the choke. Draw the tip of the knife blade across just below the choke to draw it out.*

*Outside of Italy I find the larger artichokes produce a result closer to the Italian ones.*

VEGETABLES

# Vucciria Market

Unlike the great markets of other cities, Vucciria Market in Palermo cannot easily be described in words; it must be "lived." For a little while, you can forget that just a few steps away there is a modern city. Vucciria is a small island resounding with the cries of vendors and buyers. More than other markets, it completely fills the air with its perfumes, as the name implies. Wherever you look, there are little shops and stands, old as well as new, overflowing with food. But the design and arrangement are always perfect. All the tails of the fish are tied to their heads, so you see rows and rows of fish seemingly alive and ready to swim again. That such an abundance can form so perfect a design is remarkable.

Vucciria is not merely a place to vend and to buy: it is also the place where people of all the social classes of the city mingle; it is filled with the people of the city. You can see a rich man in a business suit picking up a fish or some produce, smelling it, carefully looking it over, while next to him a craftsman who could be his own employee is doing the same to select the best-quality food at the best price.

Shopping in a food market in the south of Italy is always the duty of the male head of the house, not his wife, and mostly done before going on to work. This is not a result of male superiority but rather of respect for the wife, who is busy at home raising the children and running the household. Late in the afternoon the market is empty, everything and everybody gone. But when the first light of dawn appears, the show starts again and the sounds recommence with the first cries of the vendors.

If you understand this market, you will understand the Sicilians and the almost religious respect they have for their food and you will appreciate their rejection of and disdain for any modern innovation. Their loyalty to the old traditions are perhaps even stronger now than at the time when the novel *The Leopard* takes place—in the mid-1800s—and the old prince tells the representative of the newly unified Italy that Sicilians cannot be improved because they are already perfect.

VEGETABLES

193

# Cavolfiore
## CAULIFLOWER

Even for a Sicilian moving from one town, small or large, to a different one, it is very difficult, and some say impossible, to understand precisely when to use the term *cavolfiore*, as the white head called "cauliflower" in English may also be called *broccoló*, *vruocculo*, *vruoccolo pieno*, or even the plural form, *broccoli*. This confusion of terminology applies to many different varieties of the cabbage family produced and used locally in the different southern regions of Italy. It is most important to know when a recipe for *broccoli* (which means literally "hard flower") calls specifically for cauliflower. The following dishes, two from Sicily and one from Sardinia, are made with white cauliflower.

What I have noticed after touring the different markets in Italy is that the heads of cauliflower are much bigger than those I see abroad, contrary to the usual Italian preference for smaller vegetables (though the baby or so-called Japanese size is completely avoided).

*Cavolfiore alle olive*, from Sardinia, has a pungent taste produced by the combination of finely chopped air-dried tomatoes and green olives, mixed at the very last moment before serving.

*Cavolfiore alla siciliana* has the classic ingredients of many Sicilian dishes: raisins, onion, garlic, anchovies, saffron and pine nuts. What gives this dish its unique taste is the addition to the combination of a large amount of fresh basil.

*Cavolfiore o broccolo in pastella* uses a very unusual batter for the frying, based on the technique for making the sponge for a dough, which is then seasoned with anchovy pieces. In one contemporary version, a little anchovy paste is also added to the batter.

## FROM SARDINIA
# Cavolfiore alle Olive
## CAULIFLOWER WITH GREEN OLIVES

SERVES 4 TO 6.

| | | |
|---|---|---|
| 1 large cauliflower<br>Coarse-grained salt | 1 ounce air-dried tomatoes, preferably imported Italian from Sardinia (not dried and packed in oil) | About 1 cup chicken or beef broth, preferably homemade |
| 1 small red onion, peeled | | PLUS |
| 1 medium-sized clove garlic, peeled | ½ cup olive oil | 20 large green olives in brine, pitted and |
| 10 sprigs Italian parsley, leaves only | Salt and freshly ground black pepper | cut into pieces (see Note) |

Clean the cauliflower, removing the outer green leaves, and let rest in a bowl of cold water for ½ hour. Bring a large pot of cold water to a boil, add coarse salt, then the whole cauliflower, and cook for 5 minutes. Using a large strainer-skimmer, transfer cauliflower to a board. Detach all the flowerets and set them aside on a serving dish, covered with a wet cotton towel. Discard remainder of cauliflower.

Finely chop onion, garlic, parsley and the dried tomatoes all together on a board. Heat the olive oil in a medium-sized casserole over medium heat. When the oil is warm, add the chopped ingredients and sauté for 5 minutes. Add the flowerets, mix with a wooden spoon and season with salt and pepper. Cook for 15 minutes more, then add ½ cup of the broth. Cover and cook over low heat for another 5 minutes, by which time the cauliflower should be properly cooked and tender. (If a little more cooking is needed, add more broth.)

Two minutes before the cauliflower finishes cooking, add the olives. Mix well and taste for salt and pepper. Serve hot or at room temperature.

NOTE: *If olives have a very strong taste, soak them in a bowl of cold water for ½ hour.*

FROM SICILY

# *Cavolfiore alla Siciliana*
## CAULIFLOWER WITH RAISINS AND ANCHOVIES

SERVES 8.

2  medium-sized cauliflower (about 2 pounds each), cleaned and left whole
Coarse-grained salt
½  cup raisins
2  medium-sized red onions, cleaned

3  large cloves garlic, peeled
½  cup olive oil
4  whole anchovies in salt, boned and cleaned (see Note, page 30), *or* 8 anchovy fillets in oil, drained
2  large pinches of ground saffron

1  to 1½ cups chicken or beef broth, preferably homemade
Salt and freshly ground black pepper
5  tablespoons *pignoli* (pine nuts)
15  medium-sized fresh basil leaves, torn into thirds

Soak the cauliflower in a bowl of cold water for ½ hour. Bring a large pot of cold water to a boil over medium heat, add coarse-grained salt to taste, then the cauliflower, and cook for 4 minutes. Transfer cauliflower to a board, cover with a wet towel and let rest until needed.

Soak raisins in a bowl of lukewarm water for ½ hour. Thinly slice onions and finely chop garlic on the board. Place a large skillet with the oil over medium heat. When oil is lukewarm, add anchovy fillets and mash them with a fork. Add onions and garlic and sauté for 5 minutes or until onions are translucent.

Meanwhile, detach the flowerets from the cauliflower and drain the raisins. When onions are ready, add flowerets and sauté for 2 minutes, mixing with a wooden spoon. Dissolve the saffron in 1 cup of the broth. Add broth and pine nuts to skillet; mix well. Taste for salt and pepper and cook until cauliflower is cooked but still firm, about 15 minutes. When almost ready, add the raisins and mix well. Transfer contents of skillet to a large serving platter, sprinkle evenly with basil and mix. Serve hot.

# Cavolfiore o Broccolo in Pastella
## CAULIFLOWER IN YEAST BATTER

SERVES 4 TO 6.

FOR THE *PASTELLA* (BATTER)
   THE SPONGE
  1 ounce compressed fresh yeast *or* 2
    packages active dry yeast
  ½ cup lukewarm water, or warm water
    if using dry yeast
    A pinch of salt
  ¾ cup plus 1 tablespoon unbleached
    all-purpose flour

PLUS
  4 anchovies in salt, boned and cleaned
    (see Note, page 30), *or* 8 anchovy fil-
    lets in oil, drained
  1 extra-large egg
  ½ cup lukewarm water
    A pinch of salt
    Freshly ground black pepper to taste
  ½ cup unbleached all-purpose flour

  1 medium-sized cauliflower
    Coarse-grained salt to taste
FOR FRYING
  3 cups vegetable oil (½ sunflower oil,
    ½ corn oil)
  ¼ cup olive oil
TO SERVE
    Salt
    Lemon wedges

Prepare the *pastella* first: Dissolve the yeast in the water in a small bowl, stirring with a wooden spoon. Add a pinch of salt. Place the ¾ cup of flour in a larger bowl, make a well in the flour and add the dissolved yeast. Mix with the wooden spoon until all the flour is incorporated. Sprinkle the remaining tablespoon of flour over the sponge mixture. Cover bowl with a cotton dish towel, put it in a warm place away from drafts and let it stand until doubled in size (about 1 hour).

Meanwhile, remove and discard all the green leaves from the cauliflower and soak it in a bowl of cold water for ½ hour.

Bring a large pot of cold water to a boil, add coarse-grained salt to taste, then the cauliflower and, counting from the moment the water returns to a boil, cook for 5 minutes. Cauliflower should not be completely cooked. Cooking time of cauliflower as for all the winter vegetables, such as cardoons and rape *(broccolirab)*, is difficult to determine because the tenderness depends on the amount of cold weather to which they have been exposed. Use a strainer-skimmer to transfer the head of cauliflower, left whole, to a plate, cover with a towel dampened with cold water and let stand until cool, about ½ hour.

Finely chop anchovies on a board.

When the sponge is ready and the cauliflower is cool, add the chopped anchovies to the sponge along with the egg and mix very well with a wooden spoon. Add the water and mix, then add salt and pepper to taste. Add the ½ cup of flour, a tablespoon at a time, continuously mixing with the wooden spoon until all the flour is well incorporated and the batter is smooth, about 10 minutes.

Place a large skillet with the vegetable oil and the olive oil over medium heat and let the oil heat until it reaches about 400 degrees.

Meanwhile, detach all the flowerets from the stem of the cauliflower and discard the stem. Line a serving dish with paper towels.

When the oil is hot, dip each floweret in the batter and place it in the hot oil. Sometimes 1 or 2 cloves of garlic, peeled and left whole, are also placed in the oil and removed and discarded once they turn dark. Add enough cauliflower pieces to fill the skillet but not crowd it. Cook on both sides until golden, about 30 seconds per side. Use a strainer-skimmer to transfer the cooked cauliflower onto the

towel-lined serving dish. Repeat until all the flowerets are cooked, then remove the paper towels and serve immediately, sprinkled with a little salt, and lemon wedges.

NOTE: *The names* broccolo *and* calvofiore *are interchangeable but very frequently we find* broccolo *"translated" for broccoli or broccoli rape.*

# Cavolo e Patate Saltate

## STEWED CABBAGE AND POTATOES

### SERVES 6 AS A SIDE DISH.

Savoy cabbage is used frequently in different soups or *minestroni* in Sardinia, though it is not a vegetable often cooked as a side course as it commonly is in the Friuli region. In this Sardinian vegetable course, once the cabbage is blanched, it loses its somewhat strong taste and then, when combined with the potatoes, becomes extremely mellow.

2 pounds Savoy cabbage leaves, cleaned and large veins removed

1 pound peeled all-purpose potatoes, cut into 1½-inch pieces
Coarse-grained salt

3 large cloves garlic, peeled but left whole

6 bay leaves

¾ cup chicken or vegetable broth

PLUS

5 tablespoons olive oil

2 large cloves garlic, peeled and cut into slivers
Salt and freshly ground black pepper
A large pinch of hot red pepper flakes

Cut the cabbage into thin strips and place in a bowl of cold water for ½ hour. Put the potatoes in another bowl of cold water.

Set a large pot of cold water over medium heat. When the water reaches a boil, add coarse salt to taste, then the garlic and bay leaves. Let boil for 15 minutes. Drain the cabbage and add it to the boiling water to cook for 5 minutes, then use a strainer-skimmer to transfer the cabbage from the boiling water to a bowl. Drain the potatoes and add them to the pot of boiling water to cook, also for 5 minutes, then transfer them to another bowl. Discard the boiling water along with the garlic and bay leaves.

Place a casserole with the oil over low heat. When the oil is warm, add the garlic and immediately top with the cabbage. Season with a little salt and pepper. Add the potatoes, season again with salt and pepper, cover casserole and cook for 10 minutes, without mixing but shaking casserole every so often so that nothing sticks to the bottom. Pour in the broth and cover again. Cook for 10 more minutes, adding the hot pepper.

Remove lid from casserole, increase the heat to medium and gently mix all the ingredients together. Cook for 10 minutes more. The cabbage should be cooked and very soft and potatoes cooked just right, not overcooked. Serve hot.

# Carote al "Vino Vecchio"

## CARROTS COOKED IN "OLD WINE"

### SERVES 4 TO 6.

Though boiled vegetables, including carrots, are often sauced with melted butter in other countries, in Italy such use of a pure butter sauce is quite rare. Carrots do have an affinity for butter, which brings out their sweet flavor, but it is used in Italy as one ingredient in a more complicated sauce for the vegetable. In one notable treatment from Lombardy, butter is combined with heavy cream, which is absorbed little by little by the carrots; in another recipe, it is combined with broth and parsley, an herb that is particularly complementary to them. This Sicilian treatment employs mellow, aged Marsala wine with olive oil (no butter), parsley and garlic to produce one of the best sauces for carrots that I know.

| | | |
|---|---|---|
| 1 pound carrots, scraped | 2 large cloves garlic, peeled but left whole | 1 cup dry Marsala |
| 4 tablespoons olive oil | Salt and freshly ground black pepper | TO SERVE |
| | | 15 sprigs Italian parsley, leaves only |

Cut carrots into disc less than ¼ inch thick and place them in a bowl of cold water for 30 minutes. When carrots are ready, heat the oil in a skillet over medium heat. When the oil is warm, add garlic and sauté for 5 minutes until lightly golden; discard garlic. Drain carrots and add them to the skillet. Season with salt and pepper and sauté for 2 minutes, constantly stirring with a wooden spoon. Add Marsala and cook, covered, for 10 minutes more, stirring every so often with a wooden spoon. If by that time the carrots are not sufficiently cooked, add a little cold water and continue until they are completely cooked but still firm. Transfer carrots to a serving dish, sprinkle with parsley and serve hot.

# Ceci alla Sarda

## STEWED CHICK-PEAS, SARDINIAN STYLE

SERVES 6 TO 8.

Chick-peas are delicious simply cooked in seasoned boiling water and served with the lightest sauce, even with just a little olive oil, salt and pepper. *Ceci alla sarda* is at the other end of the spectrum, a more elaborate presentation containing aromatic vegetables, prosciutto and three herbs: parsley, basil and the one which perhaps gives it its particular Sardinian character, bay leaves. A complex dish, it becomes almost a main course.

2 cups dried chick-peas
 Coarse-grained salt

FOR THE SAUCE

15 sprigs Italian parsley, leaves only
1 medium-sized carrot, scraped
2 celery stalks

1 small red onion, cleaned
3 ounces pancetta or prosciutto, in one piece
5 tablespoons olive oil
1 pound fresh tomatoes *or* 1 pound drained canned tomatoes, preferably

imported Italian
 Salt and freshly ground black pepper
5 bay leaves

TO SERVE

15 fresh basil leaves, left whole

Soak the chick-peas in a bowl of lukewarm water overnight. Next morning place a medium-sized pot of cold water over medium heat. Drain and rinse the beans and add them to the pot. Let simmer for about 1 hour, by which time chick-peas should be cooked but still have a bite. Add coarse salt to taste and cook for 5 minutes more.

Finely chop parsley, carrot, celery and onion all together on a board. Coarsely grind or cut into small pieces pancetta or prosciutto. Place a skillet with the oil over medium heat. When the oil is warm, add the chopped ingredients and the pancetta. Cook for 10 minutes, stirring every so often with a wooden spoon.

If fresh tomatoes are used, cut them into pieces. Pass fresh or canned tomatoes through a food mill, using the disc with the smallest holes, into a crockery bowl. Add tomatoes to skillet and cook for 5 minutes more, seasoning with salt and pepper. Drain the chick-peas, saving some of the cooking water, and add drained beans to skillet. Arrange all the bay leaves over the beans. Cover skillet and cook for at least 15 minutes. Peas should be completely soft and a rather thick sauce formed. If the sauce becomes too thick, add some of the cooking water from the beans.

Transfer contents of skillet to a large serving platter; remove and discard bay leaves. Sprinkle evenly with the basil and serve.

OPPOSITE:
*The Sardinian interpretation of classic Pisan architecture is evident in this church. Another part of the same church is pictured on pages 260 and 261.*

# Cipolline in Casseruola

## BUTTON ONIONS IN SWEET AND SOUR SAUCE

SERVES 4 TO 6 AS AN APPETIZER.

1 pound button onions, cleaned
  Coarse-grained salt

FOR THE SAUCE

2 small cloves garlic, peeled
1 tablespoon capers in wine vinegar,
  drained

½ small red onion, cleaned
2 celery stalks
15 sprigs Italian parsley, leaves only
5 basil leaves
4 tablespoons olive oil

1 tablespoon tomato paste
½ cup red wine vinegar
2 tablespoons granulated sugar
  Salt and freshly ground black pepper
  to taste

Soak the onions in a bowl of cold water for ½ hour. Bring a large pot of cold water to a boil, add coarse salt to taste, then drain the onions and add them to the pot. Cook for 2 minutes, then remove onions from the water and rinse them in cold water but do not let them soak. Set aside until needed.

Prepare the sauce: Coarsely chop garlic, capers, onion, celery, parsley and the basil all together on a board. Heat the oil in a medium-sized skillet over medium heat. When the oil is hot, add the chopped ingredients and sauté for 5 minutes, mixing with a wooden spoon. Add the onions, gently sauté for 2 minutes, then dissolve tomato paste in the vinegar. Pour in the vinegar and cook for 5 minutes. Add ½ cup of water with the sugar and cook for 15 minutes more. Season with salt and pepper, then add more water and continue cooking for about 25 minutes. The onions should be cooked but still quite firm and the sauce rather thick. Serve hot.

*The baked onions are sold in the market.*

# Cipolle al Forno
## BAKED ONIONS

SERVES 12 AS APPETIZER OR 8 AS SIDE DISH.

Nothing is simpler than this preparation. The secret lies in the slow, even heat, which develops the sweetness at the core of the onions. The addition of a few simple seasonings produces a wonderful result that must be tried.

5 pounds medium-sized white onions, not cleaned

PLUS

6 tablespoons olive oil

Salt and freshly ground black pepper
A large pinch of dried oregano
White wine vinegar to taste

TO SERVE

Fresh basil and Italian parsley leaves

Preheat the oven to 375 degrees. Lightly wash the unpeeled onions in cold water and dry them with paper towels. Place the onions in a single layer in a baking pan and bake for 1½ hours or until onions are wrinkled.

Transfer onions to a board and clean them. Discard outer layers, then slice inner ones and arrange them on a serving dish. Season with olive oil, salt, pepper, oregano and white wine vinegar. Serve as an appetizer or a side dish with fresh basil and parsley.

VEGETABLES

206

# *Fagiolini all'Aglio*
## STRING BEANS IN GARLIC SAUCE

### SERVES 8.

The use of the long beans in place of the thin string beans for this dish is quite common, even though the latter have a more delicate taste and texture. This preference may be due to the strong flavorings which perhaps favor the more substantial long beans, recommended here as a second choice only because they are not always available. The sharp taste of the anchovies is balanced well by the sweetness of the butter and the basil, which complement either kind of bean.

1 pound cleaned string beans or long beans, cut into 4-inch pieces
Coarse-grained salt
2 large cloves garlic, peeled
20 sprigs Italian parsley, leaves only

15 large basil leaves, fresh or preserved in salt (see page 294)
2 whole anchovies, preserved in salt, boned and cleaned (see page 30), *or* 4 anchovy fillets in oil, drained

4 tablespoons olive oil
1 tablespoon (½ ounce) sweet butter
Salt and freshly ground black pepper to taste

TO SERVE
Fresh basil and Italian parsley leaves

Soak the beans in a bowl of cold water for ½ hour.

Bring a medium-sized stockpot of cold water to a boil over medium heat, add coarse salt to taste, then drain the beans and add them to the pot. Cook for 10 or 12 minutes (for long beans the time will be at least twice as long). Beans should still be quite firm. Transfer beans to a colander and cool them under cold running water.

Finely chop garlic, parsley, basil and anchovies all together on a board.

Place a skillet with the oil and butter over medium heat. When the butter is melted, add the chopped ingredients and sauté for 5 minutes, stirring constantly with a wooden spoon. Add the beans to the skillet and mix very well. Season with salt and pepper and cook for a few minutes more or until the beans are tender and evenly coated with the sauce.

Transfer the contents of skillet to a serving platter, sprinkle evenly with basil and parsley leaves and serve.

*Fresh borlotti beans, shelled*

# *Fagioli*
## BEANS

Both of these recipes come from Sardinia, but there is a big difference between them. The first is from Gallura, the region with the most celebrated beaches on the island, such as the *Golfo degli Aranci* and the famous *Costa Smeralda*, where the cooking has transformed Gallura's everyday ingredients into something more "continental." A little inland, however, in the mountains, where the native cooking has endured, the people love to have just one elaborate dish for dinner, even if it contains little or no meat. This first bean recipe includes cabbage, fennel seasoning, onion and garlic, which are further enriched by pancetta. The use of the poaching broth with some *carta da musica* bread turns one basic preparation into a two-course dinner: first the soup and then the fully satisfying bean and vegetable main course.

The second recipe, *Fagioli al tegame,* is more typical in its simplicity, with few ingredients, and one especially dominant flavor—rosemary.

# Fagioli alla Gallurese

## BEANS COOKED WITH SAVOY CABBAGE

SERVES 6.

1 cup dried beans, cannellini or borlotti
1 pound Savoy cabbage leaves, cleaned
2 fresh wild fennel stalks *or* all the leafy tops of 2 fennel bulbs and 1

medium-sized dried wild fennel stalk (see Note, page 94)
1 medium-sized red onion, cleaned
2 tablespoons tomato paste
4 ounces prosciutto or pancetta, in one piece

2 large cloves garlic, peeled
Salt and freshly ground black pepper
TO SERVE
Freshly ground black pepper
Olive oil

Soak the beans in a bowl of cold water overnight. Next morning place a medium-sized stockpot with 3 quarts of cold water over medium heat. When the water reaches a boil, drain the beans, add them to the pot and simmer for 30 minutes.

Meanwhile, cut the leaves of the cabbage into 1-inch strips and the wild fennel into 1-inch pieces. If, instead, you are using the leaves of the fennel bulbs along with the dried stalk of wild fennel, cut the leaves of the fennel bulbs into 1-inch pieces, but leave the dried stalk whole. Coarsely chop the onion on a board. Place all the cut-up vegetables in a bowl of cold water and let stand until needed.

Drain vegetables and add them to the pot with the half-cooked beans. Simmer for 5 minutes more, then add the tomato paste and keep simmering until beans are almost cooked (about 20 minutes).

Finely grind prosciutto and garlic together, using a meat grinder. When beans are almost done, add the ground pprosciutto and garlic with salt and pepper to taste; simmer for 2 minutes more.

Remove pot from heat and let rest for a few minutes before transferring the solids with a slotted spoon to a serving dish. Remove and discard the dried stalk of wild fennel if used. Serve hot. Sprinkle each serving with some freshly ground black pepper and drizzle with olive oil.

NOTE: *The broth may be used to cook pasta or served with some broken up* carta da musica *bread (page 242).*

# Fagioli al Tegame

## CANNELLINI BEANS WITH PROSCIUTTO

SERVES 8.

1 pound dried cannellini beans
1 tablespoon fresh rosemary leaves
2 tablespoons olive oil
   Coarse-grained salt

PLUS
   2 ounces prosciutto or pancetta, in one piece
   3 large cloves garlic, peeled
   1 tablespoon fresh rosemary leaves
   5 tablespoons olive oil

Salt and freshly ground black pepper
About ½ cup of the bean cooking water

TO SERVE
   Freshly ground black pepper
   Rosemary sprigs

Soak the beans in a bowl of cold water overnight. Drain the beans and rinse under cold running water. Place a medium-sized casserole with 3 quarts of cold water over medium heat. Add the beans, rosemary and olive oil and simmer for about 45 minutes. Beans should be almost cooked and quite soft. Add coarse-grained salt to taste and simmer for 5 minutes more. Strain the beans, discarding the rosemary leaves but saving the cooking water. Let the beans cool, covered, in a crockery or glass bowl.

When beans are ready, cut prosciutto or pancetta into tiny pieces and finely chop garlic and rosemary together on a board. Place a medium-sized casserole with the oil over low heat. When the oil is lukewarm, add prosciutto and chopped ingredients. Lightly cook for 2 minutes, stirring with a wooden spoon. Add the beans, season with salt and pepper and simmer, covered, without mixing for 3 or 4 minutes. Add ½ cup of cooking water and mix well. Cover casserole and cook for about 15 minutes, always on low heat. The water should be absorbed by the beans.

Transfer beans to a large warmed serving platter and serve with freshly ground black pepper over each portion.

# Melanzane in Forno
## BAKED EGGPLANT, SARDINIAN STYLE

SERVES 8.

Sardinia's version of baked eggplant is more complex than that of the Puglia region or even Sicily itself. Here the eggplant tastes very highly seasoned, which results not from many ingredients, but rather from aromatic ones, garlic and especially air-dried tomatoes, which impart an emphatic, definitive taste.

4 medium-sized thin eggplants (about 2 pounds total), but not baby ones
Coarse-grained salt
5 medium-sized cloves garlic, peeled

15 sprigs Italian parsley, leaves only
1 ounce air-dried tomatoes
8 tablespoons olive oil

Salt and freshly ground black pepper
TO SERVE
15 sprigs Italian parsley, leaves only

Clean the eggplants, discarding the stems. Cut each eggplant lengthwise in half. Place eggplant halves on a serving platter with the cut side facing up. Sprinkle evenly with coarse salt and let rest for ½ hour.

Preheat oven to 400 degrees.

Use a blender or food processor to finely grind garlic, parsley, tomatoes and 4 tablespoons of the oil until a paste forms. Transfer to a crockery or glass bowl and season with salt and pepper. Mix very well and set aside until needed.

Rinse the eggplants very well under cold running water, then dry them with paper towels. Use a sharp knife to make several slits in the pulp of the eggplants and insert in each slit some of the prepared "stuffing." Lightly oil a baking dish. Arrange all the eggplants in the dish, drizzle with the remaining 4 tablespoons of the oil and bake for 30 minutes.

If the eggplants are thin and young, they should be very soft after ½ hour and ready to be served, sprinkled with some of the parsley leaves; otherwise bake them until soft. The eggplants also may be eaten at room temperature, drizzled with a little more olive oil.

## *Patate*
### POTATOES

It might seem that potatoes do not occupy the preeminent position in Italy that they do in some northern countries, where for many the principal meal of the day must have some potato side dish with the main course. But we should not underestimate the role the vegetable plays in Italian cooking. It appears as an appetizer in fritters or in a potato salad flavored with olive oil, garlic and parsley (never with mayonnaise); as a first course such as *gnocchi*, in soups, *minestroni*, pasta, even in a dessert dish.

Roasted or fried, potatoes, like other vegetables, are often a course by themselves. Boiled, whole or puréed, they more often accompany a main dish of boiled meats or steamed fish. Some of the dishes in which potatoes create the perfect balance are the classic *cotechino* (large boiled sausage) or *zampone* (stuffed pork foot) with mashed potatoes, or those in which the potatoes are roasted with meats to absorb their juices or placed below a spit to absorb the drippings from the turning skewers.

The first recipe, *Patate al tgame*, which is flavored with Sicily's beloved saffron, oregano, garlic and parsley, is the perfect side dish for any of the island's meat or fish courses. The second, also from Sicily, may be served at room temperature as an appetizer or warm as an accompaniment for boiled or other simple main courses that could use a lift from the garlic, green olives and capers in the potatoes.

### FROM SICILY
# *Patate al Tegame*
## POTATOES IN CASSEROLE

### SERVES 4 TO 6.

2 pounds all-purpose potatoes
20 sprigs Italian parsley, leaves only
2 large cloves garlic, peeled
¼ cup olive oil

Salt and freshly ground black pepper
2 large pinches of dried oregano
¾ cup lukewarm water with a large pinch of ground saffron dissolved in it

TO SERVE
10 sprigs Italian parsley, leaves only, left whole

Peel the potatoes, cut them into 2-inch cubes and place them in a bowl of cold water until needed.

Finely chop parsley and garlic together on a board. Heat the oil in a heavy medium-sized casserole over medium heat and preheat the oven to 375 degrees.

When the oil is warm, add the chopped ingredients and sauté for 1 minute. Drain potatoes and add them to the casserole. Mix very well, season with salt, pepper and the oregano and cook for 5 minutes. Add the lukewarm saffron water, cover the casserole and bake for 35 minutes. By that time potatoes should be cooked and almost all the water absorbed. Sprinkle with fresh parsley leaves and serve.

# *Patate in Salsa o Condite*
## POTATOES IN CAPER/OLIVE SAUCE

### SERVES 4.

1½ pounds all-purpose potatoes

FOR THE SAUCE

  1 large red onion, cleaned

  ½ cup olive oil

  2 ounces pitted green olives in brine, drained

  2 ounces capers in wine vinegar, drained

 15 sprigs Italian parsley, leaves only

    Salt and freshly ground black pepper

  1 tablespoon red wine vinegar

TO SERVE

  2 ounces pitted green olives in brine, left whole

Peel the potatoes, cut them into 2-inch cubes and soak them in a bowl of cold water until needed.

Finely chop the onion on a board. Place a medium-sized casserole with the oil over medium heat. When the oil is warm, add the chopped onion and sauté for 15 minutes, stirring every so often with a wooden spoon.

Meanwhile, finely chop olives, capers and parsley all together on a board. Drain potatoes and add to casserole; mix very well. Add ⅓ cup cold water, cover casserole and cook for 5 minutes. Add another ⅓ cup cold water, mix again, cover and cook for 5 minutes longer. Keep adding very small amounts of cold water, mixing and covering, until potatoes are almost cooked. Add the chopped ingredients, season with salt and pepper and cover casserole again. After a few minutes potatoes should be ready. Add the vinegar and keep mixing constantly for 30 seconds. Potatoes should be cooked but not mushy. Transfer contents of casserole to a serving dish, sprinkle evenly with the whole olives and serve.

This dish is still very good a few hours later.

# Patate e Funghi in Forma
## BUDINI OF POTATOES AND MUSHROOMS

SERVES 8.

The humble potatoes do a bit of social climbing in Elba, where they are combined with wild *porcini* mushrooms and then shaped into small timbales, to become, in Cinderella style, quite a refined dish.

¾ ounce dried *porcini* mushrooms
2 cups lukewarm water
1 pound all-purpose potatoes
   Coarse-grained salt
½ pound fresh mushrooms
10 sprigs Italian parsley, leaves only

2 cloves garlic, cleaned
5 tablespoons olive oil
1 tablespoon tomato paste
   Salt and freshly ground black pepper
PLUS
4 extra-large eggs
½ cup freshly grated *Parmigiano*

6 tablespoons heavy cream
   Enough butter to coat 8 custard cups
   About ½ cup unseasoned very fine bread crumbs, lightly toasted, preferably homemade

Soak the dried *porcini* mushrooms in the lukewarm water for ½ hour. Meanwhile, peel potatoes and place them in a bowl of cold water until needed.

Place a medium-sized pot of cold water over medium heat. When the water reaches a boil, add coarse salt to taste, then drain potatoes, add them to the pot and boil for 30 minutes or until very soft. Drain boiled potatoes and rice them with a potato ricer into a crockery or glass bowl.

Drain the *porcini* mushrooms, saving the soaking water. Clean the mushrooms, removing all the sand attached to the stems, and strain the soaking water by passing it through paper towels.

Clean the fresh mushrooms and coarsely chop them on a board. Coarsely chop parsley and garlic together. Heat the oil in a medium-sized casserole. When the oil is warm, add the chopped parsley and garlic and sauté for 2 minutes.

Meanwhile, coarsely chop *porcini* on a board and add them to the casserole; sauté for 5 minutes, stirring every so often. Dissolve the tomato paste in the mushroom water. Add fresh mushrooms to casserole, season with salt and pepper and sauté for 5 minutes more. Start adding the mushroom water, a little at a time; cover casserole and cook for about 20 minutes, adding all the remaining water as liquid is needed. Transfer the contents of the casserole to a crockery or glass bowl and let cool completely.

When ready, preheat the oven to 375 degrees and place several layers of paper towels or a cotton towel on the bottom of a baking pan to prepare a water bath (*bagno Maria*).

Mix the cooled mushroom mixture with the riced potatoes, taste for salt and pepper and add eggs, *Parmigiano* and the heavy cream; mix very well.

Butter and lightly line with bread crumbs 8 custard cups. Divide the stuffing equally among the cups. The mixture should fill about three-quarters of the cup. Place cups in the baking pan, then pour in enough lukewarm water to reach almost to the level of the mixture. Bake for 40 minutes.

Remove from oven, transfer the cups to a rack and let cool for 5 minutes before unmolding them onto individual plates.

A very light tomato sauce may be served with the *budini*. Prepare sauce with 1½ pounds of tomatoes, 4 basil leaves and 3 tablespoons of olive oil, cooked all together, then passed through a food mill and seasoned with salt and pepper.

# *Peperonata alla Siciliana*

## PEPERONATA, SICILIAN STYLE

SERVES 6 TO 8.

It was difficult to select just one *peperonata* recipe to include in this book. The variations are endless; the preparation varies from one part of the island to the other, and each is regarded locally as the "classic" *peperonata*.

This proprietary feeling about a category of dishes that as much as any other is a signature of the island once again raises doubts about the formative influence of the Arabs, as peppers were brought to Sicily and the rest of Europe from the New World centuries after the Arabs left the island.

In this recipe, one of the most straightforward, the taste of the peppers, the main ingredient, is not dominated by a large number of seasonings and other ingredients that are used in other wonderful but more complex versions.

| | |
|---|---|
| 8 large sweet bell peppers of different colors | imported Italian |
| | ½ cup olive oil |
| 2 medium-sized red onions, cleaned | 3 tablespoons red wine vinegar |
| 1½ pounds fresh tomatoes or 1½ pounds drained canned tomatoes, preferably | Salt and freshly ground black pepper |

½ pound green olives in brine

5 leaves basil, fresh or preserved in salt (see page 294)

TO SERVE
Several fresh basil leaves

Roast the peppers and remove tops, skins and seeds. Cut the peppers into 1-inch strips and put them between layers of paper towels to dry. Let stand until needed.

Coarsely chop the onions on a board. If using fresh tomatoes, blanch them in boiling water (see Note, page 40), then skin them and remove all the seeds; cut into large pieces. If canned tomatoes are used, it is better to pass them through a food mill, using the disc with the smallest holes, instead of trying to remove all the seeds; otherwise too much pulp will be discarded.

Heat the oil in a large skillet over medium heat. When the oil is warm, add the onions and sauté for 5 minutes, or until translucent. Add the vinegar and let evaporate for 2 minutes, then add the tomatoes and let cook for 15 minutes more. Add the peppers and cook for 10 minutes. Taste for salt and pepper. Pit the olives and cut them in half or thirds, depending on their size, then add them with the basil, torn into thirds. Taste again for salt and pepper, then cook for 10 minutes more, mixing all the ingredients together several times. Remove from heat, transfer to a large platter and serve with fresh basil leaves.

*Peperonata* may be eaten immediately or later at room temperature. It may even be prepared one day in advance and reheated at the last moment. If refrigerated, be sure to remove *peperonata* from the cooking skillet and to store it, covered, in a crockery or glass bowl.

# *Piselli*
## PEAS

I have selected just a few of the many recipes for peas that are used everywhere on these islands, though mainly in Sicily. The choice was restricted to those dishes served as side courses; otherwise the list would be much longer. The vegetable is included as an important or defining ingredient in sauces and stuffings, and once in Sicily I even ate a dessert based on peas. Though you might think I was being punished for my unlimited curiosity, I am sure that if the opportunity arose to repeat the experience—and it was a real experience—I would try it again.

I have chosen to include from Sicily *Piselli in umido*; *Piselli alla menta*, peas cooked in broth with fresh mint leaves and served with fresh basil; and *Piselli alla lattuga*, the remarkable dish in which peas are cooked with lettuce and scallions. From Sardinia I include *Piselli allo zafferano*.

FROM SICILY
# *Piselli in Umido*
## STEWED PEAS

### SERVES 6 TO 8.

1 medium-sized yellow onion, cleaned
¼ cup olive oil
1¼ pounds shelled fresh peas *or* 2 10-ounce packages  frozen "petite" peas (see Note, page 219)
15 sprigs Italian parsley, leaves only

5 large basil leaves, fresh or preserved in salt (see page 294)
2 medium-sized cloves garlic, peeled but left whole
½ teaspoon granulated sugar
Salt and freshly ground black pepper

About 1½ cups chicken broth, preferably homemade

TO SERVE
5 sprigs Italian parsley, leaves only
5 large fresh basil leaves, torn into thirds

Finely chop the onion on a board. Place a skillet with the oil over low heat. When the oil is warm, add the chopped onion and sauté until translucent, about 5 minutes. Add the frsh or still-frozen peas and cook for about 5 minutes, stirring every so often with a wooden spoon.

Coarsely chop the parsley and basil together on the board and add them to the skillet along with the whole cloves of garlic. Season with the sugar and salt and pepper to taste and sauté for 2 minutes. Pour in the broth and simmer for about 15 minutes, by which time the peas should be cooked, but still retain their shape, and most of the broth should be absorbed. Taste for salt and pepper.

Discard the garlic and transfer peas and sauce to a large serving dish. Sprinkle evenly with the parsley and basil and serve hot.

# Piselli allo Zafferano
## PEAS WITH SAFFRON

SERVES 6.

1 medium-sized red onion, cleaned
¼ cup olive oil
1¼ pounds of shelled fresh peas *or* 1¼ pounds (2 10-ounce packages) frozen "petite" peas (see Note, page 219)
1 cup chicken broth, preferably homemade, completely defatted
2 large pinches of ground saffron, preferably Sardinian
Salt and freshly ground black pepper
TO SERVE
Several fresh mint leaves

Finely chop the onion on a board. Place a medium-sized casserole with the oil over medium heat. When the oil is warm, add the onion and sauté for 5 minutes, stirring every so often with a wooden spoon. Add the fresh or still-frozen peas, mix very well, then add ½ cup of the broth with the saffron dissolved in it and salt and pepper to taste. Simmer for 15 minutes or until the peas are cooked and the sauce rather thick, adding the remaining broth as needed.

Transfer peas and all the sauce to a serving platter, sprinkle evenly with the mint leaves and serve.

# Piselli alla Menta
## SWEET PEAS WITH FRESH MINT

SERVES 6 TO 8.

1¼ pounds of shelled fresh peas *or* 1¼ pounds (2 10-ounce packages) frozen "petite" peas (see Note, page 219)
1 small red onion, peeled
6 tablespoons olive oil
Salt and freshly ground black pepper
½ to 1 cup lukewarm chicken or beef broth, preferably homemade
30 fresh mint leaves, left whole

Finely chop the onion on a board. Heat the oil in a medium-sized casserole over low heat. When the oil is warm, add the chopped onion and sauté for 5 minutes or until translucent. Add the fresh or still-frozen peas to the casserole, raise the flame to medium and sauté for 1 minute. Season with salt and pepper, then add the ½ cup of broth and the mint leaves. Cover and cook for 20 to 35 minutes, adding more broth if needed. (If large peas are used, you will need the entire cup of broth.) The peas should be completely cooked but still firm and the broth completely absorbed. Transfer to a warmed serving dish and serve.

# Piselli alla Lattuga
## PEAS COOKED WITH LETTUCE

SERVES 8.

1¼ pounds of shelled fresh peas *or* 1¼ pounds (2 10-ounce packages) frozen "petite" peas (see Note)

1 tablespoon unbleached all-purpose flour (if using large peas)

10 scallions

½ cup olive oil

1 large head Boston lettuce

Salt and freshly ground black pepper

If using fresh peas, soak them in a bowl of cold water for ½ hour. If peas are not small, add a tablespoon of unbleached all-purpose flour to the water to help tenderize them, and parboil them (see Note).

Clean the scallions, discard the green tops and coarsely chop the remaining white parts. Place chopped scallions in a medium-sized casserole, then pour in the oil. Drain and rinse the peas if fresh and add the fresh or still-frozen peas to the casserole. Place casserole over medium heat and cook for 5 minutes.

Meanwhile, clean and wash the lettuce very well, discarding the dark outer leaves. Then cut leaves into thin strips and soak them in cold water until needed.

Stir the peas, add salt and pepper to taste, then drain the lettuce and arrange it over the peas. Cover, lower heat and cook, without stirring, for 20 minutes, by which time the peas should be cooked but still firm. Mix well and taste for salt and pepper. If peas are large and need additional cooking time, add ¼ cup lukewarm water, cover and let cook for 10 minutes more or until ready. Transfer to a warmed serving dish and serve.

NOTE: *Outside the spring season of small fresh peas, cooks have two options in making this and other recipes based on peas:*

1. *Use the large fresh ones obtainable out of season, but boil them first with a clove or two of garlic, peeled but left whole, and coarse-grained salt for about 15 minutes. Then they may be sautéed for the same cooking time as the small fresh ones.*
2. *Use the excellent "petite" or "tiny tender" peas sold frozen in 10-ounce packages. Do not defrost or precook them at all. Sauté them for the same amount of time as the small fresh ones. (They are perhaps the only frozen items I sometimes use, because the result is totally without compromise.)*

Some of the most important ancient Roman mosaics are at Piazza Armerina in the heart of Sicily. They form the
floors in the reconstruction of an entire Roman villa. Against the mosaic of the "Ten Maidens"
we see a basket containing two of Sicily's most important fruits, lemons and the famous southern Italian
plum tomatoes. In recent centuries lemons and oranges have been introduced into Sicily and have become
almost the signature fruit.

VEGETABLES

220

# Pomodori in Forno

## TOMATOES BAKED WITH THREE HERBS

SERVES 6.

We cannot omit a stuffed tomato recipe when we want to present a vegetable from these islands off the Campania coast. Simple, easy to prepare, wonderful tasting, these may be served with a large variety of main courses, as an appetizer or even as part of a buffet.

6 large ripe but not overripe tomatoes
  Coarse-grained salt
50 large sprigs Italian parsley, leaves
  only
25 large fresh basil leaves
8 mint leaves

1 medium-sized clove garlic, peeled
4 tablespoons olive oil
  Salt and freshly ground black pepper
OPTIONAL
3 tablespoons unseasoned very fine

bread crumbs, lightly toasted, prefer-
  ably homemade
TO BAKE THE TOMATOES
  About 6 tablespoons olive oil
TO SERVE
  Fresh basil leaves

Carefully wash tomatoes and cut them crosswise into 2 pieces. Remove all the seeds and sprinkle a little coarse salt in each cavity. Place tomatoes upside down on paper towels and let rest for about 20 minutes.

Preheat the oven to 375 degrees and use 2 tablespoons of the oil to heavily coat a ceramic or glass baking dish.

Finely chop parsley, basil, mint and garlic all together on a board. Transfer chopped ingredients to a crockery bowl, add the 4 tablespoons of oil and season with salt and pepper; mix very well with a wooden spoon.

Lightly wash the cavities of the tomatoes and dry them with paper towels. Fill up all the cavities of the tomatoes with the chopped herbs. Place tomatoes in the baking dish, top with some oil and the bread crumbs, if using, and bake for about 1 hour. Tomatoes should be very soft. Sprinkle tomatoes with basil leaves and serve hot or at room temperature after a few hours.

*A vendor proudly presenting the long zucchini at his stand in the Vucciria market.*
*These zucchini are mainly used for frying.*

VEGETABLES

# Zucchine in "Cassarola" al Forno
## BAKED ZUCCHINI CASSEROLE

### SERVES 8 TO 10.

If you are able to get the thin, pale, variegated zucchini, you can skip the step of soaking them in cold water with a little salt because there is no bitterness to remove; they are already sweet. If you are using the dark green, smooth-skinned ones more often found outside of Italy, it is necessary to soak them to remove the bitterness, as when cooking eggplant. This dish is usually a side course, but it may also be used for a light lunch or at room temperature as an appetizer.

2 pounds small zucchini, but not baby ones
Coarse-grained salt
1 medium-sized red onion, cleaned
5 fresh basil leaves

1 pound ripe tomatoes *or* 1 pound drained canned tomatoes, preferably imported Italian
½ cup olive oil
Salt and freshly ground black pepper
PLUS
3 extra-large eggs

3 teaspoons freshly grated *Pecorino Romano*
Salt and freshly ground black pepper
TO BAKE
2 tablespoons olive oil
TO SERVE
Fresh basil leaves

Remove and discard both ends of the zucchini and peel the zucchini, yielding a net weight of about 1½ pounds. Place the whole zucchini in a bowl of cold water with a little coarse salt added and let soak for ½ hour.

Drain zucchini and rinse them under cold running water, then pat them dry with paper towels. In Sardinia the zucchini are very small, about 4 inches long and 1½ inches thick. With larger zucchini, cut them into pieces of about that length and width.

Finely chop onion and basil on a board. Heat the oil in a casserole large enough to contain the zucchini in a single layer over medium heat. When the oil is warm, add the chopped ingredients and sauté for 10 minutes, stirring every so often with a wooden spoon.

If fresh tomatoes are used, cut them into large pieces. Pass fresh or canned tomatoes through a food mill, using the disc with the smallest holes, into a crockery or glass bowl.

Arrange zucchini over the cooked vegetables in a single layer, season with salt and pepper and sauté for 10 minutes, turning the zucchini over 3 times. Add the strained tomatoes and simmer for about 15 minutes more or until zucchini are soft.

Preheat the oven to 375 degrees and oil a glass or ceramic baking dish.

Transfer the contents of the casserole to the baking dish. Lightly beat the eggs and the cheese together and season with salt and pepper. Pour the egg mixture over the zucchini and bake for 15 minutes. Remove from the oven and serve hot, slicing the batter-covered zucchini into squares and lifting them out with a spatula. Serve with fresh basil leaves.

# Zucchine Fritte alla Sarda
## FRIED ZUCCHINI, SARDINIAN STYLE

SERVES 4 AS SIDE DISH.

This Sardinian style of frying zucchini is used frequently with the other vegetables served on the island, such as mushrooms, eggplant and the ever popular fennel bulbs. Coating the moist vegetables with very fine semolina and frying them immediately (without eggs) will produce a very crisp and quite dry crust without absorbing the oil that makes fried vegetables coated with flour or bread crumbs, with or without eggs, often greasy. Another advantage of using semolina is that the food will remain perfectly crisp without becoming soggy. This particular method is found only here in Sardinia, where semolina is used more frequently in cooking than in other regions of Italy.

6 very small zucchini, but not baby ones
Coarse-grained salt
About ½ cup very fine semolina flour

OPTIONAL
A large pinch of ground saffron
TO COOK THE ZUCCHINI
2 cups vegetable oil (½ sunflower oil, ½ corn oil)

¼ cup olive oil
TO SERVE
Salt
Lemon wedges

Remove and discard both ends of the zucchini and soak the zucchini in a bowl of cold water with a little coarse salt added for ½ hour. Soaking the zucchini in lightly salted water will lift or diminish any slightly bitter taste they might have.

Rinse zucchini very well under cold running water, then slice them lengthwise into quarters. Then cut each quarter into 2- or 3-inch pieces. Place the semolina flour in a bowl and, if using, add the saffron and mix very well.

Heat the oil in a large skillet over medium heat. Line a serving dish with paper towels. When the oil is hot (about 400 degrees), place the zucchini pieces in a strainer and put them first under cold running water for a few seconds, then into the bowl with the semolina. Mix very well so the zucchini will have a nice coating. Fry them, a small number at a time, in the hot oil until golden all over. Transfer zucchini to the towel-lined serving dish. When all of the zucchini are cooked, quickly remove the paper towels, sprinkle with some salt and serve hot with lemon wedges.

# Zucchine al Cartoccio
## ZUCCHINI IN A PAPER BAG

SERVES 6.

Traditionally, for this dish, the damp zucchini were wrapped in brown paper and placed under the lukewarm ash to rest for at least 2 hours. In the "modern" version, the zucchini are wrapped in aluminum foil and cooked in the oven. Certainly the taste and texture do suffer a little from this adjustment, but the result is more than acceptable. The unusual and almost exotic aromatic herb used is lemon verbena—a "remembrance of things past" even in Italy. Not so many years ago, no vegetable garden or even flower garden was complete without a bush of lemon verbena, either for its perfume, for use in cooking, usually in place of mint, or for making an infusion as an herbal remedy.

6 small zucchini, but not baby ones
Coarse-grained salt
Salt and freshly ground black pepper
1 tablespoon olive oil

FOR THE SAUCE

3 tablespoons capers in wine vinegar, drained
3 large cloves garlic, peeled
15 sprigs Italian parsley, leaves only
3 teaspoons dried lemon verbena

leaves, or 15 fresh mint leaves, torn into thirds
Salt and freshly ground black pepper to taste
½ cup olive oil

Clean the zucchini, removing the two ends. Place the zucchini, whole, in a bowl of cold water with 1 tablespoon of coarse salt added and let them soak for ½ hour. Drain zucchini and rinse them very well under cold running water, then dry them well with paper towels.

Preheat the oven to 400 degrees. Brush each of the zucchini with a little oil, sprinkle them with a little bit of salt and pepper and wrap each zucchini in a piece of aluminum foil with the shiny side on the inside. Place the prepared zucchini in a baking dish, if using a normal oven; in a brick oven, place them directly on the bricks or tiles. Bake for 30 minutes. If zuchcini are thin and young, by that time they should be cooked, but still retain a bite. If less young, bake them as much longer as necessary.

Meanwhile, finely chop capers, garlic and parsley all together on a board. Transfer chopped ingredients to a crockery or glass bowl, crumble the dried verbena over or sprinkle the mint leaves over, season with salt and pepper, then add the olive oil and mix very well.

When zucchini are ready, unwrap them and place on a serving dish. Cut zucchini into 2-inch-thick discs, pour the prepared sauce all over and serve either hot or at room temperature after a few hours.

# Torta di Zucca

## SAVORY SQUASH TORTE

### SERVES 8 TO 10.

Squashes are not used a lot in Tuscany, but Elba, the largest of the Tuscan islands, is home to this surprising dish, which makes you think you must be in a different region. True, the combination of garlic, sage and nutmeg is very Tuscan, but not the squash itself, which so strongly suggests the cooking of northern Italy, especially that around the old city of Mantua.

1 large (about 3½ pounds) butternut squash
Coarse-grained salt

2 ounces (4 tablespoons) sweet butter

4 large sage leaves, fresh or preserved in salt (see page 294)

2 large cloves garlic, peeled but left whole

15 ounces ricotta, drained

½ cup freshly grated *Parmigiano*

4 extra-large eggs
Salt and freshly ground black pepper
A pinch of freshly grated nutmeg

PLUS

2 tablespoons (1 ounce) sweet butter
About ½ cup unseasoned very fine bread crumbs, lightly toasted, preferably homemade

TO SERVE
Fresh sage leaves

Clean the squash, removing and discarding the skin, seeds and all the inner membranes. Cut the squash into large pieces and measure out 2 pounds. Save the remainder for another use, such as soup.

Place the 2 pounds of squash in a medium-sized stockpot, add enough cold water to cover and coarse salt to taste. Set pot over medium heat. When the water reaches a boil, simmer for about 20 minutes. Squash should be very soft. Drain it, discard the water and pass the squash through a food mill, using the disc with the smallest holes, into a crockery or glass bowl.

Melt the butter over medium heat in a large skillet, add the sage and the whole cloves of garlic and sauté for a very short time, 30 seconds to 1 minute; garlic and sage should be not even lightly golden. Add the riced squash, lower the heat and sauté for 15 minutes, stirring constantly with a wooden spoon. Transfer the contents of the skillet to a crockery or glass bowl to cool completely, about ½ hour.

Preheat the oven to 375 degrees. Heavily butter a 10-inch spring-form and line it with bread crumbs.

Remove garlic and sage from the bowl and add the ricotta to the cooled squash; stir very well until the mixture is completely smooth. Add *Parmigiano*, eggs, salt and pepper to taste and the pinch of nutmeg; mix very well. Transfer the mixture to the prepared form and bake for 70 minutes. The top part of the torte should be golden and quite firm.

Let spring-form rest on a rack for 15 minutes before opening it and transferring the torte to a round serving platter. Serve by slicing like a pie. Each serving should be topped with a few sage leaves.

# BREADS · FOCACCE

*I*n both Sicily and Sardinia bread plays an important role in custom, folklore and religion as well as in diet. In Sardinia and the countryside, bread and sometimes even the flour that goes into it is still made at home. The woman of the house, even if she can afford servants, regards it as almost a religious duty to supervise all steps of the bread making, beginning with the grinding of the wheat. The shape of the bread changes from one small village to another and according to the time of year and various festivities and special occasions. Some celebrated types are the ring-shaped, called by many different names in different regions, and *coccoas*, a bread made in remembrance of the dead. For religious festivals, there are the rooster-shaped *galletti*, boat-shaped *barchette* and *ometti*, which is made in the form of a small man.

In Sardinia, there are many variations of round flat breads of the *schiacciata* type, called *fresa*. Some of these, even the very flat ones, are made with yeast. But there are others, made of wheat or barley flour, that are prepared without yeast, like the biblical unleavened bread, called in Italian *pane azzimo*. Many think that the famous Sardinian *carta da musica* bread (see page 242), though now made with yeast, was originally a *pane azzimo*. This is an example of the survival in Sicily and Sardina of foods that in ancient times belonged to the entire Mediterranean world ruled by Rome. It would be as questionable to attribute the *pane azzimo* of Sardinia to direct Jewish influence as to attribute many of the ancient surviving dishes in Sicily to direct Arab influence.

Sicilian bread is generally of very high quality because of the wonderful nutty flavor of the famous Sicilian wheat. Forms vary from oval, loaf-shaped, round and flat, to ring-shaped (called *vasteddi*), crown- and garland-shaped, half moon and special children's bread that is shaped like horses, puppets and dolls. Generally the bread is dusted with sesame or fennel seeds.

The island has a wide variety of stuffed pizzas and *focacce*, called *scacciate* or *panate*.

Also part of the repertoire is rectangular or oval flat pizza topped with cheese; *ricotta salata*; sausages; anchovies; sautéed tomatoes; vegetables, such as spinach or cauliflower; or meat, such as cooked lamb, pork or goat. The pizza is then rolled up before baking, so that the topping becomes a stuffing. The typical western Sicilian pine nuts and raisins are often included.

We include the following sampling of breads: from Sicily, focaccias with garlic, with rosemary, with sausages, with escarole and an unusual one from Enna; from Sardinia, the celebrated *pizzette* from Cagliari and *focaccia* or *pizza alla Sarda*; and we end with the famous *carta da musica*.

*The elaborate designed breads of Sardinia.*

# Focaccia con l'Aglio

## GARLIC *FOCACCIA*

SERVES 12 AS AN APPETIZER.

**FOR THE SPONGE**

1 cup plus 1 tablespoon unbleached
all-purpose flour
1 ounce fresh compressed yeast *or* 2
packages active dry yeast
¾ cup lukewarm water, or warm water
if using dry yeast
A pinch of salt

**FOR THE DOUGH**

3¾ cups unbleached all-purpose flour
2 tablespoons olive oil
Salt and freshly ground black pepper
to taste
1 cup lukewarm water

**TO BAKE THE *FOCACCIA***

4 tablespoons olive oil
Salt and abundant freshly ground
black pepper
5 medium-sized cloves garlic, peeled

**TO SERVE**

3 tablespoons olive oil

Prepare the sponge: Place the cup of flour in a small bowl and make a well in
the center. Dissolve the yeast in the water, stirring with a wooden spoon. Add
the pinch of salt. Pour the dissolved yeast into the well and mix very well
with the wooden spoon until the flour is incorporated. Sprinkle the additional tablespoon of flour over the sponge, then cover the bowl with a cotton
dish towel and let rest, in a warm place away from drafts, until the sponge has
doubled in size, about 1 hour. (Signs that the sponge has doubled in size are
the disappearance of the tablespoon of flour or the formation of large cracks
on top.)

Prepare the dough: Place the 3¾ cups of flour in a mound on a board,
then make a well in the center. Place the sponge in the well, along with the
olive oil, salt and pepper to taste and the water. Mix together thoroughly all
the ingredients in the well, then start incorporating some of the flour from
the edges. When a ball of dough is formed, start kneading it, with the palms
of your hands, until the dough becomes very elastic, about 2 minutes.

Use 2 tablespoons of the oil to grease a 15-by-10½-inch jelly-roll pan.
Use a rolling pin to stretch the dough to the same size as the pan and place
the dough in the pan. Prick dough with a fork in several places and drizzle
with the remaining 2 tablespoons of the oil. Sprinkle with a little salt and
abundant ground black pepper. Cut the garlic into thin slivers and arrange
them all over the dough. Cover the *focaccia* first with a piece of plastic wrap,
then place over it a cotton dish towel and let rest, in a warm place away from
drafts, until doubled in size, about 1 hour.

Preheat the oven to 400 degrees. When dough is ready, remove plastic
wrap and dish towel and bake for about 40 minutes or until golden all over.
Cut *focaccia* into squares, transfer to a large serving platter and drizzle with the
olive oil. Serve hot.

# Pizzette alla Cagliaritana
## SMALL PIZZAS, CAGLIARI STYLE

MAKES 14.

FOR THE SPONGE
- 1 cup plus 1 tablespoon unbleached all-purpose flour
- 1 ounce fresh compressed yeast *or* 1 package active dry yeast
- ¾ cup lukewarm milk, or warm milk if using dry yeast
- A pinch of salt

FOR THE DOUGH (SECOND RISING)
- 4 ounces all-purpose potatoes
- Coarse-grained salt
- 4 cups unbleached all-purpose flour

- 1 extra-large egg
- 1 cup lukewarm milk
- Salt to taste

FOR THE DOUGH (THIRD RISING)
- About ½ cup unbleached all-purpose flour

FOR THE TOPPING
- 8 ounces mozzarella, cut into 14 slices
- 2 large tomatoes, blanched (see Note, page 40), seeded and cut into small pieces

- 7 whole anchovies, preserved in salt, boned and cleaned (see Note, page 30), *or* 14 anchovy fillets, packed in oil, drained
- 14 teaspoons freshly grated *Pecorino Romano*
- 14 pinches of dried oregano mixed with ½ teaspoon of salt and ½ teaspoon of freshly ground black pepper
- 14 teaspoons olive oil

FOR BAKING
- 3 tablespoons olive oil

Prepare the sponge: Place the cup of flour in a small bowl and make a well in the center. Dissolve the yeast in the milk, stirring with a wooden spoon. Add the pinch of salt. Pour the dissolved yeast into the well and mix very well with the wooden spoon until the flour is incorporated. Sprinkle the additional tablespoon of flour over the sponge, cover the bowl with a cotton dish towel and let rest, in a warm place away from drafts, until the sponge has doubled in size, about 1 hour. (Signs that the sponge has doubled in size are the disappearance of the table-spoon of flour or the formation of large cracks on top.)

Meanwhile, bring a medium-sized pot of cold water to a boil. Add coarse salt to taste, then the unpeeled potatoes, and cook until they are very soft, about 25 minutes. Peel the potatoes and pass them, still very hot, through a potato ricer into a bowl.

Prepare the dough: Place the 4 cups of flour in a mound on a board, then make a well in the center. Place the sponge in the well, along with the riced pota-toes, the whole egg, the milk and salt to taste. Mix together thoroughly all the ingredients in the well, then start incorporating some of the flour from the edges. When a ball of dough is formed, start kneading it with the palms of your hands until the dough becomes very elastic and all the flour is incorporated, about 2 minutes. Place the dough in a very lightly oiled bowl, cover the bowl with plastic wrap and let rest, in a warm place away from drafts, for about ½ hour. By that time the dough should have risen, but not doubled in size.

Preheat the oven to 400 degrees. Oil 2 15-by-10½-inch jelly-roll pans.

Place the ½ cup of flour for the third rising on a board. Transfer the dough to the board and start kneading, incorporating more flour for at least 10 minutes. Divide the dough into 14 pieces and knead each piece for a few seconds. Roll out each piece of dough into a disc about 5 inches in diameter. Transfer the *pizzette* to the prepared pans. Cover pans with plastic wrap and top with a cotton dish towel. Let rest for 10 minutes.

Remove plastic wrap and dish towel and top each *pizzetta* with a slice of moz-zarella, then sprinkle with some cut-up tomato, 1 anchovy fillet cut into small pieces, a teaspoon of the grated cheese and then a teaspoon of the oil. Sprinkle with a little of the oregano mixture. Bake for 25 minutes and serve hot.

# Focaccia al Rosmarino

## FOCACCIA WITH ROSEMARY

SERVES 12 AS AN APPETIZER.

FOR THE SPONGE

- 2 cups plus 1 tablespoon unbleached all-purpose flour
- ½ ounce fresh compressed yeast *or* 1 package active dry yeast
- 1½ cups lukewarm water, or warm water if using dry yeast
  A pinch of salt

FOR THE DOUGH

- 2 cups unbleached all-purpose flour
- 4 tablespoons olive oil
- ¼ cup lukewarm water
- ½ teaspoon salt
- 3 tablespoons rosemary leaves, fresh or preserved in salt (see page 294)

TO BAKE THE *FOCACCIA*

- 7 tablespoons olive oil
  Coarse-grained salt

TO SERVE

  Coarse-grained salt
  Olive oil

Prepare the sponge: Place the 2 cups of flour in a large bowl and make a well in it. Dissolve the yeast in the water, then pour it into the well with the salt. Use a wooden spoon to incorporate the flour little by little until it is all incorporated. Sprinkle the remaining tablespoon of flour over the sponge, cover bowl with a cotton dish towel and let rest until the sponge has doubled in size, about 1 hour. (Signs that the sponge has doubled in size are the disappearance of the table-spoon of flour or the formation of large cracks on top.)

When the sponge is ready, spread out the 2 cups of flour on a board and place the sponge in it. Make a well in the sponge, then pour in the oil and water and add the salt. First mix all the ingredients in the well together, then start incorporating the flour until a ball of dough is formed. Knead the dough in a folding motion until all the flour is incorporated and the dough is elastic and smooth. Add the rosemary leaves and knead the dough for 2 seconds more. Use 4 tablespoons of the oil to coat a 15-by-10½-inch jelly-roll pan. Use a rolling pin to roll out a sheet of dough large enough to fit pan. Place the dough in the pan, spreading it out to reach the sides. Drizzle evenly with the remaining olive oil, then sprinkle with coarse-grained salt to taste. Prick the dough all over with a fork, then cover the pan with plastic wrap and let rest, in a warm place away from drafts, until doubled in size, about 1 hour.

Preheat the oven to 400 degrees.

When the dough is ready, remove plastic wrap and bake for 30 minutes. Remove *focaccia* from oven and cut into slices. Sprinkle with more coarse salt all over and drizzle with more olive oil. Serve hot.

# Focaccia o Pizza alla Sarda

## TOMATO *FOCACCIA*

SERVES 12 AS AN APPETIZER.

FOR THE SPONGE

1½ cups plus 1 tablespoon unbleached
  all-purpose flour
1½ ounces compressed fresh yeast *or* 3
  packages active dry yeast
1¼ cups lukewarm water, or warm water
  if using dry yeast
A pinch of salt

FOR THE DOUGH

6 ounces all-purpose potatoes
  Coarse-grained salt
1 ripe fresh tomato (about 5 ounces)
5 whole anchovies in salt, boned and
  cleaned (see Note, page 30), *or* 10
  anchovy fillets, drained
1 tablespoon olive oil
  Salt and freshly ground black pepper

A large pinch of dried oregano
3½ cups unbleached all-purpose flour
½ cup lukewarm water

TO BAKE THE *FOCACCIA*

4 tablespoons olive oil

TO SERVE

3 tablespoons olive oil
  Coarse-grained salt
  Fresh basil leaves

Prepare the sponge: Place the 1½ cups of flour in a bowl and make a well in the
flour. Dissolve the yeast in the lukewarm or warm water and pour it into the well
along with a pinch of salt; mix with a wooden spoon until all the flour is incorporated. Sprinkle the additional tablespoon of flour over the sponge, then cover
the bowl with a cotton dish towel and put it in a warm place away from drafts.
Let it stand until the sponge has doubled in size, about 1 hour. (Signs that the
sponge has doubled in size are the disappearance of the tablespoon of flour or
the formation of large cracks on top.)

Meanwhile, boil the potatoes with the skin on in salted water until very soft,
about 40 minutes. Skin the potatoes and pass them through a food mill, using the
disc with the smallest holes, into a bowl.

Cut tomato into tiny cubes without removing skin or seeds. Transfer tomato
to a crockery bowl. Cut anchovies into 1-inch pieces and add them to the tomatoes along with the tablespoon of oil, salt and pepper to taste and the oregano;
mix well. Let rest until needed.

Prepare the dough: When the sponge is ready, place the 3½ cups of flour in a
mound on a board, then make a well. Place the riced potatoes along with the
sponge and the lukewarm water in the well. Thoroughly mix all the ingredients in
the well. Add the tomato mixture and stir again. Using your hands, start incorporating the flour from the rim of the well until almost all the flour is incorporated.
Knead the dough with the palms of your hands until it is homogeneous and quite
smooth, about 4 minutes.

Use 2 tablespoons of the oil to coat a 15-by-10½-inch jelly-roll pan. Stretch
out the dough with your hands, then transfer it to the pan. Use your fingers to
stretch the dough to reach the sides of the pan. Drizzle dough with the remaining
2 tablespoons of oil, then cover with plastic wrap and let rest until *focaccia* has
doubled in size, about 1 hour.

Preheat the oven to 375 degrees. When ready, remove plastic wrap and bake
for about 50 minutes. Remove the *focaccia* from oven, drizzle with the oil and
sprinkle with coarse salt and some fresh basil leaves. Serve hot.

*Did Napoleon eat this* focaccia *while in exile on Elba?*

# *Focaccia alla Ricotta*

## FLAVORED RICOTTA *FOCACCIA*

SERVES 12 AS AN APPETIZER.

FOR THE SPONGE
- 1¾ cups plus 1 tablespoon unbleached all-purpose flour
- 2 ounces compressed fresh yeast *or* 4 packages active dry yeast
- 1 cup lukewarm water, or warm water if using dry yeast
- A pinch of salt

FOR THE DOUGH
- 3¼ cups unbleached all-purpose flour or more if ricotta is not very well drained
- ½ cup lukewarm water
- 8 ounces ricotta, drained very well
- 1 tablespoon olive oil
- Salt and freshly ground black pepper
- A large pinch of ground cinnamon

TO BAKE THE *FOCACCIA*
- 6 tablespoons olive oil

TO SERVE
- 3 tablespoons olive oil
- Fresh rosemary leaves

OPTIONAL
- Coarse-grained salt

Prepare the sponge: Place the 1¾ cups of flour in a bowl and make a well in the flour. Dissolve the yeast in the lukewarm or warm water, then pour it into the well with a pinch of salt. Mix with a wooden spoon until all the flour is incorporated. Sprinkle the additional tablespoon of flour over the sponge, cover the bowl with a cotton dish towel and put it in a warm place away from drafts. Let stand until the sponge has doubled in size, about 1 hour. (Signs that the sponge has doubled in size are the disappearance of the tablespoon of flour or the formation of large cracks on top.)

Prepare the dough: Place the 3¼ cups of flour in a mound on a board, then make a well. Place the sponge in the well along with the water, ricotta, olive oil, salt and pepper to taste and the cinnamon. With a wooden spoon, carefully mix together all the ingredients in the well, then using your hands, start incorporating the flour from the inside rim of the well until almost all the flour is incorporated. Knead the dough with the palms of your hands until it is homogeneous and smooth, about 5 minutes.

Use 3 tablespoons of the oil to coat a 15-by-10½-inch jelly-roll pan. Using a rolling pin, stretch the dough to the same size as the pan. Transfer the dough to the prepared pan. Use a fork to prick the top all over. Drizzle the *focaccia* with the remaining 3 tablespoons of oil, then cover it with plastic wrap and let stand until doubled in size, about 1 hour.

Preheat the oven to 375 degrees. When ready, remove the plastic wrap and bake the *focaccia* for 45 minutes. Remove from oven and cut into pieces. Drizzle with more oil and sprinkle with fresh rosemary leaves and a little salt, if using.

# Focaccia di Enna

## FOCACCIA WITH HOT SAUSAGES

SERVES 12 AS AN APPETIZER.

FOR THE SPONGE

- 1 cup plus 1 tablespoon unbleached all-purpose flour
- 1 ounce fresh compressed yeast *or* 2 packages active dry yeast
- ¾ cup lukewarm water, or warm water if using dry yeast
  A pinch of salt

FOR THE DOUGH

- 3 cups unbleached all-purpose flour
- 2 tablespoons (1 ounce) sweet butter, at room temperature
- ½ cup lukewarm water
  Salt to taste
- 1 tablespoon olive oil

PLUS

- 4 teaspoons plus 1 tablespoon olive oil
- 8 ounces Italian hot sausages, without fennel seeds
- 1 large ripe tomato, cut into 12 slices
  Salt and freshly ground black pepper

Prepare the sponge: Place the cup of flour in a small bowl and make a well in the center. Dissolve the yeast in the water, stirring with a wooden spoon. Add the pinch of salt. Pour the dissolved yeast into the well and mix very well with the wooden spoon until the flour is incorporated. Sprinkle the additional tablespoon of flour over the sponge, then cover the bowl with a cotton dish towel and let rest, in a warm place away from drafts, until the sponge has doubled in size, about 1 hour. (Signs that the sponge has doubled in size are the disappearance of the tablespoon of flour or the formation of large cracks on top.)

Prepare the dough: Place the 3 cups of flour in a mound on a board, then make a well in the center. Place the sponge in the well along with the butter, the water and salt to taste. Mix together thoroughly all the ingredients in the well, then start incorporating some of the flour from the edges. When a ball of dough is formed, start kneading it with the palms of your hands until the dough becomes very elastic and almost all the flour is incorporated.

Oil a 15-by-10½-inch jelly-roll pan and roll out the dough to the same size as the pan. Cover pan with plastic wrap for 5 minutes.

Meanwhile, remove the casing from the sausages and divide the meat into 12 small balls.

Remove the wrap from the pan and use your index finger to make 12 pockets (depressions) in the dough. Into each pocket pour ½ teaspoon of olive oil, then place a sausage ball over the oil and top it with a slice of tomato. Repeat the same procedure with all the other pockets. Drizzle with the remaining tablespoon of oil and sprinkle with salt and pepper. Cover pan with plastic wrap until dough has doubled in size, about 30 minutes.

Preheat the oven to 400 degrees. When ready, remove plastic wrap and bake *focaccia* for about 40 minutes. Remove from oven and serve hot.

# *Focaccia con la Salsicce*

## *FOCACCIA* WITH SAUSAGES

SERVES 12 AS AN APPETIZER.

FOR THE SPONGE
- 2 cups plus 2 tablespoons unbleached all-purpose flour
- 1½ ounces compressed fresh yeast *or* 3 packages active dry yeast
- 1½ cups lukewarm water, or warm water if using dry yeast
  A pinch of salt

FOR THE DOUGH
- 3½ to 4 cups unbleached all-purpose flour
- 2 Italian hot sausages (about 3½ ounces each), without fennel seeds
- 15 large fresh basil leaves, torn into thirds
  Salt and freshly ground black pepper to taste
- 2 tablespoons olive oil
- ½ cup lukewarm water

TO BAKE THE *FOCACCIA*
- 4 tablespoons olive oil

TO SERVE
- 3 tablespoons olive oil
  Coarse-grained salt
  Fresh basil leaves

Prepare the sponge: Place the 2 cups of flour in a bowl and make a well in the flour. Dissolve the yeast in the lukewarm or warm water and pour it into the well along with a pinch of salt; mix with a wooden spoon until all the flour is incorporated. Sprinkle with the additional tablespoon of flour, then cover bowl with a cotton dish towel and put it in a warm place away from drafts. Let it stand until the sponge has doubled in size, about 1 hour. (Signs that the sponge has doubled in size are the disappearance of the tablespoon of flour or the formation of large cracks on top.)

Prepare the dough: When the sponge is ready, place the 3½ cups of flour in a mound on a board, then make a well. Remove the skin from the sausages and break the meat into pieces. Place the sausages, basil leaves, salt and pepper, olive oil and water in the well. Combine all the ingredients in the well thoroughly, then add the sponge and stir again. Using your hands, start incorporating the flour from the rim of the well until almost all the flour is incorporated. Knead the dough with the palms of your hands until it is homogeneous and quite smooth, about 4 minutes.

Use 2 tablespoons of the oil to coat a 15-by-10½-inch jelly-roll pan. Stretch the dough with a rolling pin to fit the size of the pan, then transfer it onto the pan. Drizzle dough with the remaining 2 tablespoons of oil, then prick it with a fork in several parts. Cover pan with plastic wrap and place a cotton dish towel over the wrap. Let the *focaccia* rest until doubled in size, about 1 hour.

Preheat the oven to 400 degrees. When ready, remove plastic wrap and bake for about 40 minutes. Remove *focaccia* from oven, drizzle with the olive oil and sprinkle with coarse salt and basil leaves. Serve hot.

# Focaccia con la Scarola

## FOCACCIA WITH ESCAROLE

SERVES 12 AS AN APPETIZER.

1 pound cleaned escarole with large
 leaves removed
 Coarse-grained salt

PLUS

2 medium-sized cloves garlic, peeled
3 tablespoons olive oil
 Salt and freshly ground black pepper
 A large pinch of hot red pepper
 flakes

FOR THE SPONGE

1½ cups plus 1 tablespoon unbleached
 all-purpose flour
1½ ounces fresh compressed yeast *or* 3
 packages active dry yeast
1 cup lukewarm water, or warm water
 if using dry yeast
 A large pinch of salt

FOR THE DOUGH

2 tablespoons olive oil

½ cup lukewarm water
2¾ cups unbleached all-purpose flour
 Salt and freshly ground black pepper
 to taste

TO BAKE THE *FOCACCIA*

5 tablespoons olive oil

TO SERVE

4 tablespoons olive oil
 Coarse-grained salt

Soak the escarole in a bowl of cold water for ½ hour. Bring a medium-sized pot of cold water to a boil over medium heat, add salt to taste, then drain the escarole, add it to pot and boil for 15 minutes. Drain the cooked greens and cool them under cold running water. Gently squeeze excess moisture from the escarole and coarsely chop it on a board.

Coarsely chop garlic on the board and heat the oil in a skillet over medium heat. When the oil is warm, add the garlic and sauté for a few seconds. Add the escarole, season with salt, pepper and the red pepper flakes and cook for 15 minutes, mixing occasionally with a wooden spoon. Transfer the sautéed escarole to a crockery or glass bowl and let rest until needed.

Prepare the sponge: Place the 1½ cups of flour in a bowl and make a well in the flour. Dissolve the yeast in the lukewarm or warm water and pour it into the well along with the salt; mix with a wooden spoon until all the flour is absorbed. Sprinkle the remaining tablespoon of flour over the sponge and cover the bowl with a cotton dish towel. Let the sponge rest, in a warm place away from drafts, until doubled in size, about 1 hour. (Signs that the sponge has doubled in size are the disappearance of the tablespoon of flour or the formation of large cracks on top.)

Use 3 of the 5 tablespoons of olive oil to coat a 15-by-10½-inch jelly-roll pan.

Prepare the dough: When the sponge is ready, pour the oil and water into the sponge and season with salt and pepper. Mix very well with a wooden spoon.

Place the 2¾ cups of flour in a mound on a board and make a well in the flour. Place the cooled escarole in the well of the flour, then add the sponge mixture. Combine all the ingredients in the well thoroughly with a wooden spoon, then start incorporating some of the flour from the rim of the well. When a rather thick dough has formed, knead it with the palm of your hands, incorporating more flour. The amount of flour absorbed varies, depending on the amount of liquid in the escarole, and sometimes the dough can be very sticky. Lightly stretch dough with a rolling pin to fit the size of the pan. Drizzle with the remaining 2 tablespoons of oil and prick the dough with a fork in several places. Cover *focaccia* with plastic wrap and let it rest until doubled in size, about 1 hour.

Preheat the oven to 375 degrees. When ready, remove the plastic wrap and bake for about 45 minutes. Remove from oven, drizzle with the last 4 tablespoons of oil and sprinkle with some coarse salt. Serve hot.

# Carta da Musica

## MUSIC PAPER BREAD

QUANTITY VARIABLE (SEE TEXT)

FOR THE SPONGE
- 1 cup plus 1 tablespoon unbleached all-purpose flour
- ¼ cup very fine semolina flour
- ½ teaspoon coarse-grained salt

- 1 cup lukewarm water, or warm water if using dry yeast
- 1 ounce fresh compressed yeast *or* 2 packages active dry yeast

FOR THE DOUGH
- 2 cups unbleached all-purpose flour plus ½ cup for kneading
- ½ cup very fine semolina flour
- ¾ cup lukewarm water

Prepare the sponge: Mix the cup of flour with the semolina flour and place in a small bowl. Make a well in the flour. Add the salt to the water, then add the yeast. When the yeast is dissolved, pour it into the well. Incorporate the 1¼ cup flour by mixing with a wooden spoon. Sprinkle the remaining tablespoon of flour over the sponge. Let the sponge rest, covered, overnight in a warm place away from drafts.

Next morning, if you do not have a brick oven, line the lower shelf of the oven with unglazed terra-cotta tiles or, as second choice, use a pizza stone. Preheat the oven to 400 degrees. Be sure to preheat the oven at least 1 hour before using it because the tiles themselves must reach that temperature.

Prepare the dough: Mix the 2 cups of flour with the ½ cup of semolina flour and make a large well in the flour. Place the sponge in the well along with the water. Carefully mix the sponge with the water, using a wooden spoon, then start incorporating the flour from the edges of the well. Gather the dough with your hands, form a ball and place the ball on a board or other work surface. Start kneading, incorporating more flour. Knead with a folding motion. At this point you will need some of the ½ cup of reserved flour. When the dough becomes very elastic, after about 5 minutes of kneading, lightly flour it, place it in a bowl and let it rest until doubled in size, about 1 hour.

The classic size of the *carta da musica* is a disc of about 18 inches in diameter. Bearing in mind the size of your oven and even your own experience in handling large sheets of thin dough, divide the risen dough into pieces of a comfortable size, remembering that the dough is to be stretched to the thickness of about 1/8 inch. Once the dough is divided into pieces, knead each piece with a little flour. Roll each piece very evenly to a uniform thickness, with no holes at all and no creases; otherwise the dough will not puff up completely in the oven.

As 2 or 3 pieces of dough are rolled out, start baking them one at a time. Place a disc on a baker's peel, transfer it onto the tile, close oven and bake for 1 minute. Open the oven, gently turn the puffed-up dough over and bake for 30 seconds more.

Remove bread from oven, transfer onto a board and immediately insert a sharp knife between the two puffed-up, separated layers of half-cooked *carta da musica*. Placing one hand over the puffed up dough, use the other hand to cut all around to detach the edges of the layers from each other.

It is best if a second person can do this cutting because the first will be completely occupied in rolling out dough and baking the remaining dough.

Stack the separated halves on a towel, being absolutely sure that all are placed with the inner side down, so that no 2 inside parts will touch. Place a light weight over the stack of prebaked *carta da musica* halves to prevent them from curling up.

When all the pieces of dough have been baked, placed under the weight and cooled, take the pieces and return them, one at a time, to the oven to bake for about 10 seconds on each side or until very crisp. *Carta da musica* should be very dry and extremely crisp. Continue until all the pieces of the bread are rebaked and crisp. Once all the layers are cold, you may wrap them in brown paper and use them for as long as several months if the humidity is not high.

The uses of this bread are described in individual recipes.

# CARTA DA MUSICA

*Carta da musica* or *carta di musica*, once baked, may be stored and used over a long period. It also forms the foundation for many dishes: broken up, it may be used in soups in place of pasta or rice; soaked and fried, it becomes either savory or sweet fritters. In its most famous transformation into a main course it becomes *pane frattau* (see page 150).

*Carta da musica* is often used by shepherds as a plate on which they place other food; however, the "plate" is eaten together with the other food, as one eats an open-faced sandwich. Occasionally *carta da musica* is dried, then ground and used in place of flour. This technique is very similar to the grinding of unleavened bread into meal, still used by Jews for Passover, and suggests that this practice started when the *carta da musica* was still unleavened. Another use that has become popular very recently is to drizzle the *carta da musica* with olive oil, sprinkle it with a little salt and warm it in the oven as a kind of *fet-tunta* or *bruschetta* to be served as an appetizer or snack.

Making this bread requires a refined and strict technique that is completely different from that used in making other flat breads that separate into two layers, such as pita, piadina or tortillas.

1: The special raw linen and hemp or flax cloth used to wrap the dough and the bread while it dries in the sun is called *"Sos Pannos de Ispicia."*

2: The dough is kneaded and rolled into a long thick rope.

3: The rope is cut into pieces.

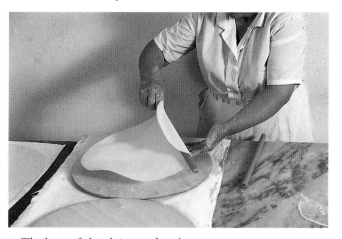

4: The pieces of cut dough: each piece, when rolled thin and baked, will produce two sheets.

5: Using a short and uniformly thin rolling pin (the ends do not taper like the classic French rolling pin)

6: Rolling up and down, then from side to side, working to achieve a round shape. This is done on a marble table.

7: From the marble table, the sheet of dough, almost completely stretched, is transferred to a special bread board. Finally it is stretched to the exact dimensions of the board.

8: The layer of dough is transferred…

9: ...to the hot oven. The classic Sardinian ovens are quite small and dome shaped. The dough starts puffing up immediately from the heat.

10: The puffed-up dough is removed and quickly turned over and it is in that moment that it is shaped somewhat like a cushion. The bread is baked for a few seconds more.

11: The bread is transferred to a board, where a young woman immediately inserts a knife to cut open the edges where the top and bottom are attached.

12: The separated layers are peeled apart.

13: The separated layers are piled one on top of the other until they cool.

14: The pieces are taken, one by one, and put back in the oven until they are very crisp. The single thin breads are then stacked in piles of 30 or 40 and wrapped. From this point on they are ready to be eaten and will last for several months without losing their crispness and flavor.

# DESSERTS

*I*n order to have optimum results with the desserts from Sicily, Sardinia or Elba, it is most important to have very high-quality basic ingredients: candied citron, orange and other fruits if possible; excellent almonds, walnuts and pistachios; superior marzipan; ricotta—if possible of sheep's milk; jasmine and orange essence imported from Italy and rosewater from Italy or the Near East; homemade bread crumbs; and a top quality Marsala wine.

Marsala, easily the best known of the wines made on the islands, is produced in the provinces of Trapani, Palermo and Agrigento. Very versatile, it makes a good aperitif when chilled and can be used for cooking dishes and desserts. It is also a pleasant after-dinner drink. I particularly like to use it in the preparation of pastries, not as a flavoring, but rather as a catalyst, because combining flour, butter and eggs with Marsala chemically creates the same flakiness as a liqueur but produces a much more distinctive aroma and texture.

When using candied fruits, be especially careful to obtain a piece of a whole candied citron, not the diced pre-packaged type, and the orange rind in large pieces, not diced. Specialty food stores, or Italian or Middle-Eastern groceries, can be good sources for these. Some ingredients may not be obtainable, but they should be your model.

These traditional desserts are older and differ from those developed in the 19th century, which are based on creams, chocolate and butter, and were themselves often French adaptations of lighter pastries from Florentine Renaissance cooking. The cakes here often retain ground nuts in the flour, as was the dominant method in pre-Renaissance Italy, and are often heavier in texture. It is best to think of these desserts, though they are often quite sweet, as food, substantial and significant in their own right, not as light, fluffy caps to the meal.

Just a few steps from the Vucciria market is a convent of Benedictine nuns. In past centuries the revolving drum—called a "turn"—we see in the photo was used for leaving foundling babies. In recent decades these still-cloistered nuns started making several types of pastries, such as cannoli, to sell and used the revolving drum to push them out to their customers.

Years ago, before the nuns specialized in desserts, I used to eat their black couscous (made with cuttlefish ink) whenever I was in Palermo. And yes, it was delivered in the same manner.

PAGES 248-249:
A display of colorful marzipan fruit, called Frutta Martorana after the nuns of the Martorana Convent who first made them. Marzipan, made from almonds originated in Sicily, which has a huge crop.

The photograph was taken in the historic cellars of Florio Marsala. The wine of the same name is very versatile and is used for everything from aperitif to dessert and is also much employed in cooking.

The green almonds with the outside hull still on. They are used to prepare a liqueur in the style of the famous nocino from Modena. When they are very fresh, green almonds may be eaten raw.

# Torta di Mandorle alla Siciliana
## ALMOND TORTE
### SERVES 10 TO 12.

Many Sicilian desserts are based on almonds, which centuries ago were a culinary staple used for thickening and, when ground, in place of flour for cakes. The Mediterranean trade in almonds was once one of the area's largest commercial enterprises. Sicily was a great center of almond production and still is.

When making this torte and other cakes, I buy unblanched almonds and blanch them myself in order to restore the full flavor of the fresh almond and to remove some of the nut's oil, which can turn rancid. When chopping the almonds, I also sprinkle them with sugar to quickly absorb still more of the oil. This *dolce* must be served with a dessert wine, never with coffee.

12 ounces unblanched almonds

16 tablespoons (8 ounces) sweet butter

8 extra-large eggs, separated

10 ounces granulated sugar

2 tablespoons confectioners' sugar
  Grated peel of 2 medium-sized oranges (see page 294)

1 teaspoon rosewater

6 ounces unbleached all-purpose flour

2 tablespoons potato starch (*not* potato flour)

2 teaspoons baking powder

TO SERVE
  Confectioners' sugar

Preheat the oven to 375 degrees. Blanch the almonds for about 2 minutes in boiling water, transfer to cold water, and remove the stems. Place the blanched almonds on a cookie sheet and toast them in the preheated oven for 10 minutes. Set aside to cool. Leave oven on.

Meanwhile, melt the butter in a double boiler and let rest until needed.

Place the egg yolks along with 8 ounces of the granulated sugar and the confectioners' sugar in a crockery or glass bowl. Stir with a wooden spoon, always in the same direction, until the sugar is completely incorporated and the egg yolks turn a lighter color. Slowly add the cooled melted butter to the bowl, mixing thoroughly.

Place half of the almonds and the remaining 2 ounces of granulated sugar in a blender or food processor and finely grind them. Then add the remaining almonds and grind those coarsely. Start adding the almond mixture, along with the grated orange peel and the rosewater, to the bowl containing the other ingredients. Mix thoroughly with a wooden spoon.

Lightly butter a 15-by-10½-inch jelly-roll pan.

Combine the flour with the potato starch and the baking powder, and mix very well. Add the flour mixture to the bowl containing the other ingredients, stirring constantly with a wooden spoon until homogeneous.

With a wire whisk, beat the egg whites in a copper bowl to soft peak and gently fold them into the almond mixture. Pour the batter into the prepared pan and spread it out with a spatula. Bake for about 35 minutes.

Remove torte from oven and transfer it to a rack to cool for about ½ hour. Cut the torte into squares, sprinkle evenly with the confectioners' sugar and serve.

# Cassata alla Siciliana

## SICILIAN CASSATA

SERVES 8 TO 10.

*Cassata* means Sicily to Italians. The special flavor of the dessert and its colorful candied fruit reflect the warmth of the people and recall the excess of the Baroque period while providing an appropriate finale for a wonderful meal.

A most unusual candied fruit, *zucca candita* is really a vegetable, candied squash, which is used primarily in this region. It is cut into very thin strips, called "angel hair" (*capelli d'angelo*), also the name of a type of pasta which is much less popular in Italy than it is abroad.

*Cassata* is traditionally the dessert for Easter.

### FOR THE *BOCCA DI DAMA* (SPONGE CAKE)

7 extra-large eggs, separated
6 tablespoons granulated sugar
6 tablespoons confectioners' sugar
Grated peel of 1 medium-sized lemon (see page 294)
5 ounces unbleached all-purpose flour
4 ounces potato starch (*not* potato flour)
A pinch of salt

PLUS

Butter and flour for a 10-inch double cake pan

### FOR THE FILLING

1½ pounds ricotta, drained very well
5 tablespoons superfine sugar
5 tablespoons confectioners' sugar
2 tablespoons Maraschino (cherry liqueur)
1½ ounces candied orange rind, cut into small pieces
1 ounce candied citron, cut into small pieces
1 ounce semisweet chocolate, cut into small pieces, *or* 1 ounce of candied cherries and more citron combined

### TO ASSEMBLE THE *CASSATA*

2 cups water
½ cup granulated sugar
½ tablespoon freshly squeezed lemon juice
3 tablespoons Maraschino liqueur *or* 1 teaspoon rosewater

### FOR THE GLAZE

1 pound confectioners' sugar
4 teaspoons milk

### TO DECORATE THE CAKE

Different candied fruits to shape into flowers, leaves, etc.

One or 2 days in advance, prepare the *Bocca di dama*: Preheat the oven to 350 degrees. Lightly butter and flour a 10-inch double cake pan.

Mix the egg yolks very well with the granulated sugar, confectioners' sugar and lemon peel until the eggs are almost whipped. You can use an electric mixer. Sift the flour and the potato starch together, then start adding the mixture to the eggs, stirring constantly. When all the flour is incorporated, add the pinch of salt.

Using a wire whisk and a copper bowl, beat the egg whites to soft peak. Gently fold the whites into the thick batter with a rubber spatula, then transfer mixture to the prepared cake pan. Bake for 35 to 40 minutes or until very spongy to the touch. Transfer to a rack and let the cake rest for 30 minutes before unmolding it onto a second rack. Let rest until the following day.

The next day prepare the filling: Be sure the ricotta is very well drained, then mix it with the superfine sugar and the confectioners' sugar. Add the liqueur or

OPPOSITE:
*Sicily's most popular dessert,* Cassata, *against one of the island's Greek temples, at Segesta. Many of the greatest ancient Greek ruins are in Sicily.*

DESSERTS

the ricotta and refrigerate, covered, for at least 3 hours before using it.

Meanwhile, prepare the syrup: Set a medium-sized saucepan with the water, sugar and lemon juice over medium heat and simmer for about 35 minutes. A very thin syrup should form. Cut a slice less than ½ inch thick off the top of the cake and save it. Form a "container" from the bottom part by inserting a sharp knife ½ inch from the edge and cutting all around, leaving a ½-inch-thick bottom. Scoop out the inside crumb of the cake, being careful not to make any holes in the bottom, and save it if you are making the Variation 3 version of the dessert (see below); set aside.

Add the liqueur or the rosewater to the sugar syrup and pour enough over the bottom part of the cake to lightly soak the "container." Pour all the filling into the hollowed-out cake, level it with a spatula and fit its "cover" back in place. Drizzle some of the syrup over the top.

Transfer the filled cake to the bottom part of a 10-inch spring-form lined with parchment paper, then line the sides of the cake with a band of parchment paper. Fit the outer side of the form in place and close the spring-form. Refrigerate, covered, for at least 3 hours before glazing it.

When ready, prepare the glaze: Sift the confectioners' sugar into a medium-sized bowl. Add the milk and mix very well with a wooden spoon until a very smooth and rather thick, not translucent, white paste forms.

Release the spring-form and transfer the cake to a cake stand. Remove the parchment band and glaze the cake, top and sides, by gently pouring the glaze all over the cake and spreading it evenly over the top and sides with a metal spatula. The layer of glaze should be rather thick and very smooth. Set aside for at least 1 hour.

Once the glaze has hardened, shape the candied fruit over the cake in whichever decoration you prefer. *Cassata* remains at its best for no longer than 2 days.

## VARIATIONS

1. For the filling: Omit the liqueur and use 2 tablespoons rosewater.
2. For glaze: Use 8 ounces semisweet chocolate melted with 4 tablespoons unsalted butter. Omit decorations with candied fruit.
3. The *cassata* may be covered with a crust instead of the glaze: Prepare a *pasta frolla* (short pastry) using the following ingredients:

   12  ounces unbleached all-purpose flour
       Grated peel of ½ lemon (see page 294)
       A pinch of salt
   4  ounces granulated sugar
   6  tablespoons (3 ounces) sweet butter, chilled
   2  extra-large eggs
   2  tablespoons very cold water

Use this pastry to line a 10-inch double cake pan. Crumble enough of the leftover *bocca di dama* crumb (which was removed to make the pastry container in the original recipe) to yield ⅓ cup of crumbs. Sprinkle these over the bottom layer of *pasta frolla*. Pour filling into the cake and top with 1 layer of the pastry.

Bake for 35 to 40 minutes or until top is golden and the pastry is completely detached from the sides. Transfer to a rack to cool.

Once it reaches room temperature, dust the cake with confectioners' sugar and transfer to a serving platter.

# Cassata al Forno

## BAKED CASSATA

SERVES 10 TO 12.

While not as elaborate as *Cassata alla siciliana*, this *cassata* has a wonderful flavor nonetheless as a result of baking the filling.

FOR THE CRUST

- 5 ounces unbleached all-purpose flour
  A pinch of salt
- 1 ounce shelled walnuts
- ½ cup granulated sugar
- 8 tablespoons (4 ounces) sweet butter
- 1 extra-large egg
- 4 tablespoons cold water or dry white wine

FOR THE FILLING

- 4 egg yolks
- 8 tablespoons granulated sugar
- 1 tablespoon potato starch (*not* potato flour)
- 3 large pieces orange rind
- 1 cup milk
- 4 tablespoons candied orange rind, cut into very small pieces
- 4 tablespoons candied citron, cut into small pieces
- 1 teaspoon jasmine extract *or* 2 drops if imported from Italy
- 30 ounces ricotta, well drained
- 1 ounce grated bittersweet chocolate

Prepare the crust: Place the flour in a mound on a board and make a well in it. Put the pinch of salt in the well. Using a food processor or blender, finely grind the walnuts and ¼ cup of the sugar. Pour the walnut mixture and the remaining ¼ cup of the sugar into the well, then mix all the ingredients together. Place the butter on the flour mixture, then use a dough scraper to chop the butter, incorporating it into the flour compound. Make another well and pour the egg and heavy cream into it. Add the water and quickly mix the liquids together. Start incorporating the flour mixture, using your hands to form a ball of dough. Wrap the dough in plastic wrap and refrigerate for 1 hour before using it.

Prepare the filling: Make a custard cream, using the egg yolks, sugar, potato starch, orange rind and the milk, in a double boiler over boiling water (see Note, page 259). Transfer the prepared custard to a crockery or glass bowl, cover the bowl with plastic for 10 minutes, then refrigerate until needed.

When ready, finish the filling: Remove the orange rind from the custard cream, then add the candied orange rind, citron and jasmine extract to the bowl with the custard. Mix very well, then add the ricotta and the chocolate. Mix again and refrigerate while you finish the pastry.

Preheat the oven to 375 degrees. Lightly butter a 12-inch cake pan with removable bottom.

With a rolling pin, stretch the pastry between 2 pieces of plastic wrap, into a disc about 18 inches in diameter. Peel off the top plastic wrap from the pastry, then flip the pastry into the lined pan. Press the sides of the pastry into the bottom and against the sides of the pan, remove the second piece of plastic wrap, then pour in the prepared filling. Use a pastry wheel to cut off the excess pastry around the sides of the pan. With the excess pieces of pastry, prepare several strips about 1½ inches wide to make the criss-cross top crust. Bake for 1½ hours.

Remove from the oven and let the cake rest in the pan for at least ½ hour before lifting it out of the cake pan. Serve at room temperature.

# *Il "Mazariso"*
## PISTACHIO CAKE
### SERVES 6 TO 10.

We are more accustomed to seeing the lovely colored pistachio nuts as little jewels in galantine and other savory stuffings than as the main ingredient of a cake, but there is one cake that is made completely of ground pistachios. It is found in Sicily, of course, where the nuts are grown and not so prohibitively expensive to use in great quantity. The best pistachios come from the small area of Bronte, in the province of Catania. *"Mazariso"* in its original cake form is now difficult to find, but as small pastries, it is still popular.

Not to be missed is the delicious pistachio *gelato* in Sicily, made from the local nuts.

8 ounces unblanched pistachio nuts
 Coarse-grained salt
1 large orange with thick skin
2 whole extra-large eggs
4 extra-large eggs, separated
2 tablespoons (1 ounce) sweet butter,
 at room temperature

5 ounces plus 2 tablespoons granulated
 sugar
4 ounces potato starch (*not* potato
 flour)
1 tablespoon baking powder
 A pinch of salt

TO BAKE
 Sweet butter and unbleached all-purpose flour for the mold

PLUS
 6 tablespoons dry Marsala wine
FOR THE ICING (*GLASSA*)
 8 ounces confectioners' sugar
 3 to 4 tablespoons orange juice
 A large pinch of ground saffron
TO SERVE
 About 20 blanched pistachio nuts,
 left whole

Preheat the oven to 375 degrees.

Shell and blanch the nuts for 1 minute in salted boiling water (see Note), then dry them on a cookie sheet in the preheated oven for 10 minutes. Leave oven on.

Meanwhile, grate the orange rind (see page 294) and place the grated rind in a medium-sized crockery or glass bowl. Squeeze the orange itself, saving the juice for later use. Add the whole eggs and egg yolks along with the butter and 3 ounces of the sugar to the bowl. Mix very well with a wooden spoon until the egg yolks turn a lighter color and all the ingredients are almost whipped.

Finely grind the nuts with the remaining sugar in a blender or food processor. Add the ground nut mixture to the bowl with the other ingredients and stir very well. Mix the salt, potato starch and baking powder together and add to the bowl, a little at a time, constantly mixing with a wooden spoon.

Lightly butter and flour a 10-inch double cake pan. Line the bottom with parchment paper and lightly butter the top of the paper.

In a copper bowl, beat the egg whites with a wire whisk until stiff and fold them into the nut mixture. Pour the batter into the prepared pan and bake for 50 minutes. Remove from oven, transfer the pan to a rack and let cool for 15 minutes before unmolding onto a round serving platter, covered with two half discs of new parchment paper. Peel off the old parchment paper, which is now on top, and pour the Marsala over the cake.

Prepare the *glassa*: Sift the confectioners' sugar into a small saucepan. Add 3 tablespoons of the reserved orange juice and the saffron; mix very well. Set pan over very low heat, stirring constantly, until the sugar and saffron are completely melted and the texture is homogeneous.

LEFT:
*A spray of the fruit of the pistachio tree*

BELOW:
*Mazara del Vallo at the southwest tip of
Sicily is one of the most active fishing ports.
The old city is rich in baroque architecture.*

Quickly spread the *glassa* over the top and sides of the cake, using a metal spatula. Be sure the icing is evenly spread. Let the cake rest for a few minutes before placing it in the still warmish oven for 1 minute to make the icing shine.

Remove from oven and gently pull out the two half discs of paper from under the cake. Make a circle of whole pistachios around the edge of the cake. Let cake cool for at least 15 minutes before serving.

NOTE: *If you do not put salt in the boiling water when you blanch pistachios, they turn yellowish and not the vivid green you want, especially if they are not very fresh.*

# Dolce di Farina di Castagne

## CHESTNUT FLOUR CAKE

SERVES 8.

In central Italy, including Tuscany's island of Elba, chestnut flour made from fresh rather than dried chestnuts is used in many dishes, from appetizers to desserts, particularly in hearty repasts of the winter season.

Pastas may be made from this flour, sometimes mixed with other flours, most notably the Ligurian *Corzetti stampati*, a coin-shaped one stamped with many different designs. When the chestnut flour is freshly made, it is rather doughy and has a smoky taste. At that point it is best used to make a special polenta that is eaten with a pork stew. When it is more seasoned and drier, the smoky taste disappears and it becomes sweeter. It is then ready to be used for desserts such as *Castagnaccio* or *Migliaccio*, made throughout Tuscany, including Elba, as well as for this dessert.

FOR THE CAKE

- 4 ounces Italian chestnut flour (see Note)
- 4 ounces unbleached all-purpose flour
- ½ cup warm espresso
- 3 tablespoons granulated sugar
- 3 tablespoons bittersweet cocoa powder
- 1 cup cold milk
  A pinch of salt

PLUS

- 5 ounces shelled walnuts
- 5 extra-large eggs, separated
- 6 tablespoons granulated sugar
- 2 tablespoons confectioners' sugar
- 3 tablespoons light rum
- 6 tablespoons (3 ounces) sweet butter, at room temperature

FOR THE PASTRY CREAM

- 4 extra-large egg yolks
- 6 tablespoons granulated sugar

- 1 tablespoon potato starch (*not* potato flour)
- ½ cup dry white wine
- 2 tablespoons light rum

FOR THE GLAZE

- 8 ounces bittersweet chocolate, in one piece
- 6 tablespoons (3 ounces) sweet butter
- 3 tablespoons superfine sugar

TO SERVE

- 5 marrons glacées, crumbled

Mix the 2 flours together, then sift to remove all the small lumps and to incorporate air. Place the flour in a medium-sized bowl and make a well in it. Pour the espresso into a crockery or glass bowl, add the sugar and cocoa and mix very well with a wooden spoon. Pour this mixture into the well of the flour. Little by little, incorporate some of the flour from the rim of the well, constantly mixing with a wooden spoon, being careful to avoid forming lumps. Start pouring in the milk, still mixing constantly, and when all the milk is incorporated, add salt and mix again. Let this batter rest, covered, until needed.

Finely grind the walnuts. For grinding the walnuts, you may use either of 2 methods: The first is to grind the walnuts along with 3 tablespoons of the granulated sugar in a food processor (if walnuts are very fresh, grind carefully so that paste does not form on the sides of the processor's bowl); the second method is to grind the walnuts in a Mouli cheese grater, but without the sugar.

Transfer the ground walnuts to a crockery or glass bowl, then add the egg yolks, saving the egg whites in a glass bowl for later use; 5 tablespoons of the granulated sugar only if the walnuts have been ground with a Mouli grater, otherwise 2 tablespoons; the confectioners' sugar; rum and butter. Mix all together very well, then add the mixture to the prepared batter; stir well with a wooden spoon.

Preheat the oven to 375 degrees. Lightly butter a 10-inch double cake pan and dust it with flour, then line the bottom of the pan with parchment paper and butter and flour the paper.

Using a copper bowl and wire whisk, beat the egg whites together with the remaining tablespoon of sugar until stiff and fold them into the batter. Transfer the mixture to the prepared cake pan and bake for 40 minutes, watching that the top of the cake does not turn too dark.

Meanwhile, prepare the pastry cream (see Note) in a double boiler with the ingredients listed above. Transfer the cooked cream to a crockery or glass bowl and let rest until completely cold, about ½ hour.

Transfer the baked cake to a rack and let rest for 10 minutes. Meanwhile, line a round serving platter with parchment paper cut in the shape of two half-moons. When ready, unmold the cake onto the lined round serving platter and let it rest for at least ½ hour.

Prepare the glaze: Bring a medium-sized stockpot of cold water to a boil over medium heat. Place the chocolate, cut into small pieces, butter and sugar in a metal bowl. When the water reaches a boil, remove stockpot from the heat and insert the bowl with the chocolate over the pot. Be sure the bottom of the bowl is not touched by the water. Let stay until the chocolate is completely melted, about ½ hour.

Slice through the cake crosswise, making 2 disc-shaped layers. Remove the top layer. Spread the cooled cream over the bottom disc on the serving dish. Top cream with the other disc. When ready, mix the chocolate glaze very well and coat the top and sides of the cake. Sprinkle the crumbled marrons all over the top. When ready to serve, slice the cake like a pie.

NOTES: *Italian chestnut flour is made from fresh chestnuts, not dried.*

*To make custard cream, pastry cream or any form of zabaione: Bring some water to a boil in the bottom of a double boiler. Put the egg yolks into a crockery or glass bowl and add the sugar and all the other solid ingredients called for by the recipes, such as potato starch, flour, etc. Stir with a wooden spoon, always in the same direction, until the sugar is completely incorporated and the egg yolks turn a lighter color. Add the liquid or liquids and stir very well; then transfer the contents of the bowl to the top part of the double boiler and insert it over the boiling water. Stir constantly with a wooden spoon. Just before it boils, the* crema *or* zabaione *should be thick enough to coat the wooden spoon. Absolutely do not allow to boil. Immediately remove the top part of the double boiler from the heat and stir the contents for 1 minute longer. Then transfer the sauce to a crockery or glass bowl to cool completely (about ½ hour).*

OVERLEAF:
*An array of the Sardinian cookies with such dialect names as* pabassinas, bianchittu *and* pirichittus, *found in all the pastry shops of the island. Many of them, as in Sicily, include ground almonds. The church is an example of the rough, rustic Sardinian version of Pisan style architecture. In the Middle Ages the island was dominated first by Pisa, then Genoa.*

# Dolce alle Pere

## PEAR CAKE

SERVES 8.

8 ounces plus 2 tablespoons granulated sugar

8 tablespoons (4 ounces) sweet butter, at room temperature

1 extra-large egg

4 extra-large eggs, separated

1 teaspoon lemon extract *or* 1 drop if imported from Italy

2 tablespoons brandy or light rum
A pinch of salt

6 ounces unbleached all-purpose flour

1 scant tablespoon baking powder

2 medium-sized Bosc pears (about 12 ounces), ripe but not overripe, cut into quarters, peeled and cored
Juice of ½ lemon

PLUS

Sweet butter and flour for the mold

TO SERVE

2 large Bosc pears (about 16 ounces), ripe but not overripe, cut into quarters, peeled and cored

2 tablespoons (1 ounce) sweet butter

2 tablespoons granulated sugar

2 tablespoons brandy
About 1 cup cold water, depending on the ripeness of the pears

*The small June pears so beloved in Tuscany, including Elba. The normal sized pear in the center gives you the sense of scale.*

Place the 8 ounces of sugar and the butter in a crockery or glass bowl and use a wooden spoon to mix the 2 ingredients together until the sugar is completely dissolved and a light creamy texture results. (An electric mixer with the whisk can be used up to the point where the flour is added.) Start adding the egg and the egg yolks, one at a time, mixing constantly, then add the lemon extract along with the brandy and the salt; mix very well. If using a mixer, transfer the batter to a large bowl, then start adding the flour mixed with the baking powder and mix very well.

Preheat the oven to 375 degrees. Butter and lightly flour a 10-inch double cake pan. Line the bottom with parchment paper and lightly butter the top of the paper.

Cut each pear quarter into very thin slivers and place them in a crockery or glass bowl with the lemon juice; mix well. Set aside until needed.

Use a copper bowl and a wire whisk to beat the egg whites until stiff, incorporating the remaining 2 tablespoons of the sugar. Gently fold the whites into the batter. Drain the pears and add them to the batter. Using a rubber spatula, carefully incorporate the pears. Pour the mixture into the prepared pan and bake for 1 hour.

Meanwhile, prepare the topping: Cut the pear quarters into thin slivers, then melt the butter in a medium-sized sauté pan over medium heat. When the butter is completely melted, add the sugar and the brandy. Mix very well for 20 seconds, then add the pears and sauté for 2 or 3 minutes or until pears are coated with the almost caramelized sugar. If pears are not very ripe, add from ¼ to ½ cup of cold water as they are cooking and cook a little longer until they are soft.

When the cake is ready, place pan on a rack and let rest for a few minutes before unmolding it onto a round serving platter. Peel off the parchment paper and let the cake rest for at least 20 minutes before serving. When ready, slice the cake, top with the pear sauce and serve. Cake may be prepared in advance and the sauce/topping reheated at the last moment before serving.

# Torta di Pane o Castagnaccio Finto
## ITALIAN BREAD PUDDING

SERVES 8.

This Italian bread pudding is made with whole-wheat bread. The addition of cocoa powder darkens the pudding to a shade close to the color of chestnut flour. Because of the way it is baked, it is thought to resemble a mock *Castagnaccio*, the famous Tuscan chestnut flour dessert, in appearance, not in taste.

½ pound day-old Italian whole-wheat bread
4½ cups milk
4 ounces raisins
1 large orange with thick skin
8 tablespoons granulated sugar
4 tablespoons (2 ounces) sweet butter, at room temperature
3 extra-large eggs, separated

3 tablespoons unsweetened cocoa powder
3 tablespoons pine nuts (*pignoli*)
PLUS
3 tablespoons (1½ ounces) sweet butter
TO SERVE
1½ cups heavy cream
2 tablespoons granulated sugar
1 teaspoon confectioners' sugar
Zest of 1 large orange

FOR THE SAUCE
12 ounces cleaned strawberries, cut into quarters
4 ounces raspberries
1 cup dry white wine
4 tablespoons brandy
½ cup cold water
4 tablespoons granulated sugar or more, depending on the sweetness of the berries

Without removing the crust from the bread, cut bread into small pieces. In a crockery or glass bowl, soak bread with 4 cups of the milk for 1 hour, mixing every so often with a wooden spoon.

Meanwhile, warm remaining ½ cup of milk in a small saucepan over low heat. Add raisins and soak for 30 minutes. Grate the orange peel (see page 294). Preheat the oven to 375 degrees. Heavily butter a 13½-by-8¾-inch glass baking dish.

When ready, drain the bread through a colander without pressing, allowing bread to retain a lot of milk. Transfer the bread from the colander to a crockery or glass bowl and mix very well to be sure there are no big pieces. Add the grated orange peel along with the sugar, butter and the egg yolks; mix very well. Add the cocoa powder and mix again. Drain the raisins and add them along with the pine nuts to the bread mixture; mix gently with a rubber spatula. Using a copper bowl and a wire whisk, beat egg whites until stiff and fold them in. Pour bread mixture into prepared baking dish. Bake for 45 minutes.

Meanwhile, using a wire whisk and a chilled metal bowl, prepare the whipped cream with the granulated and confectioners' sugars. Zest the orange and place the strips in a bowl of cold water until needed.

Combine strawberries, raspberries, wine, brandy, water and sugar in a medium-sized casserole over medium heat and bring to a boil; then lower heat and simmer for 25 minutes. Ten minutes before the sauce is ready, taste for sweetness, adding more sugar as necessary.

Remove the *torta di pane* from the oven and let cool for at least 15 minutes before serving. Cut the bread pudding into squares and gently transfer them to individual plates. Spoon some berries with their sauce over each square. Some sauce will fall to one side of the plate. On the other side, place some of the whipped cream and sprinkle it with some orange zest. The sauce may be prepared in advance and reheated.

# Torta di Noci

## WALNUT TORTE

### SERVES 8.

A flourless cake, this torte uses "flour" made from ground walnuts mixed with bread crumbs, a combination found in Friuli as well as in Sicily, where bread crumbs have a very important place in the culinary repertoire. Aside from desserts, bread crumbs are used a great deal in savory dishes, often with the addition of oregano, anchovies, saffron, parsley, salt and pepper. Instead of grated cheese, they are often sprinkled over pasta dishes before serving.

10  ounces granulated sugar

6  ounces shelled walnuts

½  of a clove
   A pinch of ground cinnamon

4  ounces unseasoned very fine bread crumbs, lightly toasted, preferably homemade

   Grated peel of ½ lemon (see page 294)

2  extra-large eggs

4  extra-large eggs, separated

4  tablespoons (2 ounces) sweet butter at room temperature

TO BAKE

2  tablespoons (1 ounce) sweet butter

⅓  cup unseasoned very fine breadcrumbs, lightly toasted, preferably homemade

1  tablespoon granulated sugar

TO SERVE

1  heaping teaspoon confectioners' sugar

Place 2 ounces of the sugar in a blender or food processor, add the walnuts and finely grind. Transfer ground walnuts to a bowl. Mix the clove, cinnamon, bread crumbs and the grated lemon rind all together, then finely grind them in a blender or food processor.

Preheat the oven to 375 degrees. Butter bottom and sides of a 10-inch double cake pan, then line the sides of the pan with bread crumbs. Line the bottom of the pan with a piece of parchment paper and butter it.

Place the remaining 8 ounces of the sugar, the eggs, the egg yolks and the butter in a crockery or glass bowl or in an electric mixer and whisk until eggs are almost whipped. Start adding the walnut mixture, little by little, then the bread crumb mixture. After all the ingredients have been combined, whisk for 5 minutes more.

Beat the egg whites to soft peak and gently fold them into the thick batter in the mixer. Transfer the batter to the prepared pan and bake for 20 minutes. Sprinkle the tablespoon of granulated sugar evenly over the top and bake for about 20 minutes more. Transfer to a rack and let cool for ½ hour, then unmold the torte onto a round serving platter and let it cool to room temperature.

Place a stencil with a diamond pattern over the cake and use a confectioners' sugar shaker to cover the exposed area. Slice the cake into wedges and serve.

# Budino o Torta di Semolino
## SEMOLINA CAKE

SERVES 6 TO 8.

3 cups milk
2 ounces very fine semolina
  A pinch of salt
1 large orange with skin
3 tablespoons raisins
3 extra-large eggs, separated

4 tablespoons (2 ounces) sweet butter
6 tablespoons granulated sugar
3 tablespoons pine nuts (*pignoli*)
FOR THE ORANGE SAUCE
1 cup cold milk
3 extra-large egg yolks

3 ounces granulated sugar
½ cup heavy cream
1 teaspoon orange extract or 2 drops if extract is imported from Italy
TO SERVE
  Orange zest

*Pantelleria Island's famous raisins called "Zibibbo" also exist on Elba under the name of "Uva Salamanna."*

Wet a medium-sized casserole with cold water so the milk does not stick to the bottom. Place casserole with the milk over medium heat and when it reaches a boil, add the semolina a little at a time, constantly stirring with a wooden spoon. When all the semolina has been added, with constant mixing, simmer for 8 minutes, adding a pinch of salt. Transfer semolina to a crockery or glass bowl and let cool completely, about ½ hour.

Meanwhile, prepare the orange sauce: Wet a heavy casserole with cold water. Add milk, bring it to a boil over medium heat and cook for 5 minutes, stirring every so often.

While milk is heating, put the egg yolks in a crockery or glass bowl and add the sugar. Stir with a wooden spoon, always in the same direction, until the sugar is completely incorporated and the egg yolks turn a lighter color. Slowly pour in the heavy cream, mixing steadily.

Place the bottom part of a double boiler over medium heat with enough water to reach just high enough not to touch the bottom of the insert. When the milk is ready, pass it through a fine strainer to remove any skin formed on top, into a bowl. Immediately transfer the strained milk to the other bowl containing the egg yolks, stir very well with a wooden spoon and add the orange extract. Then transfer the contents of the bowl to the top of the double boiler and place it over the bottom part containing the boiling water. Stir constantly with a wooden spoon, always in the same direction. Just before reaching a boil, the cream should be thick enough to coat the spoon. Absolutely do not allow it to boil. Immediately remove the top part of the double boiler from the heat. Continue to stir the contents for 2 or 3 minutes longer, then transfer cream to a crockery or glass bowl to let cool for about 15 minutes, mixing every so often with a wooden spoon. Pour the cream into an empty wine bottle, cork it and place on the bottom shelf of the refrigerator for about 1 hour or until needed.

Preheat the oven to 375 degrees. Butter a 10-inch spring-form and dust it with flour. Cut out a disc of parchment paper to fit the bottom of the spring-form and press it in. Butter and flour the surface of the paper.

When semolina is ready, grate the orange peel (see page 294) and soak the raisins in a bowl of lukewarm water for about 15 minutes.

Add the egg yolks to the semolina, along with the butter and sugar, and mix very well. Butter should be completely absorbed by the semolina. Drain the raisins and add them to the bowl along with the pine nuts and orange peel; mix again.

Using a copper bowl and a wire whisk, beat the egg whites until stiff and gently incorporate them into the thick batter. Pour the batter into the prepared pan and bake for 40 minutes.

Transfer cake to a rack and let rest 15 minutes before releasing form. Unmold the *torta* onto a round serving platter, gently peel off the paper, and let the *torta* cool slightly before cutting.

Each serving should be prepared with a thin layer of the cooled orange sauce, topped with a square of the cake, and garnished with orange zest. The cake is good even after several hours, but it is best when still warm.

FROM SARDINIA

# Budino agli Amaretti
## BITTER-ALMOND CUSTARD

SERVES 10.

3 cups whole milk
1 (2-inch) piece vanilla bean
3 extra-large eggs
3 ounces granulated sugar

4½ ounces amaretti cookies
    Grated peel of ½ lemon
TO SERVE (OPTIONAL)
1½ cups heavy cream

1 tablespoon granulated sugar
2 teaspoons confectioners' sugar
1 teaspoon orange extract or 2 drops if
    extract is imported from Italy

Set a medium casserole with the milk and vanilla bean over low heat and simmer for 4 minutes, removing the film that forms over the milk as it appears.

Meanwhile, preheat the oven to 400 degrees and prepare a large roasting pan with lukewarm water to be used later for the *bagno Maria* (water bath). Lightly butter a 5-by-9-inch non-stick loaf pan.

Place the eggs in a crockery or glass bowl, add the sugar and mix with a wooden spoon until the sugar is completely dissolved and the eggs turn a lighter color. Use a mortar and pestle or food processor to finely grind the amaretti together with the lemon peel.

When the milk is ready and still hot, pour it little by little into the egg mixture, constantly stirring with a wooden spoon, to prevent the eggs from curdling. When all the milk is incorporated, add the amaretti and mix again. Pour the contents of the bowl into the prepared loaf pan. Put a cotton towel or some paper toweling on the bottom of the roasting pan containing the water, set loaf pan in it and place in the preheated oven. Bake for 1 hour.

Remove the loaf pan from oven, let cool for 30 minutes, then refrigerate for at least 1 hour before unmolding it onto a serving dish.

Serve custard by cutting it in half lengthwise, then widthwise into fifths, making 10 servings. If serving with the optional whipped cream, whip the cream using a chilled metal bowl and wire whisk, adding the sugar and the lemon extract.

*Caltagirone is famous for its ceramics, which are considered among the best not only in Sicily but in all of Italy. From May 20th to the 31st the city has its very folkloric festival of Maria Santissima di Conadomini. All the elegant carriages and ordinary cars are "dressed up" with flowers, lace, feathers and a host of other decorations.*

# FESTIVITY

# Cannoli alla Palermitana

## CANNOLI FROM PALERMO

### MAKES ABOUT 20.

These *cannoli* differ from those of Naples, which contain rosewater and a little ground cinnamon in the filling. The crust of the Sicilian *cannoli*, from Palermo, is very light and crisp, with small bubbles created by the wine, either white wine or dry Marsala, in the dough. It is difficult to duplicate the exact taste and texture of real Sicilian sheep's milk ricotta; some cooks use ricotta mixed with cocoa powder, but in doing this, you lose the classic taste of the jasmine extract in the filling, which I feel is more important for the dessert.

These *cannoli* are the traditional dessert of the carnival season. In the photo the *cannoli* are facing the complex of a *quadriglia* by Mario Rutelli on top of Palermo's Pompeian-style Politeama Theater.

FOR THE FILLING

2 pounds whole-milk ricotta

3 ounces candied orange rind, cut into small pieces (see Note)

⅔ cup confectioners' sugar

1 teaspoon orange extract *or* 2 drops if imported from Italy

5 ounces semisweet chocolate, coarsely chopped

FOR THE CRUST (THE SHELLS)

½ pound unbleached all-purpose flour, sifted

½ cup dry white wine

A pinch of salt

4 tablespoons (2 ounces) sweet butter, at room temperature, cut into pats

4 tablespoons granulated sugar

TO FRY THE SHELLS

3 cups vegetable oil (½ sunflower oil, ½ corn oil) or olive oil

TO SERVE

Confectioners' sugar

Several pieces of candied orange rind

Let the ricotta drain overnight in the refrigerator in a strainer lined with cheesecloth.

Prepare the pastry for the shells to be used the next day: Mix the flour with the wine, salt, butter and sugar. Knead the pastry for at least 15 minutes, then enclose it in plastic wrap and refrigerate overnight.

Next day, unwrap the pastry and knead it for 10 minutes more. Use a rolling pin to roll out a layer of dough into a square or rectangle on a floured pasta board. The thickness of the layer should not be more than ⅛ inch. Cut the pastry into strips using a jagged pastry cutter. The width of the strips should be a little less than the length of the *cannoli* molds. Cut the strips into squares. Turn a pastry square diagonally to resemble a diamond. Place the *cannoli* mold at one point and roll it on the mold, being careful not to press the pastry with your fingers. Brush the opposite point of the diamond with cold water to seal the pastry together.

Heat the oil in a deep-fat fryer over medium heat. When the oil is heated to about 365 degrees, which is not as hot as for normal deep-frying, put in 3 or 4 *cannoli*. Let the *cannoli* fry slowly, 2 to 3 minutes or until golden all over.

*Palermo style* cannoli *with the neo-classic* Teatro Politeama *in the background, near Palermo's famous botanic gardens*

Prepare a serving dish by lining it with paper towels. With a large strainer-skimmer, transfer the *cannoli* from the pan to the towel-lined serving dish and let cool completely (about 20 minutes).

To remove the *cannoli* from the mold, contract the mold by gently pressing it together at one end where the metal is not covered with pastry. The contracted mold will detach from the pastry and can be removed. Let the shells sit on paper towels to be sure all the excess oil is drained off.

Finish the filling: Transfer the drained ricotta to a bowl and add the orange rind, confectioners' sugar and jasmine extract. Let rest, covered, in the refrigerator until needed.

When ready to serve, remove filling from refrigerator and mix in the choco-late pieces. Fill a pastry bag with the filling and squeeze it into both open sides of each *connolo*. Transfer the stuffed *cannoli* to a serving dish. Using a strainer, sprinkle evenly with the confectioners' sugar and serve with candied orange rind placed over.

The shells may be made in advance and stored in plastic. Leftover shells may be stored in the same way.

NOTE: *In Sicily a candied squash called* zuccata *is used but is unavailable elsewhere, so I suggest this substitute.*

# *Focaccette Ripiene*

## SWEET SMALL *FOCACCE* FOR BREAKFAST

MAKES 12.

You might be taken aback at the idea of first baking these pastries and then frying them, but do not assume that they turn out heavy or greasy. Instead they are very light, with a wonderful paper-thin crust of a crispness that would be impossible to attain with any other method of cooking. The fruit filling is just perfect for the pastry covering.

FOR THE CRUST
- 1 cup whole milk
- 2 tablespoons (1 ounce) sweet butter
- ½ cup unbleached all-purpose flour
- 2 extra-large eggs

FOR THE FILLING
- 2 large red or yellow Delicious apples, peeled, cored and cut into small pieces

- 2 tablespoons granulated sugar
- ¼ cup dry Marsala
- ¼ cup water
- 3 tablespoons raisins

TO COOK THE *FOCACCETTE*
- 1½ cups cold milk
- 1 cup unbleached all-purpose flour
- 2 extra-large eggs

- 1 cup very fine unseasoned bread crumbs, lightly toasted, preferably homemade
- 2 cups vegetable oil (½ sunflower oil, ½ corn oil)

TO SERVE
- 4 tablespoons granulated sugar

Put the milk and the butter in a medium-sized casserole and set casserole over medium heat. When the milk reaches a boil and the butter is completely melted, remove casserole from the heat and immediately add the flour. Mix very well with a wooden spoon until a quite uniform ball of dough forms, about 3 minutes. Place casserole over low heat and constantly stir the dough, using a wooden spoon, for 2 minutes.

Transfer the dough to a crockery bowl and let rest for about 15 minutes.

Meanwhile, put the apples, sugar, Marsala, water and raisins in a small saucepan and cook, mixing every so often until the apples are quite soft, about 15 minutes. If apples are underripe you will need to add a little more water and cook longer; the apples should be not quite completely cooked but all the liquid should be evaporated.

Preheat the oven to 300 degrees and lightly butter and flour a baking sheet.

Add eggs, one at a time, to the dough, mixing vigorously with a wooden spoon after each egg is added. Put the dough in a pastry bag without a tip and push the dough through, onto the baking sheet, to make 12 small mounds. Use the back of a fork to flatten down the dough a little. Bake for 30 minutes, then lower the heat to 250 degrees and bake for 20 minutes longer.

When the filling is ready, transfer it to a crockery or glass bowl and let rest until cool, about 15 minutes, then use a fork to mash it a little. Remove the baked rolls and let them rest not more than 15 minutes before filling them.

Put the filling in a pastry bag with a round tip and insert some of the filling into each roll. Pour the milk into a bowl and soak the rolls one at a time for 3 seconds each, then place them on a rack. After 10 minutes dust them gently with flour all over.

Line a serving dish with paper towels. Lightly beat the eggs with a fork. Heat the oil in a medium-sized skillet over medium heat and when the oil is hot (about

*We can see the blood red orange juice against the background of the cathedral in Palermo. During the photography we had one of those experiences that happen in Sicily. We saw the sign "Grand Hotel" on one of the buildings and proceeded to climb the stairs to look for a room, but the building was empty. We searched around until a lady approached and asked why we were still there, hadn't we finished making the film? The building was actually a school, and a film company had transformed the facade into a hotel for one of their scenes.*

400 degrees), dip the stuffed rolls one by one in the eggs, then gently coat with the bread crumbs and fry them on all sides for 1 minute, or until lightly golden. Transfer the rolls to the lined serving dish to absorb extra oil.

When all the *focaccette* are on the serving dish, remove the paper, sprinkle evenly with the granulated sugar and serve hot. These sweet *focaccette* are eaten for breakfast, usually accompanied by a glass of the blood orange juice from Sicily's *tarocchi* oranges.

DESSERTS

# "*Brioscia*"

## BRIOCHE ROLLS FOR *GELATO* OR ICE CREAM

MAKES 24 OR 36.

Small rolls made with not very sweet, orange-flavored brioche (*bomboloni*) pastry are very popular opened and stuffed. The most typical stuffing is a dessert *gelato*, as Sicilians absolutely refuse to eat *gelato* in a cone.

Sicilian *gelati*, *sorbetti* and *granite* are all incredibly delicious and justly famous. Once you taste a Sicilian coffee ice topped with whipped cream, you will never forget it.

Also popular are *brioscia* rolls stuffed before baking with such savories as cooked vegetables, meat, poultry or cheese, with or without the addition of prosciutto or *prosciutto cotto* (boiled ham), and eaten warm. Most of the pastry shops and coffee shops carry them during the day and they are a favorite snack.

FOR THE SPONGE

1 cup plus 1 tablespoon unbleached all-purpose flour
1½ ounces fresh compressed yeast *or* 3 packages active dry yeast
3¾ cups lukewarm milk, or warm milk if using dry yeast
A pinch of salt

FOR THE DOUGH

4 tablespoons (2 ounces) sweet butter

4 extra-large egg yolks
2 tablespoons granulated sugar
1 teaspoon orange extract or 2 drops if imported from Italy
¾ cup lukewarm or warm milk, depending on the type of yeast used
A large pinch of ground saffron
2 cups unbleached all-purpose flour or 3 cups (see Note)

TO BAKE THE ROLLS

Enough butter to coat the muffin tins or the cookie sheet

PLUS

2 extra-large eggs

VARIATIONS

FOR THE DOUGH

1) Use orange juice instead of milk.
2) Add 1 teaspoon of rosewater.

Prepare the sponge: Place the cup of flour in a bowl and make a well in the flour. Dissolve the yeast in lukewarm or warm milk, depending on the yeast, and pour it into the well of the flour with the salt. Mix with a wooden spoon, incorporating all the flour. Sprinkle the remaining tablespoon of flour over the sponge, cover the bowl with a cotton towel and let rest, in a warm place away from drafts, until the sponge has doubled in size, about 1 hour.

Meanwhile, melt the butter in a double boiler and let it rest until needed.

When ready, transfer the melted butter to a large bowl or to the bowl of an electric mixer with the paddle on. Using a wooden spoon, if mixing by hand, or an electric mixer, add 1 egg yolk at a time without adding the following one until the previous one is completely amalgamated with the butter. When all the yolks are incorporated, add the sugar, orange extract and lukewarm milk. Add the risen sponge with the saffron and keep mixing steadily. Start adding the flour a little at a time. When almost all the flour is used up, stop mixing, cover bowl with plastic wrap and let rest until doubled in size, about 1 hour.

When the dough is ready, if you want to bake the rolls in molds lightly butter 2 regular muffin tins or 3 mini-muffin tins. Mix the dough with a wooden spoon, then scoop out a heaping tablespoon or ½ tablespoon of the dough and

*The opened roll serves as a container for the* gelato

place it in the regular-size muffin tin or the mini-muffin tin, respectively. Let the rolls rest, covered with plastic wrap, for 30 minutes.

Lightly beat the eggs with 1 tablespoon of water and quickly brush the top of each roll. Bake about 20 minutes for the large size and about 15 for the small size.

Remove rolls from the oven, let rest a few minutes in the mold, then unmold and let the *briosce* rest until cool before using them.

NOTE: *If preparing small individual* panini, *or rolls, without a mold, the flour should be increased to almost 3 cups instead of 2, so when the dough has doubled in size, there will be more than 1 cup of flour left to knead and roll out the dough itself. Once the dough has doubled in size, work this extra cup of flour into the dough until you are able to divide the dough into pieces of about 3 ounces. You will make 14 rolls.*

*Butter and lightly flour a cookie sheet. Knead each piece of dough, shape it into a small roll and place it on the cookie sheet to rise, covered, for 30 minutes. Bake rolls for about 20 minutes. Remove from oven and let rest until cool before using them.*

# Sorbetto al Gelsomino
## JASMINE SORBET

SERVES 8 TO 10.

A few drops of jasmine extract give this *sorbetto* a really exotic and unusual flavor. I first ate this dessert in the small baroque town of Noto, not far from Siracusa, where the fantastic show of palaces and churches built upon each other like terraces made me feel that I was not only experiencing baroque architecture, but even eating a *gelato* with a baroque flavor.

4 cups cold water
¾ cup granulated sugar
4 tablespoons fresh lemon juice

4 teaspoons jasmine extract or 8 drops if imported from Italy

TO SERVE
Fresh mint leaves

*Eating a very expensive* gelato *in a piazza of the not very Sardinian Costa Smeralda*

*All the baroque balconies in Noto have different motifs in the
stone work, even in the balconies of the same palace*

Pour the water into a medium-sized saucepan, add the sugar and mix very well
with a wooden spoon to completely dissolve the sugar. Set pan over medium heat
and simmer for about 45 minutes. A thin syrup should form.

Transfer syrup to a crockery or glass bowl and let cool completely, about 1
hour, then refrigerate for at least 2 hours more.

When ready, add lemon juice and jasmine extract to the syrup, mix very well,
then pour it into the bowl of a *gelato* maker and churn for about 25 minutes.

Transfer *sorbetto* to a tin *gelato* container and place it in the freezer for at least 1
hour before serving. Scoop the *sorbetto* into chilled glasses and serve with a fresh
mint leaf.

# Frittelle di Ricotta alla Sarda

## RICOTTA FRITTERS WITH ROSEWATER

SERVES 8 TO 10.

15 ounces whole-milk ricotta, very well drained

3 ounces granulated sugar

3 ounces unbleached all-purpose flour

4 ounces amaretti cookies (bitter-almond cookies)

2 extra-large eggs

1 extra-large egg yolk
Grated peel of 1 lemon (see page 294)

1 teaspoon rosewater

TO COOK THE FRITTERS
About 1 cup unbleached all-purpose flour

3 extra-large eggs

About 1 cup unseasoned very fine bread crumbs, lightly toasted, preferably homemade

3 cups vegetable oil (½ sunflower oil, ½ corn oil)

TO SERVE
Granulated sugar

Place ricotta in a medium-sized crockery or glass bowl, add the sugar and the flour and mix very well. Finely crumble the amaretti and add to bowl along with the eggs, egg yolk, grated peel of the lemon and the rosewater; mix very well with a wooden spoon to form a very smooth, thick batter. Using tablespoonfuls of the mixture, form into individual balls and lightly flour them.

Lightly beat the eggs in a crockery or glass bowl and spread out the bread crumbs on a board.

Heat the oil in a skillet over medium heat. When the oil is hot enough to make an inserted wooden spoon sizzle (about 375 degrees), dip each ball in the beaten egg, coat it with bread crumbs and fry until golden all over, about 1 minute. Transfer balls to a serving platter lined with paper towels to drain excess oil.

When all the fritters are on the serving platter, remove the paper towels and sprinkle with some granulated sugar. Serve hot.

The texture of the fritters should be very crusty on the outside and extremely creamy on the inside.

*In Sicily fritters were also made with* carrube, *a fruit from unusual trees that grow in southwest Sicily. The long pods are sometimes boiled, then chopped and fried. They may also be toasted and ground and used as a coffee substitute.*

FROM ELBA

# *Frittelle di Farina Dolce*

## CHESTNUT FLOUR FRITTERS

MAKES 18.

1 cup Italian chestnut flour, sifted (see Note, page 259)

¾ cup milk

1 tablespoon granulated sugar

A pinch of salt

2 heaping tablespoons raisins

PLUS

1 quart vegetable oil (½ corn oil,

½ sunflower oil)

TO SERVE

½ cup granulated sugar

Place the flour in a crockery or glass bowl, make a well in the flour and start adding the milk a little at a time, mixing constantly with a wooden spoon to prevent lumps from forming. When all the flour is incorporated and the batter is smooth, add sugar, salt and the raisins. Mix very well and let rest as you heat the oil in a medium-sized skillet over medium heat. When the oil is hot (375 degrees), spoon 1 tablespoon of the mixture into the hot oil, being careful to prevent fritters from touching one another. Cook for a few seconds or until lightly golden on both sides. Use a slotted spoon to transfer the cooked fritters to a serving platter lined with paper towels. When all the fritters are ready, remove the paper and sprinkle with the sugar. Serve hot.

*The two versions of seadas, baked and fried*

# Seadas al Forno
## SARDINIAN SOUR-CHEESE HONEY TARTS

SERVES 18.

FOR THE FILLING
- 2 cups cold water
- 1 pound sour cream (see Note)
- 5 tablespoons very fine semolina
  A pinch of salt
- 1 extra-large egg yolk

Grated peel of 2 lemons with thick skin (see page 294)

FOR THE CRUST
- 2 cups unbleached all-purpose flour, plus ½ cup for kneading and stretching

- 7 tablespoons (3½ ounces) sweet butter, at room temperature
- ½ cup lukewarm water
  A pinch of salt

PLUS
- ½ pound bitter honey (see Note)

Prepare the filling: Pour the water into a medium-sized saucepan, then add the sour cream and mix very well. Add the semolina and incorporate it well with a wooden spoon. Set pan over medium heat, stirring continuously until a smooth and velvety cream is formed, about 15 minutes, adding a pinch of salt at the end. Transfer "cheese" to a crockery or glass bowl and let rest for 30 minutes, mixing every so often.

Wet a large cotton dish towel with cold water and spread it over a wooden board. When the "cheese" has cooled, add the egg yolk and the lemon peel and mix very well. Make small ¼-cup mounds of the "cheese" on the wet towel and let rest for at least 1 hour.

Meanwhile, prepare the crust: Place the 2 cups of flour in a medium-sized bowl, make a well and put in the butter, water and the pinch of salt. Use a wooden spoon to incorporate the butter completely into the flour, then transfer the pastry to a board and knead it for 30 seconds or until a ball of dough is formed. Wrap dough with plastic wrap and refrigerate for at least 30 minutes.

Preheat oven to 375 degrees and lightly butter 18 2-inch tartlet molds with removable bottoms. Spread remaining ½ cup flour over a board, then knead pastry for 30 seconds. With a rolling pin or hand pasta machine, roll out pastry to a thickness of ¼ inch. Use a scalloped pastry wheel to cut out 18 5½-inch discs. Fit each disc into the prepared mold, then with a metal scraper, transfer about 2 heaping tablespoons of the "cheese" to each mold. Bake for 35 minutes.

Meanwhile, warm the honey in a small saucepan over low heat. Remove *seadas* from oven, unmold them and serve with some of the lukewarm honey used as topping.

NOTES: *If sour cream is freshly made, it may require 1 tablespoon each of granulated and confectioners' sugar plus 1 additional tablespoon of semolina.*

*The authentic bitter honey would be from the strawberry tree (*arbitus unedo*)—corbezzole in Italian —or substitute chestnut flower honey or another not very sweet honey.*

# Amaretti di Oristano
## BITTER-ALMOND COOKIES FROM ORISTANO

MAKES ABOUT 24.

3 ounces blanched almonds
3 ounces unblanched almonds
3 ounces packaged amaretti cookies

6 ounces granulated sugar
3 pinches of ground cinnamon
3 pinches of freshly grated nutmeg
3 large egg whites

FOR BAKING
3 teaspoons (1 ounce) unsalted butter, melted in a double boiler
3 teaspoons confectioners' sugar

The commercial amaretti cookies are used as an ingredient to intensify the bitter-almond taste that the unblanched almonds give to the Sardinian amaretti cookies from the town of Oristano. Be sure the almonds are very dry, otherwise place them in a preheated 375-degree oven for 10 minutes. Place the blanched and unblanched almonds in a blender or food processor along with the commercial amaretti and the sugar and season with the cinnamon and nutmeg. Grind everything together to form a "flour."

Preheat the oven to 250 degrees. Lightly butter 2 large pieces of parchment paper and place them over 2 cookie sheets.

Beat the egg whites in a copper bowl with a wire whisk until soft peaks form, then add the almond/amaretti mixture, 1 tablespoon at a time, constantly mixing. The result will be a very thick batter.

Place the batter in a pastry bag with a large plain tip and pipe it onto the prepared paper, making "lines" about 3 inches long. Be sure to leave enough space between rows. Sift the confectioners' sugar over the unbaked batter and let rest for 15 minutes before baking the cookies for 30 minutes. Lower the heat to 200 degrees and bake for 30 more minutes.

Remove cookie sheets from the oven and let rest for ½ hour before detaching the new Oristano-type of amaretti from the parchment paper. These amaretti may be prepared 1 week in advance.

# Dolce di Farina Gialla

## WALNUT/CORN MEAL CAKE

SERVES 8 TO 10.

8 tablespoons (4 ounces) sweet butter
¾ cup plus 2 tablespoons granulated
   sugar
6 tablespoons *aleatico* wine or *vinsanto*
   (see Note)
5 extra-large eggs, separated
PLUS
½ cup very fine yellow corn meal,

preferably imported Italian
4 ounces shelled walnuts
2 tablespoons granulated sugar
1 tablespoon confectioners' sugar
¼ cup potato starch (*not* potato flour)
2 teaspoons baking powder
   Peel of 1 large lemon

1 teaspoon lemon extract or 1 drop if
   imported
   A pinch of salt
TO SERVE
1 cup heavy cream
1 tablespoon granulated sugar
1 teaspoon confectioners' sugar
   Zest of 1 lemon

Place the butter with the ¾ cup of the sugar in a mixing bowl or in a mixer and mix until the butter is almost whipped. Add the *aleatico* or *vinsanto* and mix again. Start adding the egg yolks, one at a time, mixing constantly, until smooth and creamy.

Meanwhile, place corn meal, walnuts, granulated sugar and confectioners' sugar, along with the potato starch, baking powder, lemon peel, lemon extract and the pinch of salt in a food processor or blender and grind until the mixture resembles a brownish flour. Start adding this "seasoned" flour to the mixer, little by little, mixing constantly. When all the flour is incorporated, mix for 5 minutes more.

Preheat the oven to 375 degrees and butter and flour a 10-inch double cake pan. Line the pan with parchment paper and butter and flour the paper.

Using a copper bowl and a wire whisk, beat the egg whites with the remaining 2 tablespoons of the sugar to soft peaks. Gently fold the whites into the batter, then transfer it to the prepared pan. Bake for about 45 minutes; the cake should be golden and a toothpick inserted in it should come out quite dry.

Remove cake from the oven, transfer to a rack and let rest for at least 15 minutes before unmolding it onto a round serving platter.

When ready to serve, whip the cream with the granulated sugar and the confectioners' sugar in a chilled metal bowl.

Cake may be cut into wedges or into 3-inch squares. Top each serving with some of the cream and sprinkle with some of the lemon zest.

NOTE: *In Elba, beside the famous Vinsato, popular in all of Tuscany, there is the unique Aleatico d'Elba. Very robust, it recalls the flavor of blackberries. Produced from the omonimous grape, it is dark in color and has a full-bodied flavor which some say reveals a hint of the island's iron mines. As a child my father often used to take me along when he inspected the vineyards in Elba, so I have fond memories of this wine, still one of my great favorites.*

# *Mele al Caramello*
## CARAMELIZED CUSTARD APPLES

SERVES 6.

FOR THE CUSTARD CREAM
- 4 extra-large egg yolks
- 4 tablespoons granulated sugar
- 1 tablespoon potato starch (*not* potato flour)
- 1½ cups whole milk or heavy cream

FOR THE APPLES
- 3 large apples, ripe but not overripe, preferably Rome apples or red or yellow Delicious apples
- 6 tablespoons muscat raisins

- 1 cup granulated sugar
  Juice of ½ lemon, plus 1 whole lemon
- 2 teaspoons orange extract or 4 drops if imported from Italy

Prepare the custard cream with the ingredients and quantities listed above, following procedure in the Note on page 259, but adding the potato starch once the egg yolks are almost whipped, just before the milk or heavy cream. Once the custard cream is cooked, transfer it to an empty wine bottle, cork the bottle and refrigerate until needed. The custard cream may be prepared a day in advance.

Carefully wash the apples and dry with paper towels. Cut apples crosswise in half. Remove the core from each half. Fill the hole with 1 tablespoon of the raisins.

Set a casserole large enough to hold all 6 apple halves in a single layer over very low heat. When the casserole is merely warm, sprinkle ½ cup of the sugar evenly over the bottom and remove casserole from heat. Place the apples, cut part facing down, in the casserole and sprinkle with the remaining sugar and the lemon juice. Cut off the ends of the whole lemon and divide it into 8 slices. Be sure all seeds have been removed. Arrange all the lemon slices in the pan, beside but not over the apples. Pour the orange extract over the contents of the pan.

One hour before serving, set casserole, covered, over medium heat. Cook for 2 minutes, gently shaking the casserole two or three times, to dissolve the sugar. Cook for 2 minutes more, being careful that the sugar remains golden and does not become too dark. Do not touch the apples, but simply shake the casserole. Depending on the size of the apples and their ripeness, they should be cooked in about 10 minutes more, carefully watching that the sugar does not become too dark.

Pour the cold custard cream over the apples, cover the casserole and let rest for at least ½ hour before serving.

Each serving will consist of one apple half and some of the custard cream, with the almost caramelized sugar and a lemon slice underneath.

# Carta da Musica come Dolce

## MUSIC PAPER BREAD AS DESSERT

SERVES 8.

4 large discs *carta da musica* bread (see page 242) *or* 8 individual small ones

FOR THE CREAM

12 ounces ricotta, well drained

1½ cups heavy cream

1 tablespoon confectioners' sugar

OPTIONAL

Grated peel of ½ lemon (see page 294)

TO SERVE

1 pint of wild strawberries or cultivated strawberries or raspberries,

cleaned, *or* 1 large ripe peach, peeled and sliced into thin wedges

8 tablespoons warmed bitter honey (see Note, page 281)

If using large pieces of *carta da musica* bread, divide them into roughly broken individual pieces, about 5-by-5 inches. Place 1 piece on each individual plate.

Combine the ricotta, heavy cream and sugar in a blender or food processor and lightly blend for 20 seconds or until the mixture has almost the texture of whipped cream. Transfer this "cream" to a crockery or glass bowl and let rest, covered, in the refrigerator for at least 2 hours before serving.

When ready, spoon the cream onto the prepared bread pieces and top cream with either the berries, whole or cut into pieces, or the peach slices. At the very last moment before serving, drizzle some of the warmed honey over everything.

The classic way to eat this dessert is to break off a piece of your portion of the bread and use it as a spoon.

# *Lemoncello*

# THE AUTHENTIC ITALIAN LEMON LIQUEUR

MAKES ABOUT 2½ CUPS.

*Lemoncello*, the Sicilian lemon liqueur, is often prepared by allowing lemon rind to steep in alcohol for several weeks before straining the liquid and adding sugar syrup. A second shortcut, all too common, consists of simply combining alcohol and a lemon extract. The true method, given in this recipe, results in a liqueur that is not bitter or too strong but very airy and perfectly balanced.

2  large lemons with thick skins
2  cups pure grain alcohol or unfla-
   vored vodka

1  to 2 cups granulated sugar, depending on the sweetness required

5  drops lemon juice

Wash the lemons very well, first in lukewarm water, then in cold water, and pat dry. Wrap the lemons in a piece of cheesecloth and tie the package together with string, leaving enough string on both sides to wrap around a mason jar.

Pour the alcohol the jar. Hang the lemon package over the alcohol, but be sure it does not touch the liquid. Wrap the string around the mouth of the jar and tie it tightly in order to keep the cheesecloth in place. Close the jar and put it in a dark place for 2 months.

After this period of time, dissolve enough sugar to produce the desired level of sweetness in 1 cup of cold water and place it with the drops of lemon juice in a small saucepan. Set saucepan over low heat until a syrup forms, about 45 minutes. Transfer the syrup to a crockery or glass bowl and let cool completely, about 1 hour.

Open the jar containing the 2 lemons, discard the lemons and pour the flavored alcohol into a bottle, adding the cooled syrup. Shake the bottle several times, then let rest for 2 hours.

Pour the contents of the bottle through a coffee filter into a clean bottle. Cork the bottle and let rest for at least 5 days before using it.

OPPOSITE:
*The kiosks that one finds throughout southern Italy sell*
lemoncello *as well as freshly squeezed lemon juice and orange juice.*

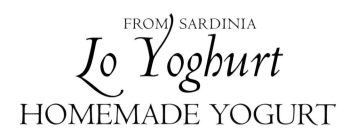

FROM SARDINIA

# Lo Yoghurt

# HOMEMADE YOGURT

MAKES 3¾ QUARTS.

I never thought of yogurt as a dessert until I tasted it homemade in Sardinia. The incredible milk has all the perfumes of this beautiful land, intensified by the spring and summer air and the sun, whose heat turns it into yogurt.

| | | |
|---|---|---|
| 8 tablespoons cold water | 4 quarts whole milk | 12 tablespoons plain yogurt |

Pour the cold water into a medium-sized casserole, then add the milk and set casserole over medium heat. When the milk is warm, transfer 6 tablespoons of the liquid to a crockery or glass bowl. Add the 12 tablespoons of plain yogurt and mix very well.

When the remaining milk reaches a boil, remove casserole from heat and add the contents of the glass bowl to it. Let rest until cool, about 1 hour.

Transfer mixture to a glass jar, cover and wrap the jar thoroughly with dish towels to keep it warm. Keep jar in a draft-free warm place, warm enough to allow the yogurt to form an even thickness after 5 or 6 hours, usually about 100 degrees.

If the yogurt does not become uniformly thick, first try moving the jar to a warmer place, again for 5 or 6 hours. Occasionally the temperature has been too warm rather than too cold, in which case you have to make a final try with a temperature cooler than the original one; this does not happen too often. In Sardinia, they place the jar in the sun in the summertime; in the winter, next to the fireplace.

*Sliced fresh citron on a ferry approaching Palermo*

# Cedro allo Zucchero
## CITRON SPRINKLED WITH SUGAR

### SERVES 6 TO 8.

| | | |
|---|---|---|
| 1 large ripe citron | 2 medium-sized lemons | ¾ cup granulated sugar |

Carefully wash the citron first in lukewarm water, then in cold water, and then dry it with paper towels. Use a sharp knife to cut the citron crosswise into slices no thicker than ¾ inch.

Arrange the citron slices on a large serving platter. Squeeze the 2 lemons and pour all their juices over the citron, then sprinkle with sugar. Let the citron marinate, covered, in the refrigerator for at least 1 hour before serving.

Very cold citron may be served in place of a fruit sorbet between courses of a very formal dinner or as a very simple dessert.

# The Cheeses of
# Sicily and Sardinia

*A selection of Sardinian cheeses: On the far left,* Brigante *or* Bianca di Sardegna; *in front, fresh* Caciottone *or* Isola Bianca; *directly behind the* Caciottone *is a* Crotone-*type or* Rigato *cheese; in the back left center is fresh* Caciotta *or Sardinian* Fresa; *the dark wheel on top of the* Rigato *cheese is* Fiore Sardo; *behind the* Fiore Sardo *is a "*Toscanello*"-type or* Sandalio *cheese; leaning against the* Sandalio *is an aged* Sandalio *cheese; the small cheese in the center of the stack is* Caciotella *or fresh* Pecorino; *below this is an aged* Semicotto; *and on the far right, another aged* Semicotto.

*On the left is the distinctive sheep's milk ricotta from Sardinia or Sicily.*

Primo Sale *for sale in a Sicilian market*

*The cheese in the center is* Canestrato *from Sicily.*

# Basic Techniques

## MAKING PASTA WITH A MANUAL PASTA MACHINE

To prepare the pasta dough, place the flour in a mound on a pasta board and use a fork to make a well in the center. Place the eggs and salt (and any other ingredients specified in the recipe) in the well and, with a fork, combine them. Still using the fork, start to incorporate the flour from the inner rim of the well with the mixture in the center, always incorporating fresh flour from the lower part, pushing it under the dough that is forming to keep it from sticking to the board. Remove the pieces of dough attached to the fork and incorporate them. Use your hands to gather the dough together.

Scrape the board with a pastry scraper, putting together all the unincorporated flour. Place the sifter on the board and using one hand, "clean" the flour by moving the sifter back and forth without lifting the sifter from the board. Discard the globules of dough that remain in the sifter. With the palm of one hand, start kneading the dough on the board, folding the dough over with the other hand, absorbing the leftover flour from the board. Do not sprinkle the flour over the dough. Continue kneading for about 2 to 3 minutes, absorbing the flour, until the dough is not wet anymore and all but 4 or 5 tablespoons of the flour have been incorporated; the remaining flour will be used for kneading the dough with the pasta machine.

Use the palm of one hand to flatten the ball of dough to a thickness of about ½ inch so it can fit between the rollers of the pasta machine. (If the pasta dough is made with more than 2 eggs, divide the dough into 1-cup portions before flattening it.) Set the pasta machine at its widest setting and feed the dough through the rollers. With your hand, remove the layer of dough from underneath the pasta machine. Holding the layer of dough with both hands, gently flour one side of the dough by drawing it across the flour on the board. Fold the dough into thirds (folding the two short sides toward the center), and press down with your fingers, starting from one open side toward the opposite open side, so that the three layers are melded together and no air remains between them. Using the same wide setting of the rollers, insert one of the open ends of the folded layer of dough through the rollers. Continue folding and feeding the dough through the rollers 8 to 10 times or less, until the dough is very smooth and elastic. The pasta dough is now ready to be stretched. Move the rollers to a narrower setting, following the manufacturer's instructions for your machine.

Flour the layer of pasta on both sides by drawing it across the flour on the board. When feeding the layer of pasta into the machine, stand sideways in relation to the table, holding the handle of the machine with your right hand. Hold the other hand up sideways, keeping the four fingers together and holding the thumb out. Let the sheet of pasta rest over your hand between the first finger and the outstretched thumb. Pass the dough through the rollers once; do not fold anymore. Move the wheel down to the next notch, passing the dough through the rollers just once. After passing each time, sprinkle the layer of pasta with a little flour. Each successive notch will produce a thinner layer of pasta. Repeat this procedure until the layer is the desired thickness, which is indicated in each recipe. Still letting the pasta hang over one hand, pull it out to its full length. Cut into the desired shape.

## GRATING ORANGE AND LEMON PEELS

Place a piece of parchment paper or thick waxed paper over the holes of a hand grater. Hold the paper in place with one hand while moving the orange or lemon back and forth on the paper with the other. Work on different sections of the paper so that the paper does not wear out. Use a rubber spatula to remove the grated orange or lemon peel from the paper. Do not use what is inside the grater or any of the bitter white part of the peel.

## PRESERVING AROMATIC HERBS IN SALT

Remove the leaves of the herbs from their stems without washing them. In a mason jar, make a ½-inch-thick layer of coarse-grained salt. Add a layer of herb leaves, then salt, and continue in this manner until all the leaves are used up or the jar is full, finishing with a layer of salt. Close the jar securely and keep in a cool place. To use the herbs, wash away the salt and any dirt that may be clinging to the leaves. Some herbs, such as basil, will lose some of their color, but they will not lose any of their flavor.

## TO PREPARE BALSAMELLA

Melt the butter in a heavy saucepan, preferably copper or enamel, over low heat. When the butter reaches the frothing point, add the flour all at once. Mix very well with a wooden spoon.

Cook until the flour is completely incorporated (1 to 3 minutes, depending on the quantities). If any lumps form, dissolve them by crushing them against the side of the pan with a wooden spoon. Remove the pan from the heat and let stand for 10 to 15 minutes.

While the butter-flour mixture is standing, heat the milk in another pan until it is very close to the boiling point. Put the saucepan with the butter-flour mixture over low heat and add all of the hot milk at once. Stir until the sauce is smooth.

When the sauce reaches the boiling point, add the salt and continue to stir gently while the sauce cooks slowly for about 10 minutes longer. Remove from the heat and transfer the sauce to a crockery bowl. According to the recipe, use it warm, immediately, or press a piece of buttered wax paper over the sauce to prevent a skin from forming and let the sauce cool completely.

## HOW TO TIE A PIECE OF MEAT LIKE A SALAMI

To tie a piece of meat like a salami, cut a piece of string six times the length of the meat to be tied. Place the string under one of the short sides of the rolled-up meat (about 1½ inches from the end) and make a knot, leaving only enough string on one side to pull over and knot the first ring in the center. Bring the long end of the string down the meat another 1½ inches, and hold the string in place with your finger. With the other hand, pull the string under and around again to the point where the string is being held by your finger. Pass the end of the string over and then under (like a sailor's knot). Remove your finger, hold the short end of the string with one hand and pull the other end tight with the other hand. Continue this process at 1½-inch intervals until you reach the opposite end of the meat. Stand the meat on one end and put the remaining string over the top end to the underside of the meat. As the string intersects with each ring of string, pull under and over, fastening in the same way as was done on the other side (it is no longer necessary to hold the string with your finger or to pull tight on this side). After the last intersections, tie a knot using the two ends of the the string. When the meat is ready, you will only need to cut the string in one place in order to remove it.

## BONING A CHICKEN AS FOR A GALANTINE

Use a boning knife to cut through the skin of the chicken around the leg joint. Cut through again to sever the tendons, then twist and push out the leg to free it from the thigh bone. Repeat with the other leg.

Turn the chicken breast-side down, then use the boning knife to cut through the skin and meat atached to the spine, cutting all the way down the back as far back as the tail so that the entire back is opened. Cut the tendons that connect the upper part of the thigh to the spine and cartilage. Cut the thigh bone free from the piece of cartilage left after the removal of the leg bone. Repeat with the other thigh.

Starting at the tail end of the back, begin to free the meat on both sides of the carcass. Continue to free all the meat around the breast, being sure that all the meat is completely detached and being careful not to make holes in the skin. At this point, the meat that remains is only attached at the tail end and to the center breast bone. Insert the knife, sharp-side up, between the meat and the end of the carcass just above the tail, and cut through. The tail will come off with it. Lift off the meat at the tail end of the carcass. Cut along the breast bone to detach the meat that is still attached to the carcass. If desired, reserve the carcass for preparing stock.

Open the whole boned chicken and remove the wishbone at the top of the breast. Detach the bone connecting the whole wing to the shoulder by cutting into the joint; then detach it at the other end, where it connects to the double bone of the second section of the wing, and discard. Scrape the meat off the double bone of the second section of the wing and cut off the bone from the attached cartilage. The chicken is now completely boned but unlike the classic galantine, all the meat is left in place, attached to the skin. Tuck in the legs and wings. (Note that to make a true galantine, the boned meat is separated from the skin and cut into cubes or strips.)

A NOTE ABOUT RICOTTA: Today most manufacturers sell ricotta in 15-ounce containers, and I have made adjustments to the recipes accordingly.

# Conversion Chart

## BUTTER

In the United States, butter is generally sold in a one-pound package, which contains four equal sticks. The wrapper on each stick is marked to show tablespoons, so the cook can cut the stick according to the quantity required. The equivalent weights are:

1 stick (½ cup) = 115 g = 4 oz
1 tablespoon = 15 g = ½ oz

## FLOUR

The recipes in this book indicate unbleached all-purpose flour. To achieve a near equivalent of American all-purpose flour, use half British plain flour and half high-gluten bread flour.

## SUGAR

American granulated sugar is finer than British granulated, closer to caster sugar, so British cooks should use caster sugar throughout.

## YEAST

Quantities of dried yeast (called active dry yeast in the United States) are usually given in number of packages:

1 package = 7 g (¼ oz) = 1 scant tablespoon

## VOLUME, WEIGHT & TEMPERATURE EQUIVALENTS

### VOLUME EQUIVALENTS

These are not exact equivalents, but have been rounded up or down slightly to make measuring easier.

| AMERICAN | METRIC | IMPERIAL |
|---|---|---|
| ¼ t | 1.25 ML | |
| ½ t | 2.5 ML | |
| 1 t | 5 ML | |
| ½ T (1½ t) | 7.5 ML | |
| 1 T (3 t) | 15 ML | |
| ¼ CUP (4 T) | 60 ML | 2 FL OZ |
| ⅓ CUP (5 T) | 75 ML | 2½ FL OZ |
| ½ CUP (8 T) | 125 ML | 4 FL OZ |
| ⅔ CUP (10 T) | 150 ML | 5 FL OZ (¼ PINT) |
| ¾ CUP (12 T) | 175 ML | 6 FL OZ |
| 1 CUP (16 T) | 250 ML | 8 FL OZ |
| 1¼ CUPS | 300 ML | 10 FL OZ (½ PINT) |
| 1½ CUPS | 350 ML | 12 FL OZ |
| 1 PINT (2 CUPS) | 500 ML | 16 FL OZ |
| 1 QUART (4 CUPS) | 1 LITRE | 1¾ PINTS |

| AVOIRDUPOIS | METRIC |
|---|---|
| 5 OZ | 150 G |
| 6 OZ | 175 G |
| 7 OZ | 200 G |
| 8 OZ | 225 G |
| 9 OZ | 250 G |
| 10 OZ | 300 G |
| 11 OZ | 325 G |
| 12 OZ | 350 G |
| 13 OZ | 375 G |
| 14 OZ | 400 G |
| 15 OZ | 425 G |
| 1 LB | 450 G |
| 1 LB 2 OZ | 500 G |
| 1½ LB | 750 G |
| 2 LB | 900 G |
| 2¼ LB | 1 KG |
| 3 LB | 1.4 KG |
| 4 LB | 1.8 KG |
| 4½ LB | 2 KG |

### WEIGHT EQUIVALENTS

These are not exact equivalents, but have been rounded up or down slightly to make measuring easier.

| AVOIRDUPOIS | METRIC |
|---|---|
| ¼ OZ | 7 G |
| ½ OZ | 15 G |
| 1 OZ | 30 G |
| 2 OZ | 60 G |
| 3 OZ | 90 G |
| 4 OZ | 115 G |

### OVEN TEMPERATURES

| OVEN | °F | °C | GAS MARK |
|---|---|---|---|
| VERY COOL | 250–275 | 130–140 | ½–1 |
| COOL | 300 | 150 | 2 |
| WARM | 325 | 170 | 3 |
| MODERATE | 350 | 180 | 4 |
| MODERATELY HOT | 375 | 190 | 5 |
| | 400 | 200 | 6 |
| HOT | 425 | 220 | 7 |
| VERY HOT | 450 | 230 | 8 |
| | 475 | 250 | 9 |

# Dictionary

| English | Italian | Sardinian | Sicilian | English | Italian | Sardinian | Sicilian |
|---|---|---|---|---|---|---|---|
| Almonds | Mandorle | Mendula | Miennula | Oil | Olio | Ozu | Ogghiu |
| Anchovy | Acciuga | Anciova | Anciova | Olive | Oliva | Ariba | Aliva or Auliva |
| Apricots | Albicocche | Baracoccu | Piricoca | | | | |
| Artichoke | Carciofo | Iscarzofa | Cacuocciulu | Onion | Cipolla | Achipudda | Cipudda |
| Basil | Basilico | Afabica | Basilicó | Orange | Arancio | Arangiu | Partuallu |
| Beans | Fagioli | Basolu | Fasola | Parsley | Prezzemolo | Pedrusimbulu | Pitrusinu |
| Bread | Pane | Pani | Pani | Peas | Piselli | Pisurci | Pisedde |
| Butter | Burro | Butiru | Buttiru | Pepper | Pepe | Pibere | Pipi Niuro |
| Capers | Capperi | Tapparas | Chiappari | Pepper (Hot) | Peperoncino | Piberoneddu Arrabiosu | Pipi Ardenti |
| Celery | Sedano | Appiu | Accia | | | | |
| Cheese | Formaggio | Casu | Caciu | Potato | Patata | Pumi di Terra | Patati |
| Cherry | Ciliegia | Cariasa | Cirasa | | | | |
| Chick-Peas | Ceci | Basolu Pitzudu | Ciciri | Rice | Riso | Arrosu | Risu |
| | | | | Ricotta | Ricotta | Arrescottu | Ricotta |
| Chicken | Pollo | Puddu | Iaddu | Rosemary | Rosmarino | Arromaniu | Rosamarinu |
| Eggplant | Melanzana | Pedringianu | Milinciani | Saffron | Zafferano | Tanfaranu | Zafarana |
| Fish | Pesce | Pische | Pisci | Sage | Salvia | Folla Salvia | Sarvia |
| Flour | Farina | Farra | Farina | | | | |
| Garlic | Aglio | Aciu | Agghiu | Salt | Sale | Sali | Sali |
| Heavy Cream | Panna | Pizzu de Latte | Rascu | Sugar | Zucchero | Tuccaru | Zuccaru |
| | | | | To Eat | Mangiare | Mandigare | Manciari |
| Honey | Miele | Meli | Meli | Tomato | Pomodoro | Pumata or Tomata | Pumaroru |
| Ice | Ghiaccio | Biddia | Ghiacciu | | | | |
| Lobster | Aragosta | Aligusta | Alaustra | Walnuts | Noci | Cocoro | Nuci |
| Meat | Carne | Petta or Pezza | Carni | Water | Acqua | Abba | Acqua |
| | | | | Wine | Vino | Binu | Vinu |
| Meat Balls (Small) | Polpettine | Bombixeddas | Purpetti | Wine Vinegar | Aceto | Axeddas | Acitu |
| Mushrooms | Funghi | Antunni | Funci | Zucchini | Zucchina or Zucchino | Corcorighedda | Cucuzzedda |

# Island recipes in other books by Giuliano Bugialli

## CLASSIC TECHNIQUES OF ITALIAN COOKING

Marzapane
Frittata con la ricotta
Lasagne con melanzane
Spaghetti all'aragosta
Spaghetti con caviale di tonno
Pasta con le sarde
Insalata di pasta II
Insalata di pasta III
Sardine di Alghero
Cavolo alla Sarda
Caponata
Torta di zucchini
Fagioli con sedano e carote
Focaccia farcita
Granita di limone

## BUGIALLI ON PASTA

Minestrone con fave
Pasta alla norma I
Pasta alla norma II
Pasta alla norma III
Melanzane ripiene di pasta
Pasta ai peperoni
Pasta con broccoli saltati
Pasta chi vruocculi arriminata
Pasta e carciofi
Pasta con i carciofi
Spaghetti al finocchio
Pasta con pesto alla trapanese
Pasta e zucchine
Pasta alle zucchine
Pasta alle sarde II
Pasta con pesce spada
Pasta con bottarga

Minestra di pasta all'aragosta
Pasta alla marinara alla trapanese
Spaghetti e gamberi
Anellini al forno
Malloreddus con sugo di pomodoro
Culingionis di melanzane
Malloreddus alla campidanese
Crusetti o rosette alla siciliana
Maccheroni inferrettati
Pasta rossa con pesto alla ragusana
Pasta di ceci al rosmarino
Pasta alla ricotta
Cuscusu
Couscous nero
Cascá
Fregola
Couscous dolce

# Index